W9-BMW-073

Contents

UPSTATE TRAVELS

A York State Book

UPSTATE TRAVELS

British Views of Nineteenth-Century New York

Edited, with an Introduction, by

ROGER HAYDON

Syracuse University Press   1982

Copyright © 1982 by ROGER HAYDON
Syracuse, New York 13210

All Rights Reserved
First Edition

This book is published with the assistance of a grant from the John Ben Snow Foundation.
Winner of the 1982 John Ben Snow Manuscript Prize
.

ROGER HAYDON received the B.A. and Ph.D. from the University of
Essex and is Associate Editor of *International Organization*

Library of Congress Cataloging in Publication Data
Main entry under title:

Upstate travels.

   (A York State book)
   Bibliography: p.
   Includes index.
   1. New York (State)—Description and travel—Sources.
2. British—New York (State)—History—Sources. 3. New
York (State)—Social life and customs—Sources.
4. Country life—New York (State)—History—19th century
—Sources. I. Haydon, Roger.
F123.U67   974.7'03   82-3312
ISBN 0-8156-2270-8   AACR2
ISBN 0-8156-0175-1 (pbk.)

Manufactured in the United States of America

Illustrations

For his assistance on illustrations, I wish especially to thank John Scherer of the New York State Museum, Albany.

The following organizations generously supplied photographs of items in their collections and permitted their reproduction here: The DeWitt Historical Society of Tompkins County, Ithaca; The New York State Museum, Albany; The McKinney Library of the Albany Institute of History and Art; The Geneva Historical Society; Cornell University Library, Ithaca; and The Broome County Historical Society, Binghamton.

Preface

O UR TRANSATLANTIC FRIENDS are morbidly sensitive as to the strictures of strangers. They hate the whole tribe of Travellers and Tourists, Roamers and Ramblers, Peepers and Proclaimers," wrote the Welsh missionary Ebenezer Davies in 1849, in his *American Scenes, and Christian Slavery*. There was an immense tribe to hate: thousands of foreign travelers visited the United States in the generation following the War of 1812. They published hundreds of accounts of their journeys, testifying to the importance the new country held for the old as an extraordinary social and political experiment. As Davies indicates, American opinion concentrated on these visitors' negative comments. The early nineteenth century was punctuated by national outcries against certain works, mainly by Britons—among them Henry Bradshaw Fearon's *Sketches of America* (1818), Basil Hall's *Travels in North America* (1829), Mrs. Frances Trollope's *Domestic Manners of the Americans* (1832), and Charles Dickens's *American Notes* (1842) were especially infamous in American eyes.

This intermittent furor about foreign criticism masked profound political struggles on both sides of the Atlantic. In the United States, cultural independence had lagged political and economic independence by half a century or more, and the country's continued reliance on British cultural norms made its citizens peculiarly aware of British strictures. British opinion, and the cultural weight it carried, was particularly important in the second and third decades of the nineteenth century. The United States, racked by radical disagreement over the shape its future should take, fought the wider political struggle between Federalists and Jacksonian Democrats in miniature, in dozens of skirmishes over the accuracy of observations and theory from the latest British visitor.

Meanwhile, on the other side of the Atlantic, Britain itself was convulsed across that same generation by demands for parliamentary and poor law reform in the 1820s, and for mass democracy in the 1830s and 1840s. Opinions of the United States were used on both sides of these British battles; the country was variously a shining example to liberal reformers and a dreadful warning to conservatives. As conservatives reluctantly yielded ground to pressures for change, they seized on every uncomplimentary account of the New World and its institutions to do down their political opponents.

Subsequent generations of readers have inherited these struggles, and republications of British accounts of North America have mainly served their ideological historians and revisionists. As a result, the bulk of travel books — the more modest, personal accounts of traveling in a massive, rapidly changing country — have tended to be overlooked. Though travel books have long been used by social historians, sheer rarity has, unfortunately, restricted knowledge of what they can tell us.

When used with discrimination they can shed new light on the early life of the United States — both in detail and when writ large — being inherently no more inaccurate (and often far closer to the truth) than contemporary American accounts. Americans, after all, thought they knew what the United States was, what it meant, and where it was going. British visitors, on the other hand, tended to start with raw prejudices of the kind described by Simon O'Ferrall in 1832, in *A Ramble of Six Thousand Miles*. "What can you possibly see there?" he asks rhetorically. "A country like America — little better than a mere forest — the inhabitants notoriously far behind Europeans in refinement — filled with wild Indians, rattlesnakes, bears, and backwoodsmen. . . ." First-hand experience of the country, though often uncomfortable, forced travelers to revise their opinions not slightly, but root and branch. As they confronted the country's achievements and its bustling energy, British tourists often made a closer pass at the truth than their American counterparts.

New York State was for the early nineteenth century the very image of the United States. The 1820 census recorded New York's taking over from Virginia the title of country's most populous state, which position it would retain until the Korean War. In land mass it was only a few hundred square miles smaller than England itself. And, between 1815 and 1845 its development, based on the building and operation of the Erie Canal, was stunning in its scale and complexity. Virtually all foreign travelers visited New York State and described it in their books; and this volume presents a sampling of those descriptions.

The first chapter gives a brief account of those who wrote about their visits to North America, whom they thought they were writing for, and the way in which both tourists' interests and the ways in which they traveled around the state helped to determine a common itinerary for visits to New York.

The bulk of the book is occupied by a selection of passages from that travel literature. The passages are all by British citizens and were written in the early heyday of New York tourism, between 1815 and the late 1840s. The extracts are organized by region and follow the broad outlines of the itinerary whose development is traced in the first chapter. No two tourists, of course, traveled exactly the same route. But their different interests were usually satisfied by one constantly reinforced itinerary. Starting in New York City (not included in this volume – it requires a book to itself), they would travel up the Hudson River, stopping at Ossining, West Point, and Catskill, perhaps, before going through to Albany. A visit to Lebanon Springs or Watervliet to stare at Shakers would be followed by a sampling of the spa waters at Saratoga or Ballston; then would come a visit to Lake George. Some would then steam north up the Champlain Valley and so to Canada; the majority returned to Albany and Schenectady. The western route, whether by road, canal, or a little later railroad, ran through the Mohawk Valley to Utica and Syracuse. A few travelers branched north here to Oswego and the Canada steamers. But the vast majority made their way west to Rochester, touching on the towns of the northern fringe of the Finger Lakes. On, then, via Lockport to Niagara Falls. Those making a tour just of the eastern states would often return by much the same route to New York City. Many made their way into Canada from Niagara, perhaps to return to New York after examining Toronto and Montreal, via Champlain and the Hudson. Those heading on into the Midwest would travel south from Niagara to Buffalo, and thence by steamer to the ports of Ohio and Michigan, and the new settlements.

This anthology is, as I have indicated, a short selection from a large literature. Personal taste has guided my selection of some of the passages (I find, for example, Richard Weston's irascibility and general bad humor almost irresistible), but there are also some more general criteria that deserve noting.

British travelers published far more about America than did other nationalities, and selections are restricted to books by nationals of the United Kingdom. Three reasons contribute to this decision. First, these nationals shared a political and social culture; there is a background of belief, practice, and assumption common to the writers represented here. Second, all wrote in English. Third, Americans of the generation covered in this book took British views of their country more seriously than the

opinions of other nationalities. By 1845 American taste was far less dominated by British models than it had been in 1815, but despite this growing
national self-confidence, Americans were still particularly sensitive to
British criticism.

The earliest date for a passage is 1815. The War of 1812 interrupted
British visits to the United States and permanently changed British perceptions of what was still deemed a new nation of dubious status. By 1845
British tourists were flocking to America in huge numbers every year,
with more to see because of improvements in transportation and the westward expansion of the nation. Their average stay, however, was considerably shorter than earlier travelers'. More sights and impressions chased
fewer pages; the book market for accounts of the eastern United States
was already glutted; and thus accounts of New York become shorter, less
detailed, and more predictable in both their choice of topics and the comments they offer.

I have deliberately sought descriptions of as many parts of upstate
New York as I could. This misrepresents the bulk of the literature to some
extent, in the sense that the descriptions of Albany appearing here are a
few from many dozens, that of Binghamton the only one that I have
found. Some areas have escaped altogether: the western Southern Tier
and the central North Country appear simply not to have been visited by
travelers who left a permanent record of their journey until later. (Adi-
rondack tourist writing, for example, would not begin to flourish until
the mid 1850s.)

The best-known writers are deliberately under-represented. Books
by authors such as Charles Dickens and Mrs. Trollope are frequently re-
printed and not difficult to obtain; the rarer the book, the more likely an
excerpt will appear here. Dickens's description of the Shakers, for instance, is appealing in a rather vicious way, but Andrew Bell's, which is
far more difficult to find, is the one I have chosen.

Finally, it should be noted that both overt British opinions about the
United States in general terms and the British fascination with American
landscape have already been served by splendid anthologies. Major collections are listed in the Bibliography. While authors' opinions shape the
passages I have chosen, it is their descriptions of the cities, villages,
farms, factories, prisons, and schools of upstate New York on which I
have concentrated.

Most of this book is in the travel writers' own words. I have provided brief biographical sketches (based on entries in county histories, the
Dictionary of National Biography, the *National Cyclopaedia of American Biography,* Lamb's and Appleton's biographical dictionaries, and

other standard sources); and I have annotated extracts sparingly, making only the most minor changes in punctuation and spelling. I have reproduced the idiosyncracies of the original texts, including their many variations in the spelling of place-names.

I record here a brief expression of thanks to the many people who have helped me in the making of this book. Margaret Hobbie and Charles L. Todd read and made valuable suggestions on various drafts and sections. The staff of Cornell University's Olin Library (especially the Inter-Library Loan and Reference divisions) helped locate numerous, often rare, and occasionally unlikely volumes. The registrars and directors of various museums and libraries throughout New York assisted in identifying and providing illustrations.

This book is dedicated with affection and gratitude to Joyce Haydon and Frederick Haydon of Ramsgate, in the county of Kent, England; and to Elizabeth Hobbie and Thomas Hobbie of Sodus, in Wayne County, New York.

Ithaca, New York   Roger Haydon
Fall 1981

British Visitors to Nineteenth-Century New York State

I N THE EARLY NINETEENTH CENTURY the recently independent United States attracted immigrants and visitors from every country in Europe. The new nation had much to recommend it to tourists: a famous—to many, notorious—social experiment in the popular control of government, manners and customs peculiar enough to enthrall and enrage Europeans, explosive growth, rapidly developing networks of transportation, and many justly famous natural wonders. Immigrants were attracted by other characteristics, prime among them being economic opportunity and comparatively cheap land.

From a distance of several thousand miles, the United States and Canada seemed remote and often mysterious. Given the number of potential voyagers and a large, more diffuse group of armchair travelers, it is not surprising that many of the hardier men and women who actually made the voyage across the North Atlantic published books about the New World and their experiences there. In the British book market, then the world's largest, impressions of North America found ready acceptance, bridging the gap in the literature of travel between commonplace accounts of western Europe and the truly exotic such as the African adventures of Mungo Park. Travel narratives had long been popular, and their popularity was compounded among those Britons who could afford books and travel for pleasure by the long Napoleonic years, during which continental Europe was forbidden as a tourist destination. North America, however, suffered no blockade. "The bibliography of travel literature reveals an ever-increasing list of visitors to these shores," writes Jane Mesick, "beginning directly after the Revolution, decreasing perceptibly during the War of 1812, and receiving a new stimulation after the

1

independence of America was fully established by the peace of 1814."[1]

Travel writing about America accumulated disagreements of fact and interpretation as well as commonplaces. As a genre it affords a lively, even rowdy, combination of notes, letters, ideas, journal entries, distortions, and downright lies. But the genre changed between the War of 1812 and the Civil War, largely because cheap lithographs and the new science of photography were beginning to make the sights of North America familiar. In terms of immediate experience, this had little appreciable effect on the tourists themselves; but cheap, accurate visual records of the continent did affect the kind of book that British publishers were willing to take on. Fact was slowly replaced by the impression that fact made on the traveler, and travel books became slowly more opaque, telling more about the individual traveler as they told less about the places that he or she had visited. Briefly, reaction replaced description, and interest in place ceded to interest in the personality of the writer.

The last mass flowering of travel writing before the personality of the author came to dominate the travel book exhibited the western world to a large, fascinated public in Britain. In this chapter I sketch briefly both the travelers themselves and the ways in which they traveled across the state. Both helped shape the accounts that they published.

Travelers disembarking in New York City, seeing North America for the first time, already had a vision of the continent, ideas about its people, and prejudices about the way in which the country was run. Noble savages, a popular control of government amounting to anarchy, unfettered economic opportunity—the lists of expectations vary with the traveler. They left the continent with impressions that depended largely on who and what they had seen, how they had traveled, and how their experience squared with the notions with which they had begun.

The accumulation of previous accounts provided many of these misconceptions and annoyed James Fenimore Cooper so much that the American novelist produced his own version of an American tour, the anonymously published *Notions of the Americans* (1828). These travelers' accounts provoked wildly differing reviews on both sides of the Atlantic until eventually the literature became so large and complex that it appears in retrospect to have taken on a life of its own, slowly floating free from the country that it claimed to represent.[2]

1. Jane Mesick, *The English Traveller in America, 1785-1835* (1922; rpt. Westport, Ct.: Greenwood Press, 1970), p. 3.
2. The wide range of British travelers in nineteenth-century America has been well

The variety of accounts of America is limited only by the diversity of characters who made the journey and published their impressions. Their works exhibit an extraordinary profusion of peeves and interests. Transcriptions of menus and cattle prices jostle carefully composed aesthetic outpourings at the sight of Niagara Falls. Private letters about the peculiarities of American speech rub shoulders with geologists' notebooks. Actors' journals contradict the reports of emigrating clergymen.

The course of British political life also shaped, sometimes radically, British views about and descriptions of the United States. The date 1832, when the passage of the Reform Act began the formal redistribution of political power in Britain by redrawing the boundaries of parliamentary constituencies, is from this perspective crucial. Before 1832 the enthusiastic supporters of parliamentary reform discovered in America evidence of the brilliant effects of democratic institutions forever obscure to their more conservative counterparts. After passage of the Act, Tory visitors outlined the excesses of Jacksonian America, which they thought awaited incautious reformers in Britain somewhere down the slippery slope of democratic change. In the 1830s and 1840s other political concerns helped fragment impressions of America. Chartists and Corn Law Leaguers found different countries lurking under the common label "United States," and a multitude of Temperance supporters, prison reformers, British Army regulars on furlough from their stations in the Canadas, and abolitionists created distinct, detailed versions of the country that only occasionally overlapped.

In more general terms, however, British travelers formed a relatively homogeneous group. Those who published accounts of their journeys were in the main financially comfortable. There were few noblemen but even fewer whose books described the extreme discomforts of crossing the North Atlantic in steerage. Once in the United States most could afford to travel without watching every penny. For a British traveler to hire an "extra exclusive," a private coach with driver, when the timetable of local public transport was inconvenient, was not uncommon. It is essentially middle-class, leisured versions of America that published accounts preserve.

Though travelers mainly come from the same class, however, their books vary according to the audience they wrote for, and the America of the run of tourist accounts differs widely from the America described by traveling British farmers.

---

served by three surveys: Mesick, *The English Traveller, 1785-1835*; Max Berger, *The British Traveller in America, 1836-1860* (New York: Columbia University, 1943); and Richard L. Rapson, *Britons View America: Travel Commentary, 1860-1935* (Seattle: University of Washington Press, 1971).

The farmer-writers understood themselves to be writing for potential emigrants from Britain, the small landowners and yeomen crushed by taxes and economic conditions. William Cobbett, as an extreme example, farmed on Long Island between 1817 and 1819; a Radical leader, he had fled England to avoid imprisonment after the suspension of habeas corpus. His account concentrates on weather and soil conditions, crops (his especial favorite being the *ruta baga*), the quality of the land he farmed, and the farming practices and traditions of his American neighbors. Cobbett's sense of audience for his book, *A Year's Residence,* was unusually precise. "In this Chapter," he notes at one point, "I wish to be regarded as addressing myself to a most worthy and public-spirited gentleman of moderate fortune *in Lancashire,* who, with a large family, now balances whether he shall come or stay" (p. 204).[3] Several other farmers wrote originally for individuals who were considering emigration: Patrick Shirreff came to check prospects for his younger brother, Robert Barclay for a relative.

These farmer-writers' intense practical interest in America links them with the dozens of pamphleteers who wrote on the desirability of emigration. Their evaluation of the United States was shaped by their intimate knowledge of the rural conditions in Britain, and underlying their works are the social upheavals attendant upon rapid industrialization, the crushing load of Poor Law rates, tithes and rents, and the sad catalog of unrest caused by high costs, low wages, and seasonal variations in rural employment.[4]

This practical concern with American conditions overrode discomforts that for other authors were enough to damn the whole country. John Fowler's travels across New York State in 1830, for instance, took him occasionally out of the traveler's usual route. He fought a running battle, which on the whole he lost, with the bedbugs and fleas of the inns of rural upstate. Yet he discriminated among areas not on the basis of the sleep he lost, but rather according to his evaluation of the capital an immigrating farmer would need and the rate of return on his investment he might reasonably expect.

The farmers who visited America were rich enough to afford investigative tours; they came from the cream of British rural society. Their reflections on the conditions of the roads related much more closely to the

3. Short references to British travelers' works about North America are given in the text throughout this volume. Full citations are to be found in the Bibliography.

4. On this background of unrest, see Eric J. Hobsbawm and George Rudé, *Captain Swing* (Harmondsworth: Penguin, 1973), and E. P. Thompson, *The Making of the English Working Class* (Harmondsworth: Penguin, 1968), especially Chaps. 7–9.

British equivalents than those by the lions of London society. And they were quite clear about the limitations of their readership, of British emigrants thinking to farm in the United States. Consistently, they recommended that British immigrants avoid new land, arguing that the long-established farms of the United Kingdom had simply not prepared Britons with the woodsman and frontier skills needed to carve a farm from the virgin forest.

Many examined farms in New York State with the express purpose of comparing conditions in the United States with those in Upper Canada — it was not only Army officers whose hearts swelled with patriotic pride when they crossed the Niagara River and stood once more beneath the Union Jack. Yet the realism of the farmer-writers usually asserted itself. As they were confident that British farmers could not handle frontier conditions, they presented Ontario as posing, at best, stiff challenges, and it received fainter praise than patriotism would have dictated. A modest acreage already under cultivation and supplied by reasonable transportation was generally thought to be worth to British immigrants the premium prices it commanded.

If farmers were interested in the conditions for farming in rural America, they were fascinated by the country's agricultural practices. The major proponents of scientific agriculture were frequently visited. In New York no farmer could leave the Albany area without visiting Jesse Buel's establishment; even more long-suffering were the ever-hospitable Wadsworths.[5] Originally from Connecticut, William and James Wadsworth settled in 1790 the area near what would develop into the village of Geneseo. James and his sons became the major landowners of the Genesee Valley, whose famed fertility drew countless British farmers.

By 1840 the primitive frontier conditions of the western states and territories had somewhat abated. Farmer-writers examined with far greater frequency the established farms of Michigan, Ohio, and Illinois. Detailed descriptions of New York conditions largely disappeared.

Farmers' accounts of New York State are unified by their focus on agriculture. They were clear about the composition and needs of their audience, and this clarity is reflected in the open, unadorned style in which they wrote. Tourists were, by contrast, a far more diverse group writing for a wide range of readers—readers who made different demands on

5. On Buel (1778–1839), see Harry J. Carman, ed., *Jesse Buel, Agricultural Reformer: Selections from His Writings* (New York: Columbia University Press, 1947); on the Wadsworths, see Alden Hatch, *The Wadsworths of the Genesee* (New York: Coward-McCann, 1959).

those who wrote for them. As a result, they provide us with a range of different Americas. A lawyer traveling in America would usually make some notes on the practice of law in the United States, he would move in a social circle containing more American lawyers than would tourists of other professions, and his impressions of New York would be to some extent shaped by his legal interests. Thus Alexander Mackay makes note of James Fenimore Cooper not purely from literary interest but because he heard him pleading one of his innumerable libel cases in court at Utica (*Western World,* 2: 201–204). But the lawyer's concern with law does not usually dominate his reflections on America to the extent farming tends to dominate the pages of the farmer-writers. (Only religious professionals achieve that degree of singlemindedness.)

Many professions are represented among the British tourists who traveled in New York State: publishers, actors, academics, lawyers, journalists, soldiers, and clergymen. Other tourists are less easily identifiable now by profession, though the meanings of "gentleman" and "lady" were far more exact and easily recognizable in the 1820s and 1830s. Each of these groups produced more or less "sectarian" portraits of America in general and of New York State in particular.

There are two commonplaces to all of these sectarian pictures. Tourists have much the same itinerary through the state of New York; and tourists are seldom concerned with the economic vitality of the state in the way that farmer-writers are. Typical is Mrs. Trollope, who suppressed the details of the commercial failure of her Bazaar in Cincinnati, preferring to present herself in *Domestic Manners of the Americans* as a genteel tourist. The common claim of these middle-class visitors, that the dollar ruled supreme in the country, is unsubstantiated by any detailed account of the commercial life of the United States. Later in the century commercial life takes on more importance in travelers' accounts as writers begin to write more frequently with an eye to the potential sales of their accounts in Britain. (No author considers the American market, for there was no international copyright agreement, and the British market was the world's largest.) The professional author, of course, chose subject matter likely to be suitable to the middle-class armchair traveler in Britain, thereby confirming the choices that commercial publishers had made on the behalf of readers throughout the first half of the century.

Tourists were conditioned by their common experience of events in Britain. Their similar social backgrounds created in them a shared understanding of the great changes of the 1820s and 1830s, though their opinions varied greatly about those changes' implications. They shared expectations about the customs and mores of polite society, and they partook of a common language of cultural fulfillment, agreeing in the most general sense about the nature of correct deportment and of the beautiful. Thus the threads of specialized interest and the more general presentation of leisured travel intertwine to form a common itinerary through New York State—a tour as predictable in its outlines as the eighteenth-century's Grand Tour made by British visitors to Europe.

The period with which this book is concerned starts immediately after the War of 1812, covers the time of the Canadian rebellions of the mid-to-late 1830s and the Maine border disputes, and ends with the Oregon border quarrels. It is, then, hardly surprising that the military history of relations between Britain and the United States attracted considerable comment. British history, after all, spoke to the importance of certain places—West Point, Saratoga, and so on. Such battle sites were in a sense "familiar" through association before the British visitor even got off the boat. And those sites not so well known were soon exhibited by American acquaintances and hosts in an understandable and tactless display of patriotic pride that occasionally annoyed the expatriate tourist.

The description of West Point, a major attraction for landscape amateurs, was usually accompanied by a meditation on the execution of Major André for his part in Benedict Arnold's attempt to betray the Hudson Highlands to the British. The visit to Saratoga was often enlivened by a visit to the battlefield of Stillwater, where General Burgoyne was defeated in 1777. The southern Champlain Valley provided sites less divisive for Britons and Americans: memories of the French and Indian War were embodied in Forts William Henry and Ticonderoga. Farther north, however, more recent events demanded notice. Few stopped for any time at Plattsburgh, as the Champlain steamers made Burlington on the Vermont shore their regular port of call, but the sight of the port on the New York shore provoked copious reflections on the naval battle and British attempts to take the city in September 1814.

At the other end of the state, the Niagara Frontier, on every tourist's itinerary, gave further evidence of previous conflict. The geography of the area cast a harsh light on the division of English-speaking nations. Buffalo had risen like a phoenix from its destruction in December 1813; meanwhile the battlefields on the Canadian bank, especially Lundy's Lane and Queenston Heights, recalled other, less spectacular atrocities. During the Canadian rebellions of the late 1830s, these memories were revived.

Accompanying this thread of military history was an interest in the current military capacity and readiness of the United States—an interest that waxed and waned with the intensity of political relations between the

two countries. Most military visitors were Army regulars, many on leave
from their regiments stationed in Canada. While interested in military
history and the tactics of their unsuccessful predecessors who had fought
in the United States, they were also professionally and socially concerned
with their American contemporaries. Furthermore, professional obliga-
tions would conspire to bring British officers into some areas of the state
otherwise scantly visited. Desertion from the British Army in Canada was
a frequent occurrence, though only an offense in the eyes of the United
States law if accompanied by theft or personal injury. The chase after deserters resulted in several accounts of the Watertown area.

Other more or less official visitors from Britain traveled through
New York. Edward Strutt Abdy, for example, made a journey with a
group examining American experiments in prison discipline and in his
book published detailed accounts of the innovative state penitentiaries at
Ossining and Auburn. Nor, indeed, was official status necessary for a
tourist to be interested in social institutions—the Auburn penitentiary
was so popular that James Stuart reports its governor defrayed some of
the prison's expenses by charging visitors twenty-five cents admission to
look through the place (*Three Years,* 1: 87). Educational experiments, especially the Female Academies of Troy and Albany, attracted attention.
But perhaps the greatest interest in current social movements was gener-
ated by the Shaker settlements at Lebanon and in Niskayuna Township
near Watervliet. Travelers usually rehashed pamphlets when describing
Shaker tenets, often mangling the Shaker creed unrecognizably. But the
organization of the community, the clothing of the sect's adherents, their
extraordinary gyrations during worship, all drew reports that ranged
from fascination through hilarity to prurience and a degree of public attention that only the Mormon settlements in Utah would match later in
the century. The other major social movements of the century, women's
rights and abolition, however, received scant attention in the context of
travels in New York: women's rights would wait until later in the century
before attracting more than cursory attention, while abolition concentrated reports in the South and the cities of the eastern seaboard rather
than in the villages and cities of upstate New York.

A distinct subset of these investigators of social movements is the
British clergymen who came in some numbers to report on the advances
made in America by their particular denominations. Some came seeking
permanent employment because they were unable to procure advance-
ment in Britain. Others came to collect donations for pet charitable proj-
ects in Britain or for missionary endeavors elsewhere. A third group came
largely convinced of the atheistical tendencies of the inhabitants of the

United States. Shocked by the absence of an Established church, these missionaries often remarked on the zealous, disputatious attachment of Americans to particular sects. The revivals that burned over the state in the first half of the century are, on the other hand, seldom mentioned; for it is the institutional church that attracted the interest of most of these clerical visitors.[6]

Another, wider stream of tourists flowed across the Atlantic, daunted only by open warfare and economic crises. This steady majority of tourists traveled for what might be termed in the most general sense "aesthetic" reasons. These reasons concentrated visitors' attention very largely on certain areas of the state to the exclusion of the rest. There were two main threads in this aesthetic interest: the literary and the pictorial.

New York State was the first part of North America to become known to Europeans through the arts. From a modern perspective the New England of Emerson, Thoreau, and Hawthorne overshadows the New York of the early nineteenth century. From the perspective of about 1835, however, the two most popular American authors were New Yorkers —Washington Irving and James Fenimore Cooper—and their works seemed to reveal whole segments of New York State to their readers. The associations built between their fiction and particular areas were strong enough, because popular enough, to affect the tourist itinerary. These associations rendered the foreign comfortably familiar to British travelers —a link with a shared literary experience was far more satisfying than some obscure battle that the British had probably lost anyway.

Irving's territory was the Hudson Valley. Many visitors passed judgment on the Dutch influence in New York's architecture and manners, mainly through a reading of his tales. *Knickerbocker's History* of the state (1809) was frequently cited; and the return of Irving from Europe to permanent residence on the Hudson was documented by one British tourist, Charles Joseph Latrobe, who traveled with the great man and accompanied him on a walking tour of the area. Thereafter, Irving's work was interrupted by countless tourists eager to converse with one of the era's authentic literary heroes.

If the Hudson was Irving's, Cooper was by common consent allowed a wider literary property. He was on the whole probably thankful about his relative lack of success in putting Cooperstown on the literary map: several tourists sought him out there after his return from Europe in 1833,

---

6. See Whitney R. Cross, *The Burned-Over District: The Social and Intellectual History of Enthusiastic Religion in Western New York, 1800–1850* (Ithaca: Cornell University Press, 1950).

but never in the numbers that disturbed Irving. But not only was the area
around Otsego Lake his; Cooper also staked out wide areas of influence
in less obviously geographical ways. The Dutch and their ways are
Irving's; the aboriginal inhabitants of New York State are Cooper's. It is a
rare tourist whose account of New York Indians does not bear evidence of
reading Cooper. His version of the Indian brings to a head two hundred
years of descriptions, capturing Indians in a simple division of good and
bad muscled by fantastic details of woodcraft and social organization.
The woodland areas of the state call Indians to the minds of tourists auto-
matically, and the Indians they recall are inevitably seen through the medium of Cooper's early novels.

New York was preeminent not merely for its literary associations
but also for its "pictorial" interest. The very language in which Britons
talked about landscape helped to focus their attention on the areas of the
United States that would offer them the greatest pictorial aesthetic satisfaction; and New York State contained the first two items on every con-
noisseur's list. The Hudson River Valley was ever being compared with the
valley of the Rhine for picturesqueness; the Rhine usually won, but only
because of the ruins and castles that studded its banks. Meanwhile, at the
other end of the state, Niagara Falls encompassed the very essence of the
word "sublime." The last years of Francis Abbott, the eccentric "Hermit
of Niagara" who took up residence next to the Falls and eventually died
there in the early 1830s, merely take the British fascination with the falls
to its lunatic extreme.

Niagara was for many visitors their journey's culmination, and
there is a sense in which crossing the state from Hudson to Niagara is
traveling through the categories of landscape—from the picturesque
through the beautiful to the sublime. It is one of the many examples of
British preconceptions shaping a view of America. The language of landscape had developed in Britain specifically for the island's manmade envi-
ronment, and it had two purposes: to describe what a person saw of the
country and to decide how valuable, in aesthetic terms, was the experience
of looking at a certain view or tract of the country. But this language,
made for and in Britain, was forced into service willy-nilly to describe the
land of America, which it fitted awkwardly if at all. Nonetheless, the language retained its power and exalted some parts of the state while con-
signing others to aesthetic oblivion.

That descriptions of New York State should be shaped by the author's personality, interests and prejudices, readership, and even the very
language in which the accounts were written, is none too surprising. But
accounts of the New World were shaped in another way—the way in

which people traveled from one place to another. It is a subject of constant comment, and the next pages summarize the complaints and occasional praises of literally hundreds of writers.

TRAVELING IN EARLY NEW YORK STATE

Traveling in the early nineteenth century could hardly be called comfortable, even at the best of times. But the period was unique in that visitors were for the first time presented with a wide array of choices for getting from place to place. At the beginning of the century, traveling in the western regions of the state had involved walking, buying a horse, or rattling around inside a coach on what all commentators agreed were atrocious roads. By 1835 or so, canal boat and railroad carriage offered relatively comfortable and cheap alternatives, and they soon established such a grip on commerce and travel that communities bypassed in the first flush of enthusiastically speculative building searched desperately for their own canals and railroads to revive their economic life.

One example illustrates the enormous effects that greater reliability and speed could make in a visitor's travel plans. After a whirlwind tour of North America in the first half of 1842, Charles Dickens found himself in New York City with five days to kill before embarking for England. He took a scheduled steamer to the river port of Hudson and there hired a private carriage to Lebanon in order to examine one of the most popular of tourist sites: the Shaker colony. The trip was abortive—the Shakers' life had been so severely disrupted by curious visitors that they had temporarily banned outsiders from their services. Dickens, annoyed at being thwarted, dashed off a few memorably vicious phrases about the sect and travestied their religious practices; he still had time for two nights at the West Point hotel before returning to New York City (*American Notes,* p. 246). By contrast, just twenty years earlier it had taken Charles Henry Wilson three full days just to travel the couple of hundred miles from New York to Albany (*Wanderer in America,* p. 35). The difference between the two journeys was the availability of regular steamship service: Wilson had only been able to travel by sloop, at the mercy of wind, tide, and weather.

But transportation involves economics as much as comfort, and the crucial economic importance of good transportation is reflected in the travels of British tourists. Such was the disparity between the new comforts of regular service and the undeveloped areas that while the canal towns from Schenectady to Lockport were frequently visited, Delaware County was largely ignored and Cattaraugus, Chautauqua, and Allegany counties were mere names in a gazeteer.

So obvious were the advantages of reliable, cheap transportation that idiosyncratic travel plans were probably discouraged, at least passively and perhaps actively, by local people. There is no direct evidence of this from the United States, but an Old World episode suggests the pressures on a visitor to use the most modern form of transportation. William Cobbett, traveling in England in the 1820s to report on agricultural conditions, noted that his need to travel off the beaten track brought him problems, and not least in getting accurate directions. Writing at Singleton, Sussex, on August 2, 1823, he says: "In cases like mine, you are pestered to death to find out the way to *set out* to get from place to place. The people you have to deal with are inn-keepers, ostlers, and post-boys; and they think you mad if you *express your wish to avoid turnpike roads;* and a great deal more than half mad, if you talk of going, even from necessity, by any other road."[7] Travelers in the United States, where canals and railroads were the focus of intense local pride, must have experienced similar reactions.

In the early decades of the century, especially the 1820s and 1830s, the newly developing transportation system largely dictated where travelers went and what they saw. Nor was this the sum of its effects, for it also helped to shape travelers' feelings about the places that they visited. As the travel-writers of the time were not on the whole self-reflective, it is rare to find a tourist thinking about the physical factors that shape his or her attitudes to the places passing by. One early exception was John Howison, who spent two and a half years in the Canadas and published a book, *Sketches of Upper Canada,* about his time there and in the United States in 1822. He summarizes the effects of different means of travel in these words: "Dr. Goldsmith somewhere observes, that the man who makes the Grand Tour of Europe on foot will make very different remarks, and form very different conclusions, from him who rolls along in a post-chaise. Nothing can be more true; and, I believe, upon this principle we may ascribe the diversities and contradictions which often characterize the accounts that different persons give of the same country, to the

7. William Cobbett, *Rural Rides* (1830), ed. George Woodcock (Harmondsworth: Penguin, 1967), p. 124.

mode in which they have travelled, and the difficulties they have encountered in the course of their journeys" (p. 64). The means of travel is never, of course, the only factor shaping the traveler's impressions, but the way in which the writer travels does have an important effect along the lines that Howison mentions.

Howison's comments suggest that a greater diversity of opinion will follow as more forms of transportation become available. The writers of the 1830s, the first to use canal boats and railroads as alternatives to coaches and horses, go some way to bearing this out. While travelers were contradicting previous writers from the earliest years of the century, the differences of opinion become sharper and more bitter in the 1830s and the better known a book, the more contrary the published reactions it would provoke. James Stuart's *Three Years in North America,* which approved greatly of most things American, is one such example. Stuart traveled in relative comfort, hiring private carriages and staying with genteel acquaintances or in the better hotels. His impressions of the United States were violently contradicted on virtually every point of substance by Richard Weston, who went to North America partly because of Stuart's glowing accounts. Weston, an Edinburgh bookseller, hated America from the very first day, when someone tried to steal his luggage from the quay in New York City. He traveled mainly on foot and could not afford the luxuries of private travel. It is partly for this reason that his experience provides a sour corrective to Stuart's cushioned optimism. Indeed, Stuart's account of the United States was so roundly attacked that he eventually published a *Refutation of Aspersions* on his original book.

Canals and railroads had other important effects on travelers' impressions of the country. As essentially public forms of transportation, they forced British tourists into close contact with a wide cross section of Americans — a section, indeed, wider than that which travelers met in Britain. More people traveled in America, and more kinds of people traveled, fostering an appearance of classlessness that revulsed conservatives and tested the theoretical approval of paper liberals. Whatever their reactions, however, travelers soon saw hints of the breadth of American society. The Quaker Abolitionist Joseph Sturge, for example, who traveled with John Greenleaf Whittier in the late 1830s, describes few of the fabled views from his Hudson River steamboat. He was too occupied talking with two of his fellow passengers, escaped slaves heading for Canada (*Visit to the United States,* pp. 52.53). And the famous were just as likely to use public transport: James Finlay Weir Johnston bumped into Henry Clay on the train between Albany and Syracuse (*Notes on North America,* 1: 154.55).

Americans were famous throughout Europe for their restlessness. The huge and sparsely populated country, masses of immigrants, the lure of western lands, and the premium wages that even unskilled labor could command there, the intensely commercial bent of American life—these and many other causes were listed by tourists avid to explain a social and geographical mobility that appeared extraordinary from the perspective of densely settled and socially stratified Britain. Authors interpreted this mobility according to their prejudices, both as symptomatic of the new country's intense, "go-ahead" vitality and as evidence of social insecurity and incipient anarchy. That Americans traveled more widely and more frequently than other nationalities, however, no one denied.

Rubbing elbows with this large, motley population disconcerted many of those British travelers who were able to purchase special treatment in Europe. Francis Marryat, in particular, was incensed by the lack of privacy. "The Americans are such locomotives themselves," he wrote in his *Diary,* despairingly, "that it is useless to attempt the incognito in any part except the west side of the Mississippi, or the Rocky Mountains" (p. 79).

The legion shocks of American democracy were eventually more important in the mass than in the particular, and close contact with large numbers of restless, curious Americans was in large part due to the use of public transport. Thus did canal packet, railroad, and stagecoach help to condition views of the country published in Britain.

Transportation also helped to change the kinds of British travelers who published reactions to America. In the era of sloops on the Hudson and carriages or packhorses in the western counties, the decision to travel in America was based on the traveler's having long periods of free time. The visitors of the earliest decades of the century tended to stay in North America for many months, even years, before returning to Britain. By the 1840s the speed and reliability of transatlantic steamships, Hudson and Champlain steamers, railroads, and canal boats allowed tourists previously limited to Europe and jaded with its familiar wonders to spend a summer exploring in America and still be back in Britain for the opening of London's social "season" in the autumn. These tourists' impressions tend to be more fragmentary and rushed, and their narrowing agenda and greater superficiality were helped by the newer, faster forms of transportation. As Marryat notes in his *Diary* about the new railroads: "Travellers proceed more rapidly, but they lose all the beauty of the country" (p. 78).

Travelers in North America, especially those who wrote for prospective immigrants and future travelers, devoted much of their writing to various ways of getting from place to place. Each had for tourists its own particular advantages and disadvantages, novelties and commonplaces; and each was affected differently by changing weather and the season in which the journey was made. Each sort of travel blocked out certain kinds of impression and stressed others, and every book published about North America results in part from the individual visitor's choice among the various forms of transport available.

Upstate Roads

Many travelers voiced their complaints, often shrilly, about the poor condition of American roads. In fairness it should be noted that roads in Britain were often just as bad. MacAdam's all-weather surface and the turnpike associations were improving the main trunks, it is true, and the Dover to Canterbury and Portsmouth to London rides were known as relatively smooth and comfortable. Away from the main roads, however, conditions varied widely. The direct route between two points often resembled a cross-country course, impossible for coaches at any time and after rain often difficult even for an unencumbered horseman.

But these considerations gave scant comfort to travelers in North America.[8] Any use of the roads posed severe problems. Walking was slow, awkward, and, in the country, it was often frustratingly difficult to identify the track at all. Richard Weston, trusting to an old and inaccurate map for a short cut across Warren County between Warrensburg and his nephew's house in the Luzerne hills, wanted to avoid the extra miles on the main road, which ran through Caldwell (now Lake George).

> The road was distinct enough at first, but became less so as I advanced. I passed several deserted houses and farms, (and a deserted log-house is really a miserable sight) till at last I came to a place where I lost all trace of the road. There was a hill, however, which I recognised to be Pot-Ash, and steered my course by it; but at times, from the undulating nature of the country, I lost sight even of this object. At length I descried a log-house on a cleared spot, which I gained by climbing over a

---

8. For a sanguine account of the turnpike movement and its effects in New York, see Joseph Austin Durrenberger, *Turnpikes: A Study of the Toll Road Movement in the Middle Atlantic States and Maryland* (Valdosta, Ga.: Joseph Austin Durrenberger, 1931), and Oliver W. Holmes, "The Turnpike Era," in Alexander C. Flick, ed., *History of the State of New York,* vol. 5: *Conquering the Wilderness* (New York: Columbia University Press for the New York State Historical Association, 1928): 255–94. British writers of the period were unanimously unimpressed with the achievement of the New York Turnpike Associations.

rail-fence, but had the mortification to find it deserted. I had now to take the woods, with no track to guide myself by; and when I got to the ridge on any of the undulating mounds (they did not deserve the name of hills), other ridges appeared beyond with a gulley between, but no Pot-Ash, nor the vestige of a house or human being. I occasionally saw cattle-tracks, which served only to mislead me. Trees I climbed, but to no purpose; in some places the direction I took seemed the right one, for I had a pocket compass, but it would bring me to nothing but a large trunk of a tree, and several times, in stepping on one of these, my foot would go right through, there being nothing but the outside bark. I proposed at last to follow a stream, as Cooper the American novelist says the Indians do, which ran in the direction I wished; but it was exceedingly serpentine, and coming to a morass on the bank before I was aware, in I plumped up to the middle. With difficulty I got myself extricated, washed my clothes in the stream, and resumed my search, leaving the faithless guidance of the river. The sun was now far past the meridian, the dark sides of the mountain had a dismal and ominous appearance, and I became full of anxiety. (*A Visit to the United States,* pp. 190–91)

After other adventures with rotting bridges, nonexistent footpaths, and unfriendly settlers, he finally met a backwoodsman who saw him safely to his destination.

Even the main highways were frequently little more than packed dirt. If anything, the discomfort was worse in town than in the country: the actor Tyrone Power, for example, gives a graphic description of the dusty streets of Saratoga in high season and suggests that the spa waters might usefully be employed on the streets to keep down the dust (*Impressions of America,* 1: 422).

So annoying could the dust become that travelers were often delighted by the prospect of rain. Too much rain, however, posed even greater problems than too little. The worst time of year for traveling overland was by common consent the time of the spring thaw. Warmer temperatures and rain rapidly transformed roads into quagmires where coaches could easily get stuck or overturn. The legacy of the thaws was felt for the duration of the main traveling season in deep ruts and potholes that resisted efforts to repair them and made a nonsense of the inflated claims of the turnpike companies.

In marshy areas "corduroy" roads were a famous characteristic of travel in America — infamous, rather, for the adjective "execrable" recurs frequently in descriptions of them. James Silk Buckingham, between Buffalo and Batavia, hit "one piece of genuine corduroy road, about a mile in length, composed wholly of logs, or trees with the bark on, laid horizontally across the road, and the interstices loosely filled up with earth, [which] shook us terribly, and gave us some idea of the misery of travelling, for any length of time, on such a rough and jolting way" (*America*, 3: 43). Yet as an ingenious solution to the problem of driving roads through swamps, corduroy roads were as fascinating to some as the great wooden bridges at Rochester and at the northern end of Lake Cayuga — one among the many species of local exotica.[9]

Indeed, American ingenuity in finding new ways to travel was noted by many British authors. Their approbation tends to focus around the great steamers of the Hudson River, though even here there were dissenters. Andrew Bell called them the "least picturesque" of vessels, a major condemnation in the eyes of the genteel traveler: "Their smoking chimneys, their ungraceful and worse than dromedary projections, give the idea of a floating foundry" (*Men and Things in America,* p. 40). But he in turn was fascinated by the solution Americans had concocted for a more local problem, how to cross the Hudson River between Albany on the west bank and Greenbush and the New England highway, on the east.

> At both sides of an immense raft, solid and broad enough to accommodate half a dozen loaded waggons, is placed a horse, each with his head turned diverse ways; they are enclosed in a kind of shed, open at the sides from about mid-height, and when the ferryman gave the word they both commenced walking, but without advancing a single inch, and continued to do so till we had got quite across the river. Every forward movement they made was immediately lost by the retrograde motion of a kind of wheels they were placed on, which all the while kept turning briskly round. Here, then, were two innocent and docile animals put to the tread-mill! This vertical movement of the side wheels is communicated by means of cranks to a kind of paddles, placed under the bottom of the raft, and thus is the thing cleverly brought about. (pp. 65–66)

(Harriet Martineau thought this cruel usage of the horses and hoped a proposed tunnel would bring the swift demise of the contraption.[10])

9. On corduroy roads see, for example, Fowler, *Journal of a Tour,* pp. 117–19, and Tudor, *Narrative of a Tour,* 1: 148–51.

10. Martineau, *Retrospect of Western Travel,* 1: 109; cf. Stuart, *Three Years in North America,* 1: 51–52.

Though a few hardy souls walked and others bought horses for their overland travel, most early tourists relied on coaches for their journeyings around New York State. Some hired extra exclusives, other depended on the scheduled runs of the mail coaches and stagecoaches. Coaches, however, had one major disadvantage for the conscientious sightseer. Here once again is the irrepressible William Cobbett, who had decided opinions about everything and detested, in the words of his editor, "canals and stage-coaches, tea and potatoes, and [he] lived long enough to lay his curse on the railways."[11] His feelings about coaches and their effects on the traveler's perceptions of the countryside are set forth in a typically vigorous passage written at East Everly, Wiltshire, on August 27, 1826. "There is no pleasure in travelling, except on horse-back, or on foot. Carriages take your body from place to place; and, if you merely want to be *conveyed,* they are very good; but they enable you to see and to know nothing at all of the country."[12]

The basic problem of visibility was compounded in the United States by the local design of carriages. The standard coach was far bulkier than English models, designed to withstand the greater shocks of American conditions. Adam Fergusson describes in detail the coaches in which he traveled.

> The American stage-coach, clumsy and unwieldy as it looks, is by no means an uncomfortable vehicle, and certainly withstands shocks, the least of which would demolish the best article ever launched from Long-Acre. It is suspended upon leather springs of great strength, and carries nine inside passengers, six of whom are seated face to face, and three upon a moveable seat in the centre, with their faces forward, and backs supported by a broad strap. On account of this middle department, you enter only on one side. The panels are open, and provided with curtains to draw close when required. The luggage is stowed away in ample reservoirs before and behind, and the only outside seat is a share of the coach-box to those who can maintain their post. For my own part, although I tried it, with a strong desire to see the country and to chat with *coachee,* I found it absolutely beyond my skill, after divers attempts, to *hold on.* (*Practical Notes,* pp. 45–46)

The sides of the coach were open, not paneled as in England, "and have pieces of leather, like curtains, which serve as weather screens [*sic*],

11. Woodcock's Introduction to Cobbett, *Rural Rides,* p. 19.
12. Cobbett, *Rural Rides,* p. 294.

and are let down and rolled up at pleasure" (Fidler, *Observations on Professions,* p. 119). Any sort of inclement weather, then, would prevent the passengers from watching the countryside roll by. Yet the leather screens were seldom adequate to save passengers from a drenching in storms, and they often made the journey oppressively stuffy (as, among others, Henry Tudor notes in *Narrative of A Tour,* p. 150).

Drawn by four horses, usually sturdy and strong, and driven by an often independently minded coachman, this pattern of one-doored, open-sided carriage was used for regular stage runs and for private hire. The springs of the vehicle deadened the worst of the shocks but, as the roads were so uneven, seldom protected passengers entirely from bruises. Fergusson's reactions are unusual. "We found our roads to-day, for the most part, very indifferent, and were kept in constant motion," he recalls of a journey between Auburn and Utica, "jolting and bumping about in high style, all taking it in good humour, and enjoying our laugh in turn, as each came in contact with his neighbour's head" (*Practical Notes,* p. 187). The vast majority of travelers failed to find amusement in such circumstances. Most, indeed, limited their praise to marveling at the skill of American drivers in avoiding fatal accidents.

Those travelers who hired an extra exclusive were able to dictate the pace and route of their journey. Most travelers, however, relied on regular coaches and were subject to the tyranny of timetables. This tyranny became worse as connections between different forms of travel multiplied. It only extended to the time of departure, however, the time of arrival at one's destination being largely a matter of luck and weather conditions. The mail coaches, for example, stopped frequently to make deliveries and, as the mail was not presorted, the resulting delays often infuriated passengers in a hurry. Frances "Fanny" Wright, however, found some amusement in the performance between driver and postmaster, as here, in a letter written in September 1819.

At Carthage [now part of Rochester] we found the postmaster, very naturally fast asleep; after much clatter against his door and wooden walls, he made his appearance with a candle, and according to custom, the whole contents of the mail were discharged upon the floor. The poor Carthaginian rubbed his eyes, as he took one letter after another from the heap before him; but his dreams seemed still upon him. 'Not a letter can I see,' he exclaimed, as he again rubbed his eyes, and snuffed his candle. 'Friend, lend me your eyes, or you may just take the whole load away with you.' 'I am none of the best at decyphering hand-writing,' replied the driver. 'Why then I

must call my wife, for she is as sharp as a needle.' The wife was
called and, in gown and cap, soon made her appearance; the
candle and the papers placed in the middle, wife, husband,
and driver, set about decyphering the hieroglyphics; but that
the wife had the character of being as sharp as a needle, I
should have augured ill of the labours of this triumvirate.
Whether right or wrong, however, the selection was soon
made, and the budget once again committed to the wagon.
(*Views of Society,* pp. 230-31)

American coaches were not the only way to travel the roads of New
York State. In winter two-horse sleighs were much used in country districts, the passengers wrapped up in buffalo hides and, to prevent frostbite,
sometimes wearing nose masks. Travelers hired packhorses occasionally,
or bought a wagon and pair, and set their own pace and itinerary. But the
wholesale migration to canal packet and railroad as they became available bears eloquent testimony to the discomforts of travel by road.

New York's Waterways

If the roads were so roundly condemned, it was at least in part because so many British tourists were introduced to New York traveling in a
vehicle both exhilarating and almost universally praised. The steamboats
of the Hudson River, though soon to be eclipsed in the popular imagination by the floating palaces of the Mississippi, revolutionized travel on the
river and brought Albany progressively closer to New York City—by 1836 a
mere ten hours' effortless journey. The Hudson River boats spawned
equally opulent services on Lakes Champlain, Ontario, and Erie. John
Fowler's reaction is typical of the astonished Briton. Boarding in New
York City, "The *Albany,*" he was moved to write, "is the most splendid
conveyance I ever moved in, in my life" (*Journal of a Tour,* p. 38). Then,
like some medieval bestiarist piling marvel on marvel, he notes that he has
heard the *North America,* which he has not seen, is an even more remarkable vessel. As a couple of fairly detailed descriptions of the *North America* survive in the pages of British tourists, the ship can stand as a type
of the Hudson steamers of the 1820s and 1830s and the reactions they
provoked.

The *North America* was launched in 1827 from William Capes's
New York shipyards. With a gross weight of 497 tons, she was 218 feet
long and 30 feet wide, riding 8 feet deep in the water and powered by 2
wood-burning beam engines. She was first owned by Robert L. Stevens
and in 1832 became part of the New York, Albany & Troy Line (the Hud-

son River Steamboat Association). A day boat on the New York to Albany run, and one of the fastest, she was eventually wrecked in the spring thaw of 1839 when the breakup of the ice carried her down river from her moorings at the Albany docks. The name, however, lived on in another steamer, one of the first of the anthracite burners, launched later that same year.[13]

Thomas Hamilton rode the *North America* from New York City to Hyde Park in early December 1830. The cold forced him below for much of the journey, and as a result he gives us a rare description of the interior of the ship.

> The accommodation . . . consisted of two cabins, which I guessed, by pacing them, to be a hundred and fifty feet in length. The sternmost of these spacious apartments is sumptuously fitted up with abundance of mirrors, ottomans, and other appurtenances of luxury. The other, almost equally large, was very inferior in point of decoration. It seemed intended for a sort of tippling-shop, and contained a *bar,* where liquors of all kinds, from Champagne to small beer, were dispensed to such passengers as have inclination to swallow, and money to pay for them. The sides of both of these cabins were lined with a triple row of sleeping-berths; and as the sofas and benches were likewise convertible to a similar purpose, I was assured, accommodation could be easily furnished for about five hundred. (*Men and Manners in America,* 1: 47–48)

The lavish scale of the meals on board, which cost a flat fifty cents per person per sitting, excited as much notice as the rapidity with which Americans consumed their food. James Stuart traveled on the *North America* early one summer in the late 1820s and spent most of his time on deck, but he also gives a vivid picture of mealtimes on the vessel.

> We had breakfast and dinner in the steam-boat. The stewardess observing, that we were foreigners, gave notice to my wife some time previous to the breakfast-bell at eight, and dinner-

---

13. Based on information in David Lear Buckman, *Old Steamboat Days on the Hudson River,* rev. ed. (New York: The Grafton Press, 1909). John Howison Morrison, in his *History of American Steam Navigation* (1903; rpt. New York: Argosy Antiquarian Ltd., 1967), p. 58, says the *North America* was sunk by ice just below Albany while on a scheduled trip from New York City in late 1839. For technical details of the early boats, see Donald C. Ringwald, *Hudson River Day Line* (Berkeley, Calif.: Howell-North Books, 1965), Chap. 1.

bell at two, so that we might have it in our power to go to the
cabin, and secure good places at table before the great stream
of passengers left the deck. Both meals were good, and very
liberal in point of quantity. The breakfast consisted of the
same articles that had been daily set before us at the city hotel,
with a large supply of omelettes in addition. The equipage and
the whole style of the thing good. The people seem universally
to eat more animal food than the British are accustomed to
do, even at such a breakfast as this, and to eat quickly.

The dinner consisted of two courses, 1. of fish, including
very large lobsters, roast-meat, especially roast-beef, beef-
steaks, and fowls of various kinds, roasted and boiled, potatoes and vegetables of various kinds; 2. which is here called
the dessert, of pies, puddings, and cheese.

Pitchers of water and small bottles of brandy were on all
parts of the table; very little brandy was used at that part of
the table where we sat. A glass tumbler was put down for each
person; but no wine-glasses, and no wine drank. Wine and
spirits of all sorts, and malt liquors, and lemonade, and ice for
all purposes, may be had at the bar, kept in one of the cabins.
There is a separate charge for every thing procured there; but
no separate charge for the brandy put down on the dinner-
table, which may be used at pleasure. The waiters will, if desired, bring any liquor previously ordered, and paid for to
them, or at the bar, to the dining-table.

Dinner was finished, and most people again on deck in less
than twenty minutes. They seemed to me to eat more at breakfast
than at dinner. I soon afterwards looked into the dining-room,
and found that there was not a single straggler remaining at his
bottle. Many people, however, were going into and out of the
room, where the bar is railed off, and where the bar-keeper was
giving out liquor.

The men of colour who waited at table were clean-looking,
clever, and active—evidently picked men in point of appearance.
(*Three Years in North America,* 1: 41–43)

The only fault that Stuart can find is—shades of Mrs. Trollope!—the universal presence of "spit-boxes."

Yet there was a darker side to steamers, which travelers occasionally
experienced. Designed for smooth waters, steamers were extremely uncomfortable when storms caught them away from the shore, and from
time to time a collision would enliven a scheduled sailing. Such accidents
were rare, and those that did occur were often the result of the several ri-
valries among captains of competing lines. But perhaps the greatest in-

conveniences were provoked by the inability of genteel travelers to avoid the crush of humanity on the classless steamers. Archibald Montgomery Maxwell is unusual in taking it all in his stride, if with a tinge of condescension. "In these steam ships, or steam towns, rather, one encounters all the world" (*A Run through the United States,* 2: 40).

By the late 1830s almost a hundred steamers plied the Hudson and another thirty Lake Ontario; and, on the whole, there was remarkable unanimity among British visitors that these vessels expressed the American genius for innovation and travel. The man-made waterways that opened the interior of the state for rapid settlement, the canals, though in many ways a greater technical achievement, stimulated a far more constrained admiration. Though many used the canals, few described them with the fervent wonder associated with the floating miracles of New York's rivers and lakes.

One of the major problems was that the canal packets were, individually, unprepossessing vessels. Only in the recitation of statistics — 8 years and 4 months to build at a cost of $9 million, 83 locks, 18 aqueducts, 363 miles — does the greatest canal, the Erie, enjoy a reflection of its central importance in the development of New York State. But such considerations were for the majority of British visitors no more than abstractions. While reassuringly smooth after the jolts administered by poorly maintained roads, a journey of any distance on the canal was to most tourists, it has to be admitted, unrelievedly dull. Landscapes from a canal boat were on the whole uninteresting, as construction costs mandated a route through the most level parts of the state. The cabins were stuffy in warm weather and the slow monotony of the journey was uncomfortably interrupted by low bridges that required outside passengers to flatten themselves to the deck on pain of decapitation.

Often other passengers were in themselves major inconveniences; more so than on the steamers, whose long decks promised some relief from the attention of bores. Harriet Martineau suffered as much as anyone. Not only did the usual heat and "the known vicinity of a compressed crowd, lying packed like herrings in a barrel" spoil her night's sleep. Sixteen Presbyterian clergymen on their way to a convention in Utica monopolized the cabin by day, inflicting their devotions on the other passengers "in a most unjustifiable manner." Martineau's being deaf gave her a slight advantage over her fellow travelers, who were forced to listen to interminable graces, scripture readings, and long-winded testimony on the joys of temperance. Still, the heat, dirt, and religious enthusiasm compounded her dissatisfaction with the boats of the Erie Canal and made the civilities of Bagg's Hotel in Utica doubly welcome (*Retrospect of Western Travel,* 1: 117–20).

The passenger packets were built to a standard pattern. Usually about sixty feet long, two-thirds of the below-decks area was by day a common cabin and after the evening meal divided into two cabins, the sleeping quarters for men and women. Most carried newspapers and a small library of light fiction and worthy pamphlets to help pass the tedious hours (Walter Scott's novels were ubiquitous). Meals were included in the price of the voyage and were generally approved.

Several writers were amused by the ingenious conversion of dining room to bedroom after supper was done. Henry Caswall notes: "Along the sides of the cabin, small narrow berths were fixed one above another, partly resting against the wall, and partly suspended by strong wires from the roof. A third row of berths was suspended from the centre of the ceiling, and ran like the two others the whole length of the gentlemen's cabin. These arrangements were made with wonderful celerity; and about fifty passengers retired in good order to repose" (*America and the American Church*, pp. 14–15). But many travelers hated the forced intimacies of communal sleeping. Actress Frances Anne "Fanny" Kemble, for instance, though not the most retiring of people and an actress by profession, refused to undress in "the horrible hen-coop allotted to the female passengers." She spent the night on a small bunk, fully clothed (*Journal,* 2: 245).

The canal boat was nevertheless by any criterion the safest form of travel. Night travel was especially dangerous in a coach or a steamer, but the canal packet traveled inexorably onward, guided by "two goose quills . . . fastened upright on either extremity of the deck, next the bow; a light from below is reflected upon the feathers, which appear to the man at the helm like two flames of fire" (Levinge, *Echoes from the Backwoods,* 1: 257). Winter closed the canals for some four or five months each year, but they still carried most of the flood of immigrants heading west and created great new cities along their banks — cities, however, that are seldom described in detail from the packets' decks because of British writers' decreasing interest in America's commercial life. The longueurs of canal travel concentrated the attention of passengers on the packet boat itself, their fellow passengers, and their boredom. Passing monotonously at some four miles an hour, the land through which the canal passed seldom received more than cursory notices.

Early Railroads

The success of the Erie Canal, whose formal opening was celebrated with great rejoicings in late October and early November 1825, spawned numerous feeder canals.[14] British visitors deserted New York's atrocious roads for the canal boats in droves. They would in turn desert the canal for the next latest thing in travel—the railroad. The 1830s, after fifteen years of state funding of canal development and expansion, saw the first movement of passengers away from the canals of New York. Bulk freight was reserved by law to the canals until 1847, and the first flimsy railroads concentrated entirely on moving people. But they moved people very well. British travel writers tended to use the railroads wherever possible for the cachet of being up-to-date, the greater speed, and the direct comparability of British and American railroads. But it was speed that was of the essence: the new, fast trains coincided with and in turn helped to spur shorter stays in the United States.

The predictability of the average tourist's journey was reinforced by the pattern of railroad building in New York State. The first line to go into operation was between Albany and Schenectady, opened on August 9, 1831. Isaac Fidler traveled on this line before its completion, when only a single line of tracks had been laid. "This was the easiest and pleasantest part of my land journey," he recalled later, "and about seventeen miles" (*Observations on Professions,* p. 119). The memory forms a springboard for a redoubled attack on the discomforts of travel by road and the clumsy design of American coaches. By 1842 sufficient short lines had been built between the cities of the canal route that the journey from Buffalo to Albany entirely by railroad was possible. By contrast, North Country towns were not open to the railroads until the 1850s, and the southern railroad, planned to run from Piermont on the Hudson to Dunkirk on Lake Erie, had, to put it tactfully, a checkered financial history. This, the Erie Railroad, went into bankruptcy during the Panic of 1837 and was moribund for a decade afterward. The line was completed and in operation by 1851 but was bankrupted again by 1857.[15] The major problem from the point of view of the middle-class British visitor was not the solvency of the company, however; it was that the Erie Railroad did not go anywhere known from previous authors to be worth visiting. The cu-

14. On the opening, see Cadwallader Colden, *Memoir . . . of the Completion of the New York Canal* (New York: W. A. Davis for the Corporation of New York, 1825). For a detailed account of the Erie and Champlain canals and their feeders, see Noble E. Whitford, *History of the Canal System of the State of New York,* vol. I (Albany: Bradford Printing Co., 1906).

15. Based on David Maldwyn Ellis et al., *A Short History of New York State* (Ithaca: Cornell University Press in Cooperation with the New York State Historical Association, 1957), pp. 250–53. For a contemporary account, see Lardner, *Railway Economy,* esp. Chap. 16.

mulation of description already favored the towns of the northerly route, from Albany to Niagara Falls and Buffalo, overwhelmingly. Though the brush-fire rapidity of railroad construction would soon present many new opportunities to the more adventurous traveler, shorter stays in the United States and a firm itinerary of sights worth seeing made the truly adventurous traveler an ever-rarer bird.

The early railroads depended largely on the carriage industry for coaches and body work, and the first trains were often oddly hybrid. Indeed, many lines started operation with horse-drawn carriages running on fixed rails, a steam locomotive only being purchased after the track had proven itself reasonably stable and the route profitable. On steep inclines horse-drawn trains survived longer, awaiting the development of more robust locomotives. Charles Augustus Murray traveled on such a railroad in the mid-thirties, between Ithaca and Owego. He thought it a token of the future. "Horse power is here used, and the road is none of the best; in some places there were only wooden rails for the wheel-track, in others the horses had to raise their feet at each step over the logs which support the rails; however, the grading, which is the chief difficulty, is overcome. The route, although but a poor railroad at present, is nevertheless an evidence of incipient improvement, and as such is commendable" (*Travels in North America,* 2: 240). The use of horses persisted in some towns: a train would become a sort of horse-drawn tram within the city limits, taking on a locomotive for the longer journeys through the countryside.

Yet railroads, unlike canals, provoked remarkably few detailed descriptions. Their speed, the brevity of early trips, and the difficulty of writing notes on the spot were certainly factors in this, but more importantly American trains were, unlike the Erie Canal and the Hudson steamers, very similar to their British counterparts. Thus the reading public's familiarity with railroad travel severely limited passages devoted to the American variety—with one exception, the lack of first-class seats and the consequent mingling of passengers without regard for social status. Those passages that did survive into print were often no more than a recitation of (often garbled) statistics. It is as though the unparalleled speed and technical complexity of railroads stunned the authors of the day: railroads differed qualitatively from earlier modes of traveling and would not develop writers who could comprehend them until later in the century. In the interim travel writing suffered in its regard for detail.

The three decades from 1815 to 1845 saw profound changes in New York State and particularly in its transportation network. The opening of the

Erie Canal and many of its feeder canals, and the rapid expansion of steamer traffic and the railroad system altered the complexion of travel in the state irrevocably. In 1815 much of upstate west of the Hudson was still a frontier area, with slow, unreliable, and uncomfortable transportation. Traveling depended heavily on the determination of the individual traveler. By 1845 the earlier gazeteers about places were being replaced by timetables, the forerunners of Bradshaw and Baedecker. The new means of transportation ran to schedules and, moreover, on fixed routes. The movement away from bad roads is, therefore, simultaneously a movement towards a more predictable itinerary.

There are numerous facets to this change from a tour to "The Tour." Those who wrote for potential immigrants had tended to stay longer in New York State and to explore it thoroughly. As their interests switched to the newly opened lands of the more westerly states, so surviving accounts of New York tended to come from an ever more homogeneous group of tourists: mainly upper middle class, mainly on holiday, mainly seeking diversion and amusement.

The dozens of accounts of America from earlier times, while varying in focus, all had turned their readers' attention to the great sights of New York, such as the Hudson and Niagara. These common highlights of early tours come to dominate the pages of later travelers to the exclusion of other destinations. The itinerary becomes firmer and more predictable.

Nor was it simply that previous authors had mapped out the route. As more visitors to New York, both British and American, traveled this one route, for whatever reasons, so the facilities for tourists along that route improved. A more genteel group of travelers was faced by 1840 or so with an ever greater disparity between the predictable comforts of the grand itinerary and the discomforts attendant on striking out on one's own. There were, of course, hotels everywhere, for Americans were notoriously great travelers. But the better hotels on The Tour improved more rapidly than those in smaller country towns; and one skirmish with bedbugs was often enough to drive the tourist back to Bagg's Hotel in Utica, the United States Hotel at Saratoga, or Delavan's Temperance House in Albany.

As public transport improved, so tourists' expectations expanded. The east coast ceased to dominate travel plans as British travelers heard of the exotic wonders of Cincinnati and Chicago; the Mormons replaced the Shakers as *the* weird sect to visit; and the steamers of the Mississippi surpassed those of the Hudson in the popular imagination. This wider appreciation of America's variety coincided with shorter visits to the western hemisphere (in themselves partly contingent upon faster, more reliable public transport). And so, by about 1850, with more to see and less time to see it in, tourists devoted fewer pages to details of life in the state, New York, that had earlier in the century provoked whole volumes and occupied at least substantial portions of almost every book about America that saw print.

The public nature of the new forms of transport also had its effects on travel writers. Greater speed, as on the railroads, meant less time to describe the passing countryside; the excision of business matters from polite journals and letters resulted in a greater concentration on the people and less on the places of the United States just as public transport was bringing visitors into inescapable contact with Americans. Ever susceptible to the tall tales of the locals, the tourist in a hurry to reach the next tourist goal on the list became increasingly gullible, more ready to accept the evaluations and opinions of a chance acquaintance as representative of the state or even the entire nation.

THE ACCURACY OF TRAVELERS' ACCOUNTS

Travelers' descriptions are at best partial. Congregating with other tourists, clannishly traveling in small groups, ignorant of commercial life, and taken with an agenda derived from British rather than American needs, tourist interests are at best tangential to those of the state's permanent residents. The Pine Orchard Hotel overlooking the village of Catskill received far more pages, and (because of the authors' knowledge of the trappings of tourism) far more informed description, than the busy industrial centers of Troy or Utica. To stay with this example a moment longer, the Pine Orchard Hotel also commanded far more consistent descriptions than the cities and villages of upstate New York. Indeed, various cities provoke deep disagreements, usually presented as a disagreement with the evaluation of a previous account.

Variety and verisimilitude are, however, not necessarily exclusive properties. While the personalities and interests of particular British visitors are of great importance in deciding what they will write about and how they will present it, variety was by no means entirely in the eye of the beholder. Writers who stayed for longer than a couple of months in New York State during the 1820s and 1830s were uniformly astonished by the rapidity of social and physical change. Rochester and Buffalo, both virtually nonexistent in 1815, were major cities by 1845. As a result of mushroom growth of this magnitude, authors separated by a mere decade, even authors of similar temper and interests, could profoundly disagree about a settlement, a social custom, or an institution without either of them necessarily being inaccurate or a liar.

It is only in comparison that the limitations of travel books about early America become clear. Given the need to move on, it is not surprising that no observer of natural history achieved the detailed excellence of a Gilbert White of Selbourne. For a companion to White it would be necessary to hunt in other fields. But the travelers' accounts of the place are not even flattered when like is compared more nearly to like. No author's work attains the high stylish rage of commitment that infuses every sentence of William Cobbett's vision of the changes in British agricultural economy. Cobbett's agricultural year on Long Island makes us conscious of what we lost in his decision not to travel but rather to stay in one place and live the life of a yeoman farmer. The mills and manufactories of the eastern seaboard find no chronicler of feverish industrial development to challenge Friedrich Engels's passionate dissection of Manchester and the effects of industrial change on people's lives. Nor does any traveler in America achieve the encyclopedic vivacity of Daniel Defoe's catalog of mercantile England.

Although no single author scales these various heights, however, even the most conventional volume of British travel in nineteenth-century New York State contains details and views of the place that are simply unavailable anywhere else. Shaped by the customs of a foreign society and foreign politics, the accounts of British travelers do not merit the oblivion to which all but a handful have been consigned. The light they throw on the changes in the life of the state extend and round out our comprehension of places apparently familiar.

The passages that follow come from the three decades between 1815 and 1845. Each is biased to some extent by the character and purpose of the traveler, each is shaped by the way in which its writer traveled. Yet, though personal character and the chosen mode of travel impose common constraints, writers frequently escape those shackles of predictability through idiosyncrasies of expression, determination, and sheer serendipity. Together they sample the response of the richest nation on earth to the most important state of the nation that both fascinated and appalled it, and that would eventually take over its global eminence.

The Hudson Valley

THE HUDSON VALLEY was universally known for scenery second in the New World only to Niagara Falls. Almost all British travelers appreciated the views and made ritual comparisons with the landscapes of the valley of the Rhine, but they generally made their observations from the decks of the Hudson steamers. Few explored life beyond the river banks in any detail.

Certain steamer halts, it is true, attracted travelers with special interests. Ossining drew its share of disembarking passengers curious about the experimental state penitentiary at Sing Sing. Tarrytown became an increasingly important port of call for literary pilgrims after 1832, when Washington Irving took up residence there. Both the military academy and the prospects from Fort Putnam made West Point a frequent resting place. The world renown of the surgery professor and botanist David Hosack lured visitors to Hyde Park; his estate, his hospitality, and his botanical collections were recorded in many accounts. Tourists made uncomfortable by the heat of summer often disembarked at Catskill, and suffered a hair-raising, three-hour coach ride up the hillside to the cool relief of the Mountain House, perhaps the most famous of all America's resort hotels. Indeed, a heat wave was not necessary to stimulate the visit — the hotel offered spectacular views of the Hudson Valley, which proved sufficient inducement to many Britons.

At the same time Americans were working, so to speak, with a different map of the river. The major halts for them were the commercial centers — Newburgh, Poughkeepsie, Kingston, and Hudson — places under-represented in the accounts of British travelers, who usually noted them, if at all, from the passing ships. Albany and New York City acted as powerful magnets, pulling most visitors away from the counties of the river bank.

Yet several books by travelers driven by more than simple tourist interests go beyond an inventory of views. Henry Fearon examined Fishkill carefully as a potential home, while of rural life in Dutchess County, among the townships east of Poughkeepsie, two descriptions by Britons have survived. Together, they provide a detailed portrait of the area in the 1830s and 1840s. By way of contrast is an account of the dominant political families, the Van Burens and the Van Rensselaers, of the Hudson Valley.

THE FISHKILL AREA IN 1817

With the end of the Napoleonic wars and the War of 1812, the latter a minor contretemps from the European perspective, economic conditions in Britain worsened to the point that people of capital, tradesmen and farmers, started seriously to consider emigration. One group of thirty-nine families commissioned Henry Bradshaw Fearon, associated with the London wine merchants of Coates and Fearon, to travel for them and "to ascertain whether any, and what part of the United States would be suitable for their residence." Fearon wrote detailed letters about rents, prices, and conditions, but his travels were cut short by the publication of Morris Birkbeck's Notes *on his English colony in Illinois. The book caused a great sensation and attracted several of Fearon's sponsors; he in turn criticized it as symptomatic of a delusive enthusiasm for the United States, and published his own reports to counteract its effects.*

Fearon was diligent in examining conditions, traveling throughout the east coast, west to Illinois, and as far south as New Orleans. He also attempted a general assessment of America, and his conclusion that the character of the Americans fell far short of their political principles angered his new world readers. "I beg leave to assure Mr. Fearon," wrote Edward Allen Talbot several years later in his Five Years' Residence in the Canadas, *"that on revisiting New York, he will meet with a very unwelcome reception" (2: 372).*

Just after his arrival in New York in early August 1817, Fearon received a letter from a Mr. De Wint offering to sell his group a considerable tract of land in Dutchess County. Fearon set out at once to investigate.

Wishing to see Mr. De Wint's property,[1] at Fishkill, . . . I took passage in the steam-boat "Chancellor Livingstone;" fare 3½ dollars, distance 60 miles, time of departure five o'clock in the evening, of arrival half past one the following morning. This vessel is, perhaps, equalled by none in the world: she may be denominated, without the charge of exaggeration, a floating palace; her length is 175 feet, and breadth 50, and she is propelled by a steam-engine of 80 horse power; there are beds for 160, and accommodation for 40 more by settees. The ladies have a distinct cabin: they seem cut off from all association or conversation with the gentlemen. On deck there are numerous conveniences, such as baggage rooms, smoking rooms, &c.; on the descent to the cabins are placed cards of tradesmen and hotels in the chief cities, and also religious tracts, which are chiefly reprints of English evangelical effusions — affording another instance of the slavish dependence of America upon British writers. The interior of this vessel is extremely splendid. The late period of the day at which we embarked, allowed me but a limited opportunity of viewing the bold and grand scenery of this majestic river. Near the banks is erected a monument to that great ornament of the federal party, Hamilton;[2] he was in the administration, and some say the director of Washington. Those who knew him best, state that he was a man far above the ordinary standard of public characters: endowed, indeed, with such talents as but few mortals are destined to possess; he was deprived of life by the celebrated Mr. Aaron Burr, thus adding another and a splendid victim to the barbarous practice of duelling — which, by the way, is very general and almost uniformly fatal in this country. A slight provocation produces a challenge, and if the parties consider themselves of what is called "equal standing," that is, of families and in worldly circumstances of equal respectability, they rarely decline the combat; and the Americans being generally good shots, and as remarkable for their cool deliberation as, too frequently, for deadly malignity, it is seldom that both parties escape with life. . . .

The boat in which I had embarked for Fishkill was well filled with passengers. The general occupation was card-playing; one or two had a book in their hands: those whose beds were in the births fitted up for that

From Henry Bradshaw Fearon, *Sketches of America: A Narrative of a Journey of Five Thousand Miles through the Eastern and Western States of America. . . ,* 3d ed. (London: Longman, Hurst, Rees, Orme, and Brown, 1819), pp. 75-77, 78-85.

1. John Peter De Wint (1787-1870) had been given a two-thousand-acre estate at Fishkill by his father, a Dutch immigrant from the West Indies.

2. Alexander Hamilton died in New York City the day after his duel with Aaron Burr on July 11, 1804 at Weehawken, New Jersey.

purpose were passengers going the entire route (to Albany), and who had taken the precaution to have their names early entered in a book kept by the captain for that purpose. Mr. Tompkins, the Vice-president of the United States,[3] was among the number going to Albany, the seat of the New York State government: he was seated among the other passengers, without assuming consequence, or receiving any particular attention. In person he is of the middle size, in complexion dark, with a countenance at that time thoughtful to an extreme; he is taller than Mr. Waithman,[4] but in other respects the latter gentleman will convey an idea of his cast of character: his solemnity may not have been habitual, for I am told by those who knew him, that he carries jocularity and lively good-nature to an extreme.

Newburgh, the town where I stopped, is 60 miles from New York; I obtained a bed after one or two unsuccessful applications at the hotels which keep open regularly for steam-boat passengers. The following morning I crossed the Hudson to Fishkill-landing. The gentleman to whose house I was going was a fellow-passenger in the ferry-boat, though at that time unknown to me. The property for sale consisted of one hundred acres of land, and fourteen small frame (not log) houses; the price for the whole is 25,000 dollars (5625l.): there is on this lot a neat frame church, which may be purchased for 2500 dollars (562l. 10s.); it is not fitted up, except a few common seats, and a pulpit of rather primitive simplicity. A credit of four years will be given, charging the interest: the present cash price is not lower.

Mr. De Wint's residence is within half a mile: I had the pleasure of dining with him in company with several ladies and gentlemen of a very superior class. The following day Judge Verplank,[5] a neighbouring gentleman and farmer, had the politeness to take me to his house. My reception at both, as well as the style of living, the substantial elegance of the furniture, and the mental talents of the company, was *essentially English*. I felt, indeed, for the first time, that I was once more in your little island.

3. Daniel D. Tompkins (1774–1825) had been governor of the state from 1809 to 1817, and was vice-president until his death. He was described by contemporaries as aged prematurely by overwork and (apparently baseless) charges of having profiteered from the War of 1812.

4. Mr. Waithman was presumably either an acquaintance or a member of one of the thirty-nine families who had commissioned Fearon to investigate America for them.

5. Daniel Crommelin Verplanck (1761–1834) had served in Congress from 1803 to 1809, and as a county judge. The farm in question had been in the family since 1682, when it had been purchased from the Indians.

That *peculiarly* British word *comfort* was well understood in these hospitable mansions. Another thing, too, was here an evident favourite, though, I lament to say, scarcely known on this side the Atlantic — *cleanliness:* the servants also were in their dress neat, and in their manners attentive, forming a striking contrast to what I have too often seen on other occasions. . . .

Servants are usually engaged by the week: enquiry as to character is not practised: blacks and whites are seldom kept in the same house; they are chiefly blacks, and, though held in the most degraded estimation, appear to do almost what they please. The condition of their kitchens is what in England would be considered very objectionable: there seem usually several black friends of the servants in this apartment. Their children I observed frequently sprawling about the floor like kittens or puppies.

Judge Verplank is a large farmer: his sheep, I think, he stated as 500, — a large flock for this country. His land appeared rather barren. — Mr. De Wint informs me that their winters are dry and severe: they commence about the 5th of December, and end by the middle of March. At this time the ice begins to break in the Hudson. The thermometer is from 56 to 70, from the 1st of April to the middle of May; in July and August it is 78 to 90; in March and April the weather is subject to sudden changes: the cold sometimes intense, with much rain and easterly winds. June is a delightful month, as are also part of September, and the whole of October. The summer heats and winter colds are usually extreme. The advance in the value of land, in this part of the State, has made many of the old settlers men of large property. The general style of living consists of a plentiful supply of the necessaries of life, but few of what in England we should call its comforts. I visited the mountain adjoining Fishkill-landing — a walk to the summit was fatiguing, but the prospect amply repaid the labour. The town from which I am now writing (Newburgh), appeared situated in a most delightful and fertile valley, with many fine roads connecting it with several parts of this immense continent. Newburgh has a population of 3000, many of whom are of Dutch descent. There are many new and excellent buildings: the genuine log house I have not yet seen. Paper currency seems to be the only circulating medium: it is of every amount, and with a reputation infinitely varied; being regulated according to the distance, and the reputation of the bank. I see no man in absolute want, nor any who appear particularly anxious about their future prospects. These are, perhaps, the natural signs of an improving country, and one whose resources, so far from being exhausted, are yet not even called wholly into action. . . .

Upon returning from my mountain excursion, I visited Vanskank's cotton manufactory.[6] It is advantageously situated on a fine fall of water, which empties itself into the Hudson. The proprietor conducted me over every part of this establishment. It was erected in 1814, has withstood the brunt of British competition, and is said to be profitable. There are sixteen hundred spindles in operation. Children perform the same kind of labour that they do with us: they receive 3s. 4½d. per week; women, 11s. 3d.; men, 31s. 6d. Every part of the machinery is manufactured on the premises. There is also a general shop or store on the ground floor, at which the work people are supplied with any thing they may want, in payment of their wages. The chief articles made are ginghams, plain chambrays, calicoes, and bed ticks;[7] the latter at a price to exclude English cotton tick. Linens are still imported. The fabric of all the articles is coarser and stronger than ours: the *finishing* department is very defective; but this will be amply compensated by the wear. This concern is modelled upon British establishments. Hearing in New York that native manufactories were ruined, I felt astonished in witnessing the prosperous appearance of Mr. Vanskank's; which may be accounted for perhaps by the able way in which it is conducted, and the excellence of the machinery. Their connection is chiefly with the southern merchants. The question as to the success of domestic manufactories, is one in which I cannot but feel personally a particular interest. My present design is to proceed to the New England States, for further information upon this and other subjects.

FARMING IN DUTCHESS COUNTY, 1830

John Fowler, having marveled at Niagara Falls, made a leisurely return to New York City and his ship back to England in the fall of 1830. He disembarked from the Hudson steamer at Poughkeepsie and stayed with friends, whose anonymity he carefully preserved in his published account, at their home near Hartsville (now Millbrook). The purpose of his tour through New York was to examine agricultural conditions for pros-

6. "Vanskank" is perhaps Peter A. Schenck, who with Philip A. Hone (a one-time mayor of New York City), J. J. Astor, and others had formed the Matteawan Company in about 1812. In 1814 the company built the area's first cotton mill on Fishkill Creek immediately above Schenck's grist mill.
7. The tick is the fabric case of a mattress or bolster.

pective immigrants, and he jotted down notes on prices and crops in a farming journal, which he used to supplement the narrative of his tour. (Another extract from his book, about Buffalo and its environs, appears later.)

September 11th. [1830] — I occupied the early part of this morning in strolling over Poughkeepsie. It stands on the east side of the river, from whence to the village is a pretty steep ascent of about three-quarters of a mile. It was first settled by some Dutch families, nearly 100 years ago, and "the Convention that met to deliberate on the federal constitution, and voted for its adoption, met in this place in 1788."[1] It now contains about 5,000 inhabitants. The streets are well laid out, the two principal ones crossing each other at right angles, and the stores and private residences have a very neat and respectable appearance. There are several churches, or meeting-houses, banks — a very handsome one is now in erection — schools, hotels, breweries, factories, printing establishments, &c. &c. The post road from New York to Albany passes through it, and its trade and intercourse with both those places, particularly the former, since the admirable facilities afforded by steam navigation, are very considerable; it has also an extensive and frequent communication with the Eastern States. In the neighbourhood are some very elegant mansions, situated either upon the bank of the Hudson, with a verdant lawn extending to the water's edge, or upon the heights around, and commanding a fine view of the river and the adjacent country. It is a place which few could see without admiring; — "taken for all in all," I have scarcely met with one, to my taste, worthy of a precedence. The name, *Poughkeepsie,* is of Indian origin, from *apokeepsing — safe harbour.*

From hence I had engaged to pay a visit to a friend, residing near *Hartsville,*[2] distant about eighteen miles in a north-easterly direction, to

From John Fowler, *Journal of a Tour in the State of New York, in the Year 1830; with Remarks on Agriculture in Those Parts Most Eligible for Settlers.* . . . (London: Whittacker, Treacher, and Arnot, 1831), pp. 174–84.

1. The New York Convention ratified the federal Constitution by thirty votes to twenty-seven on July 26, 1788. This unacknowledged quotation comes from Fowler's favorite guidebook, Horatio Gates Spafford, *A Gazetteer of the State of New-York . . .,* rev. ed. (Albany: B. D. Packard, 1824), p. 426. Of Hartsville, Spafford notes the village is "of about 25 buildings, and some mills, on the E. branch of Wappinger's C[reek]" (p. 546).

2. Hartsville became part of Millbrook. Fowler maintains the anonymity of his hosts throughout the passage.

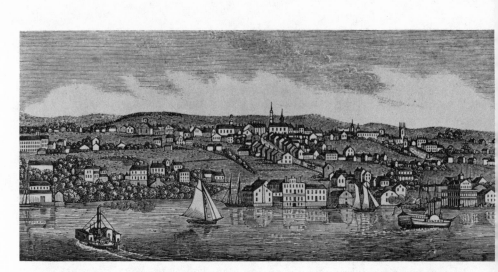

Poughkeepsie: a western view of the city, c. 1840. From John W. Barber and Henry Howe, *Historical Collections of the State of New York* (New York, 1841). Courtesy of the DeWitt Historical Society of Tompkins County, Ithaca

whom I had received no other address — a very customary and certainly a very comprehensive one — than "_____ _____, *Nine Partners*". . . . Fortunately, the family were extensively known, but, *un*fortunately, I missed the morning and only regular coach passing by Hartsville, having been deceived as to the time of its starting, and was conveyed as far as *Pleasant Valley,* seven miles on the road, in a very neat one-horse car, by a person who carried the mail to *Pine Plains,* &c., at the northern extremity of the county. The road was excellent, and the country on either side had a rich and fertile appearance, reminding me much of Herefordshire, and some other counties in England, — but of this anon.

At *Pleasant Valley,* a small village of no particular interest, not meeting with any conveyance to my mind, I determined to walk the remaining eleven miles; a mode of travelling which, notwithstanding my partiality for it, the heat of the day rendered much more fatiguing than agreeable, obliging me to raise my umbrella to protect me *from the rays of the sun;* a thing I have only had occasion to do *once for rain* since I landed. Under these circumstances I was well pleased to gain the door of my friends, where I was received with all the sincerity of an American welcome.

With this kind and hospitable family I spent nearly a week, variously but always agreeably engaged, and each member of it solicitous to add to my pleasures, and promote to the utmost the objects I had in view in visiting the county.

One of our excursions was to *Dover Falls,* east about fifteen miles from Hartsville, which though not of the magnitude of some I have seen, are well worthy of notice; but I mention the circumstance the more from a little feat which on this day it fell to my lot to perform, viz. the slaying of a *rattle-snake.* We were at the time in a very thick part of a wood, and I was just in the act of stepping over a log, on the opposite side of which the creature was lying, coiled up. I had so nearly set my foot upon it, that had it not been a young one I suppose I should not have escaped its envenomed fang; as it was, it was probably large enough to have inflicted a fatal wound, but its disposition seemed to be to retreat with all possible despatch. I had not pursued it far when I was so fortunate as to strike it, and thus capture the prize. It had one rattle perfectly formed, by which I supposed it was two years old, as I believe they have none before that age, and one annually afterwards. When I exhibited it at Dover, on our return, it appeared to excite almost as much curiosity as if such reptiles had never existed in the country; and it was generally determined that one had not been seen in those parts for twenty years or more. . . .

The shades of evening were drawing on ere we took our departure for Hartsville, and I may almost say that we travelled by *starlight,* such was the irradiating brilliancy with which they shone: nothing can surpass the purity of the atmosphere in this county: I have seen skies and sunsets of the richest beauty and splendour, such as England never knows; such as the favoured land of Italy *may equal,* but not outvie; the concurrent testimony of those who have seen both.

On several other days, or parts of days, one of our party and myself were occupied in perambulating the neighbouring country with our guns. We met with little other game than woodcock, which, had we been provided with a brace of good English pointers or setters, would have afforded us excellent diversion: as it was, we killed a considerable number. . . . Whoever designs to sport here, though as I have said it will bear no comparison with English shooting, should take care to provide himself with good dogs; they are scarce, and frequently sell for extravagant prices. I should think a cargo of them would answer better than many another shipment. I know not what amount of commissions in this way I was *favoured* to receive; certainly more than I either promised or should find it very convenient to execute.

Upon these and other occasions during my visit at Hartsville, or

_____ _Cottage,_ I had an opportunity of seeing a good deal of the soil, agriculture, &c. of the county, and of any part of the State in which I have
been—and I think I have been in the best—upon the whole, as a farming
situation, I must now say I should give a decided preference to this. It has
been long settled, and to a considerable extent is well cleared and drained
—the roads are good—the climate remarkably fine—rather more temperate than any other on the Hudson—and, not a trifling recommendation,
the water is excellent, which cannot be said of that of any of the Western
Counties, as I have but too frequently had occasion to notice.—I might
mention other inducements—or which so appear to me—but opinions
differ, and some, I have no doubt, would think the western part of the
State greatly preferable.

There is but a small proportion of land in the county that may not be
converted to the raising of grain, though, perhaps, in general, not more
than one-sixth is under the plough at a time. The produce of all the different kinds of grain is much as in Long Island, and the prices very little
lower; and, though fruit is not grown, as there, for the New York market,
it is the opinion of those to whom I have mentioned the subject, that it
might be, to a very good account.

(_Mem._—From eight to ten bushels of apples will yield thirty gallons
of juice. The value of good sweet cider in New York, in the summer
months, is from 3 to 5 dollars per barrel. The barrel (new) costs 87½
cents; freight to New York, 20 cents. The cartage from the different parts
of the county to the river varies, of course, with distance, from 6 cents to
40 cents.—When the fruit is purchased, what is called _grafted cider_ fruit
(in contradistinction to the natural or indigenous) is from 15 to 40 cents a
bushel. _Table fruit,_ from 25 to 50 cents, and the _natural fruit_ from 6 to 12
cents.)

Wool is considered as the staple produce of the county, and there has
been grown this year about 400,000 lbs.: the price from 50 to 60 cents a
pound. The quality is generally fine, averaging about 3 lbs. to the fleece.

Some flax is raised in the county: price of the seed 125 cents per
bushel; of the flax, cleaned, 12½ cents a pound. Both yard manure and
plaster[3] are much used; the latter article in the quantity of 200 pounds to
the acre; cost on the land 50 cents per acre. Some quantity of manure is
also obtained from the swamps, &c.

Fallowing is but little practised, though, by good farmers, the system is quite approved of.

_____

3. Plaster is sulphate of lime, better known as gypsum, used as a fertilizer to dress
the sandy soil of the region.

Wheat is generally sown after a summer crop of oats or barley.

Farms, in Dutchess County, are to be purchased at from 30 to 60 dollars per acre; much, as elsewhere, depending upon situation, &c.

But little land is rented.

The *halving system* is practised to a limited extent, as in Oneida County.[4]

Labourers' wages the same as in Long Island.

The fences consist of stone and wood: the expense of raising them estimated at from 50 to 70 cents a rod.

Excepting two or three turnpikes, which are not here "the King's highways," but belong to private companies, the roads are repaired by the inhabitants: cost to the farmer about 5 dollars per 100 acres per annum.

Dutchess County is well and respectably populated; the inhabitants chiefly of English and Dutch extraction. Its trade and manufactures are considerable, and in a very thriving state. No mines are in working; but iron, and lime-stone, and marble are found in the county.

The usual times of *seed time* and *harvest,* throughout the State (varying, as in England, a week or two in different parts) are as follow, namely: — Wheat is sown the latter end of September, and cut in July: — Barley the latter end of April, and cut in July: — Oats the latter end of April, and cut in August: — Indian Corn is planted about the middle of May, in the quantity of one peck to the acre, or four grains to the *hill,* in hills three and a half feet apart, and gathered in October.

The *Farm Houses* in general are smaller than in England, and built of wood; the cost of a good one, to erect it, would be from 1,500 dollars to 2,000 dollars. To English taste there is a sad want of neatness observable about them, and even where the establishment is upon an extensive scale, they will be found, in this respect, to fall many degrees below what we are accustomed to see, the *occupier* being merely a *tenant,* and not, as is nearly always the case here [England], the *proprietor:* — as to gardening, laying out ground, &c., with the idea of embellishment, 'tis out of the question. "Here," say the Americans, "the English miss it when they come to this country — these things *don't pay*". . . .

September 18*th.* — On this morning I left _____ *Cottage* for Pough-keepsie, to which place I was accompanied by several of my kind friends, and from thence by some of them down the Hudson to New York. We had a delightful ride.

4. A form of sharecropping. "The terms of this contract are: — the tenant finding half the seed and the teams, doing the whole of the work, and dividing the produce with the landlord" (Fowler, *Journal of a Tour,* pp. 76–77).

MILL AND HARVEST: WORK IN DUTCHESS COUNTY, 1841

In July and August 1841, a Scottish woolcarder and spinner named William Thomson worked at his trade and on the harvest in the vicinity of Washington Hollow. Thomson, bred to the wool trade, had sailed from Liverpool to join his two brothers in Beaufort, South Carolina, in 1840, having been advised that a change of climate would cure a pulmonary disease from which he was suffering. Recovering rapidly during the winter, he set out in February of the following year to travel the United States and Canada as a working man. His account, published in 1842 after his return to Scotland, is a unique compendium of business conditions and information on prospects for skilled workers who intended emigrating from Britain. Fascinated by machinery and the social customs of the areas through which he passed, he managed in his recollections of Dutchess County to portray everyday working life in the rural Hudson Valley, a life invisible to virtually every other writer about America in the first half of the nineteenth century.

Around Poughkeepsie, a town of 10,000 inhabitants, on the banks of the Hudson — where there is plenty of water-power, and where there are several carpet-works within twenty miles of the place — there are at least thirty . . . small establishments. Some of these have as many as eight broadlooms employed, partly on country work, and partly manufacturing for the New York market; at one of them, near Washington Hollow, I wrought for a few weeks, spinning on a hand-jenny of eighty spindles, after a condenser.[1] This place was altogether for country work. A short time ago it was a satinett manufactory. There were eight very good power-looms, but they are not in operation now. The farmers brought the work to the mill in their riding waggons; and when it was for rolls, carried it home with them again to be spun, as in Scotland; but the principal part of the wool brought to mill was left to be manufactured into cloth — flannel, satinett, and broad-cloth. Some paid money, but more wrought on shares; that is, the farmer brought 100 lbs. of wool, which was manufac-

From William Thomson, *A Tradesman's Travels in the United States and Canada* (Edinburgh: Oliver and Boyd, 1842), pp. 124–30, 145, 174–79.

    1. The condenser rolls combed raw wool from the carding-machine into loose bulky threads, ready for spinning.

tured into cloth; the manufacturer receiving one half of the finished goods in payment for his work, and the farmer, who supplied the wool, getting the other half: and this plan is followed very generally through the different states where I have been. Cash is generally paid for carding rolls. The manufacturer pays his store accounts with cloth or yarn; and when he rents the mill of another, part of the rent is not unfrequently paid in kind. Another very common plan is to pay the workmen one half in money and the other in goods. Workmen, after they get acquainted in a neighbourhood, do not dislike this plan so much as might be supposed; for they can generally pay their own store accounts with goods. If they want a pair of shoes, they can give the shoe-maker a piece of satinett that will make a pair of trousers in payment for them, and so on.

I shall now describe how we got on at the place above alluded to. The mill was a frame house, three stories high; the power a bucket-well wheel; in the lower flat[2] were the fulling-mill, scouring-rollers, cropping-machine, &c.; in the next flat there were three carding-machines (two for carding rolls), and one condenser; the third flat was full of power and hand-looms, and the jenny I wrought on—all as good as if John Sugden, of Leeds, had made them.[3] Here we were paid in money, my own wages and that of the others varying from five to seven dollars a week. We boarded with the *Boss* (at two dollars per week, including washing), who had a family of grown-up daughters; commenced work at sun-rise, and were always called to breakfast before we had wrought one hour. Our breakfast-table was covered with a white cotton Osnaburg cloth;[4] there was always some kind of meat—sometimes roast fowls, hot bread, raw onions (dished up with vinegar and pepper), mush,[5] pickles, buck-wheat cakes (smoking hot, which were very good when buttered on both sides, and eaten with molasses). We returned to work immediately on finishing breakfast; and were called to dinner at twelve, which was not very different from breakfast, only the tea-things were not paraded with so much show. The workmen sat at table without their coats, with their shirt sleeves rolled up; and I never saw them sit down without washing their hands, and their face, too, if it was dirty. After dinner we rested an hour; had supper at six o'clock—pretty much the same as at breakfast, and we then wrought till dark. Although the man who rented and carried on the place was a poor hard-working man, the same politeness and good feeling

2. By flats is meant the floors of the building.
3. John Sugden of Leeds was a Yorkshire manufacturer of mill equipment and weaving machinery noted for its quality.
4. Osnaburg is a coarse linen named for Osnabrück in Germany.
5. Mush is Indian corn stripped from the cob and boiled in milk or water.

prevailed in the family that I have spoken of as characteristic of the Americans generally. Our Sundays were spent in lounging about; some went to meeting, but more went to gather cherries and huckle-berries. The first Sunday I was there, while sitting at the door, remarking to myself on the gay parties that were driving along the road in their waggons, the *Boss,* thinking, I suppose, I felt lonesome, asked me to go into the room, where his daughters were chattering, laughing, and amusing themselves. When they understood that I liked music, they sung to me the "Braes of Birniebousle," and "Jessie of Dunblane," as pleased and as innocent-like as young lambs. This was rather a different way of spending the Sunday afternoon from what I had been taught in my father's house: yet such is the effect of example, and the influence of bright eyes and sweet voices, that I was pleased.

There are numerous hand-loom weavers throughout all these states, who make a very comfortable living. The way they carry on their work is pretty much the same as that of the country weavers in Scotland, only they have longer webs, and are rather better paid. The kind of work most common is wincey, satinetts, and flannel; the latter article is very generally used by the country people, for shirts to the men and petticoats to the women. It is always woven white, and the yarn is very good. An ordinary hand with the fly-lay can weave ten or twelve yards easily; the usual price is about sixpence sterling per yard; no allowance for warping or gearing. In the agricultural districts, any man that can do this kind of work may get through the world very easily. Many of the farmers have looms in their own houses; but this is more a matter of necessity than choice, and they consider a weaver in the neighbourhood an acquisition; will help him to build a house, sell him a few acres of land, and take an interest in his success. I have been told by weavers and people about the mills, that a good many leave their places and buy—even sometimes get—a few acres of land, and commence in this way. I have seen several who were very comfortable; their houses literally crammed with bundles of yarn, and their children filling bobbins—and who owned a cow or two, a pig, some chickens, lots of Indian corn, and potatoes.

Emigrants of the handicraft class come crowding to the manufacturing towns and well-known districts, where they frequently cannot get work until their means are expended: besides, they glut the labour market, when other places are in want of them: instead of which, if they would just shut their eyes, and walk twenty miles straight into any ordinary well-settled district, they would find profitable employment in this and many other ways. . . .

I observed that there is in universal use amongst the farmers in the

States, and in Canada too, a decidedly-improved wheel for spinning wool. It is of the "muckle" wheel species;[6] and the improvement consists in its lightness, its proportion, general finish, but mostly in a simple mode of increasing the speed of the spindle. At the head of the wheel there is a small iron shaft, about the size of a quill, on which there are two pullies, one about an inch diameter, the other four — the band from the large wheel working on the smallest one. The spindle is placed about seven inches below the shaft, on which there is a pully, one inch diameter, which is driven with a band from the four-inch pully on the small shaft above it, increasing the speed of the spindle four times, and enabling the spinner to perform, at least, one-half more work when spinning warp or small yarn. . . .

The houses are built of wood, painted white, clean and comfortable, roomy and airy; very good for summer, but not well calculated for the extreme cold of winter. They are carpetted, have sofas and sideboards; many of them have silver table spoons; their wives and daughters dressed in silk, surrounded with all the comforts of civilized life. It is worth while being a farmer's daughter here; for they do no out-door work — not even milking the cows, — never think of walking on foot, even for short distances, — driving their elegant waggons frequently themselves. I have seen the farmers' daughters sitting in the shade of the piazza, that forms part of every house, sewing or amusing themselves, while he himself was busy milking the cows.

Mr. Mitchell, a neighbouring farmer, sent to me one day, asking if I would help him to cut down some oats. This was a business I knew very little about; however, as the mill was stopped for want of water, and as I was always anxious to gather information, away I went. I shall describe exactly how I got on. It was midday when I arrived at the house, which was beautifully situated on the side of the turnpike, surrounded by an orchard; and just before the door, on the green sward, Uncle Mitchell[7] was lying in the shade of a cherry-tree, resting an hour in the heat of the day. He was lying on his back, a broad-brimmed straw-hat over his face; his neck was bare; had on a coarse cotton shirt, a pair of cotton Osnaburg trousers, mended about the knees; a pair of roughlike half boots, half shoes, that had never been brushed or greased; without stockings; with a chew of tobacco in his mouth: and this man owned 120 acres of land,

---

6. The muckle or mickle is the great wheel of a spinning wheel.

7. Uncle does not denote a blood relationship here. The term was a common honorific in rural America, "a mode of salutation, from youth to age" according to Fowler (*Journal of a Tour,* p. 52).

worth L. 18 or L. 20 per acre. He told me "he was very glad to see me, for he guessed he was pretty well used up." I sat down beside him, and ate some apples and some cherries that the children brought us. I told him I could not cradle,[8] but was willing to do anything I could. We went in to dinner; but first into the kitchen, which was large and clean, with a pump-well in one corner, and a neatly-painted trough before it, where we washed our hands. It may be worth while to notice that the well was dug about twenty feet from the house, and the neatly-made pump inside was connected with it by a one-inch leaden pipe: and in this way in a town I have seen two or three houses, each with a pump inside, and all supplied from the same well. We sat down to dinner in a comfortable little parlour, with a painted floor, a Yankee clock, and cane-bottomed chairs. The wife was a clean "tidy" body; there were two half-grown boys and a little girl. Before us there was a well-spread table, a clean table-cloth (made of coarse cotton cloth), a piece of boiled pork, a piece of cold beef, cold mush (very good), flour bread, green Indian corn (smoking hot), cucumbers, pumpkin pie, silver spoons, clean knives and forks, water in clean tumblers, and a cup of tea after. This pleased me well; but not more than the good-breeding of all, and their attention to me.

After dinner, the farmer, his two sons, and I, went to the field; and it was arranged that I should rake and bind for the old man: the two sons were to work together. At first I could not keep up; but before the horn sounded to call us home to supper, I was getting into the knack of it: really it was very hard work. Next day I was able to keep up pretty well, and tried my hand at the scythe; and between their flattery and my own anxiety to learn, I would not have been long in mastering it — not, indeed, to anything like the same perfection they had arrived at; — the old man laid his grain as straight in the swath as a bunch of candles.

They use the cradle scythe; and a good hand can cut four acres a day. But the crops are light, compared to those of the Carse of Gowrie[9]; and there is no grass in the bottom. We did not put it up in *stooks,* but built it in small cocks, in the evening after we had done cutting. I wrought here three days and a half, and got seventy-five cents a day; an ordinary hand would have got at least one dollar in good money.[10] In the course of

8. A cradle is a light wooden frame attached to a scythe, "having a row of long curved teeth parallel to the blade, to lay the corn more evenly in the swath" (*OED*).

9. The Carse of Gowrie is the north bank of the River Tay in Scotland, between Perth and Dundee, a stretch of flat, alluvial land famous for its fertility.

10. Good money probably means in specie; American banks were notorious for issuing worthless paper money, a practice that Dickens refers to ironically in the title of his account of America — *American Notes, for General Circulation.*

this harvest I was up and down the neighbourhood more than fifty miles, and did not see a woman working in the field. I was told, that on the west side of the river, which is settled to some extent by the Dutch, the females work out of doors in about the same way as they do at home — or in Scotland. In travelling about I have joined many parties in the harvest field; and although no women are to be seen, the conversation carried on is far more befitting their presence than the "cracks" on the harvest rig in moral Scotland. I never saw them eating in the field, or heard of them sleeping in such places as *bothies*.[11]

Farmers here have no difficulty in getting labourers; and twelve or fourteen dollars, with board at the farmer's table, are the highest wages in summer. It is not common to hire for more than a month at a time. Most of them have thrashing-machines: some of those who have not, employ men who go about with portable machines on a waggon. They are much smaller than those used in Scotland; and instead of having beaters on the cylinder, it is filled with iron spikes about two inches long, one fourth square, about two or two and a half inches distant from each other. The arrangement for feeding is the same, but they have no shaker attached. They are very effective, and require little power; and I believe grain is easier thrashed out here than in Scotland. At first they had the cylinder with beaters; but they have thrown it aside, as requiring too much power. I observed that the spiked cylinder cuts the straw a little; but they do not consider that of much importance.

HIGH SOCIETY, 1836

Charles Augustus Murray (1806–1895) spent some two years in the United States between 1834 and 1836. Son of the fifth Earl of Dunmore and a qualified lawyer, he was twenty-eight years old when he arrived armed with letters of introduction to the British legation in Washington. But he did not limit himself to the social life of the eastern seaboard. He praised American hospitality after catching and being nursed through cholera in Cincinnati (he might have praised it more: his grandfather, the fourth Earl, had been the last colonial governor of Virginia and had torched Norfolk in 1776), and hunted for three months with a Pawnee band in the

---

11. Bothies (cf. the word "booth") were one-roomed huts in which unmarried male farmhands were lodged.

Missouri Territory. He even fell in love, with Elizabeth, daughter of
James Wadsworth of Geneseo. Her father disapproved of the match, but
they were eventually married in 1850 after his death, though Elizabeth
would die in childbirth the following year.

Murray maintains a tactful silence about his romance in Travels in
North America, *which was published three years after his return to*
England. He became Master of the Queen's Household in 1838, and in
1844 entered on a thirty-year diplomatic career that would take him to
Persia and Egypt, and half the capital cities of western Europe besides;
and which would bring him a knighthood in 1866.

In 1836 he made the last of several journeys up the Hudson, renew-
ing acquaintances among the cream of society on the river's banks and in
Albany. Aiming to visit Niagara once more before sailing for England
and remembering the discomforts of American stages, he took his horse,
Polly, with him.

After remaining in New York a few days longer, I prepared again to turn
my steps to the westward, and accordingly embarked my baggage and
Polly on a steam-boat, which conveyed me as far as Newburgh, where I
was to pay another short visit to my friend on the Hudson river. I also
took up with me a pair of black ponies which I had lately purchased, and
which I proposed carrying back with me to Britain. I took this opportunity of revisiting West Point for a few hours, and found that my former
impressions of the extreme beauty of its situation were fully confirmed.

After spending a day or two with Mr. A___,[1] I started on horseback for Albany; crossing to the eastern bank of the Hudson, the first
town which I reached was Poughkeepsie. This is a thriving handsome
town, built on a slope considerably above the river. The bales and pack-
ages in the streets, as well as the shingles, and brick, and mortar in the
suburbs, speak plainly as to the industry and enterprise of the inhabitants. A little above the town, and commanding a fine view of the Hudson and surrounding country, is a large tavern or boarding-house, which

From Charles Augustus Murray, *Travels in North America During the Years 1834, 1835, and*
1836. . . , 2 vols. (New York: Harper and Brothers, 1839), 2: 229–34.

1. Edward Armstrong, son of a British colonel who had served in the Revolutionary
War, married the Carolina heiress Sarah Ward in 1822 and built Danskammer in the classical
style in 1834. The property had two miles of Hudson frontage, from Roseton to Cedar Cliff
in northern Orange County. Armstrong, who died in 1840 of scarlet fever, was best known
for raising racehorses.

struck me as being the most neat, quiet, and comfortable establishment of the kind which I had ever seen in America. The bar was separate from the house; the bedrooms and parlours, though not large, were decorated and furnished with good taste; and altogether the house wore a most inviting appearance to a traveller long accustomed to hotels, which are so full of noise, tobacco, and bustle, as are those of American cities in general.

From Poughkeepsie I continued my course to the northward, and was aware of a merry party coming in the opposite direction; I reined in my pony to see them pass, and soon found that they were under the combined influence of Comus, Hymen, and Bacchus; and a more mirthful assemblage can hardly be imagined. A marriage had apparently been solemnized between two (if not more) of the persons present, who seemed to be in the humbler ranks of trades people. The "cortége" consisted of twenty or thirty wagons and gigs; the horses and the ladies' heads were all adorned with flowers, and each squire had his dulcinea by his side. With a splenetic sigh over my own celibate condition, I let them go by, and rode on.

I soon came to the lodge of a country seat, which has been celebrated by almost every British traveller in America, Hyde Park, the residence of the late venerable and hospitable Dr. Hosack. I had never found an opportunity of delivering my letters of introduction to him during my former stay in New York, and I first heard of his death, which took place last winter, when I arrived at New Orleans.[2] Of course his widow received no company, so I resolved to ride through the grounds and see the prospect from them, merely leaving my card, accompanied by an apology for the liberty I had taken.

The ground between the road and the house is very bold and undulating, and affords the means of making a pretty small lake, round which the approach winds its course. The house is spacious and comfortable, without any pretensions to architectural beauty. Dismounting at the door, I sent in my card, requesting permission to walk round (what is called in Scotland) "the Policy;" and in a minute or two was agreeably surprised at hearing my name pronounced by a gentle female voice. On looking up, I recognized the daughter-in-law of Dr. Hosack, to whom I had been presented during an accidental meeting at a morning visit in New York.[3] She invited me into the house and very kindly offered to show me the "lions;" among the principal of which, in doors, was the library, a most comfort-

2. David Hosack (1769–1835), surgeon and botanist, died of apoplexy in New York on December 22, 1835. His third wife, Magdalena Coster, a wealthy merchant's widow whom he had married in 1825, survived him.

3. Elizabeth (née Leger), whom Hosack's fourth son, Alexander, had married in 1829.

able apartment, containing some tolerable pictures of the Italian and Flemish schools. I soon followed my fair conductress to the other side of the house, where might be seen a picture more glorious than ever mortal pencil designed. Below us flowed the Hudson, studded with white-sailed sloops as far as the eye could reach, even until they looked no larger than the edge of a seagull's wing; the opposite bank, which slopes gently from the river, is variegated with farms, villages, and woods, appearing as though they had been grouped by the hand of taste rather than by that of industry; while on the northwest side the prospect is bounded by the dark and lofty outline of the Catskill range. I had only intended to remain here a few minutes, as I had a long ride before me, and the shades of evening were already approaching; but, alas! W. Spencer has truly sung, how often it is that "noiseless falls the foot of time;"[4] and surely if there is any situation in which one may be forgiven, if "unheeded fly the hours," it is when enjoying the luxury of so glorious a landscape, under the guidance of a fair and amiable *chaperone,* who is herself not the least attractive feature in the scene. At length, however, I jumped on my pony, and gently admonished it that its activity must make up for my lost time, and bear me before night to some place where we might both find bed and supper. . . .

[Murray stayed overnight in Redhook, and the following day made for Albany in a rainstorm.] My progress was neither pleasant nor fast; for the mud in some places reached nearly to Polly's knees, and the small streamlets, which I was obliged to cross, were swelled to the size of turbid angry brooks. All these trifles were forgotten by seven o'clock, when she had her nose dipped into a peck of good oats in a warm stable, and I found myself again dry-clothed, with a cigar in my mouth and a cup of hot coffee at my elbow.

Albany is a very striking town, both as regards its situation and public buildings; of the latter a great many had been erected since my last visit, nearly two years before; some of them were still in progress, and promised to be very handsome, the material wherewith they are built being generally marble, the greater part of which is brought from Sing-Sing. The streets are wretchedly paved; but this is an evil which it is not very easy to remedy, as some of them are extremely steep and hilly; and as the quantity of rain which falls here is very great, the water rushes down them with incredible force, and carries away everything which contributes to support or bind the pavement.

4. Murray notes: "See his little poem, 'Too late I stayed,' &c." William Robert Spencer (1769–1834), a London wit and poet, fled England in debt and lived his last years in Paris.

Hyde Park: view of the Hudson from Hyde Park, 1837. By William Henry Bartlett, from N. P. Willis, *American Scenery* (London, 1837–40). New York State
Museum, Albany

The second day of my stay being Sunday, I went in the morning to
the Dutch Reformed Church. This sect numbers in its ranks the Van Rensselaers, the Vanderpoels, and many others of the best and oldest families
of Dutch origin residing in or near Albany. As regards its tenets and
ritual, I can perceive no difference between it and the Presbyterian
church. The building is spacious, but not remarkable for any decorations,
external or internal, except the candelabras, which are the most massive
and handsome that I have seen in this country. I am told they were presented by the Patroon, but forgot to inquire whether they were of American or foreign manufacture. The sermon was somewhat tedious, and too
illustrative of the proverb that "a good thing cannot be too often repeated;" at least it appeared to me, on leaving the church, that some men
could have put into an argument of five minutes all that was contained in
a sermon of forty. In the afternoon I went to the Episcopal church, which

is not remarkable for architectural beauty, and heard the beautiful servic
and a harmless sermon tamely read.

On the following day I received and accepted an invitation to dir
with General Van Rensselaer, generally mentioned by American travelle
as the Patroon.[5] In the morning I rode out with Mr. T. Van Buren (the sc
of the Vice-President,[6] who showed me every kind of attention and civi
ity during my stay in Albany), to see the Falls of Cohoes, on the Mohaw
river, a few miles above Troy. We could not have enjoyed a more favou
able opportunity for seeing this celebrated cascade, inasmuch as it raine
the whole day, as it *had* rained for three weeks previously. We were the
spared the annoyance of dust on the road—were cooled and refreshe
during our ride by the "gentle dew from heaven," and saw the Mohaw
pouring forth his turbid and discoloured waters, in a mass of nearly twic
his usual magnitude. The scene at the falls is very grand, but it should t
seen by one who has not seen Niagara. It is well to say that comparisor
are odious—they are so; nevertheless, the "great wonder of waters" wi
recur to memory—its wreaths of spray and boiling cauldron will fill tl
eye, and its terrible roar, the ear of fancy—despite argument, and propr
ety, and philosophy.

An observant traveller must be struck by the activity and stirrin
spirit that is everywhere discernible in this neighbourhood: villages, mill
and factories, are springing up on all sides, and it is probable that Trc
and Albany, now seven miles apart, will in a few years be one continuot
town. Half way between the latter place and the Falls of Cohoes, is an a
senal of the United States, the commander of which politely pressed h
hospitality upon us;[7] but we were obliged to hurry forward in order to t
in time for dinner. This gentleman was of courteous agreeable manner
and a brave and distinguished officer; he was severely wounded in the la
Anglo-American war;—may it remain the last for centuries yet to com

The Patroon's house stood at the north-western extremity of Alban
and is separated from it only by a few fields, which he, very naturally, wi
not allow to be covered with buildings. The house is comfortable, and c
moderate extent, but not remarkable for its architecture. The fami
party consisted of the venerable head of the house, his lady, and four c
five sons and daughters. It is difficult to believe that Mrs. Van Rensselac

5. Stephen Van Rensselaer (1764–1839), the last Patroon, was a major-general in tl
state militia in the War of 1812. Murray had been introduced to him at Saratoga in 1834
6. Smith Thompson Van Buren, third of Martin Van Buren's four sons.
7. Watervliet Arsenal, in the village of West Troy (incorporated 1836). The officer
probably Lt.-Col. William Jenkins Worth (1794–1849), severely wounded at the battle
Lundy's Lane in 1813 and commander of cadets at West Point 1820–1828.

is really the mother of the handsome young ladies beside her, she appears so youthful, and her conversation denotes a fresh, lively, and highly cultivated mind.[8] Altogether I have been admitted to few domestic circles more agreeable; and it is gratifying to see the vast possessions of the Van Rensselaers in the hands of a gentleman so liberal, and so well calculated from his character and manners to make a sensible and generous use of them, as their present possessor.

8. Stephen Van Rensselaer's second wife was Cornelia, née Paterson, whom he married in 1802 and who bore him nine children.

Albany and Its Environs

A LBANY WAS the great clearing house for travels in upstate New York. Most visitors traveled north from New York City, on the sloops and later the steamships of the Hudson. Others came overland from Boston and New England, while a few made their way south from the Canadian border, down the Champlain Valley. Albany receives much attention in the pages of their recollections.

Albany merchants had concentrated upstate trade and transportation in their own hands from the settlement's earliest days, when it held a monopoly on the fur trade. In the eighteenth century the farming of the Mohawk Valley resulted in rapidly increasing, long-distance shipments of agricultural produce. Albany's geographical location and its merchants' expertise captured most of this trade; but other settlements on the upper Hudson, and especially the manufacturing center based on water power at Troy, looked to compete more vigorously for Albany's lucrative markets. The city's preeminence, apparently certified by its choice as the legislature's permanent home, had to adjust to many economic dislocations in the early nineteenth century.

The opening of the canals in the 1820s threatened the city's control of the passenger and bulk goods trades. Troy seemed likely to siphon off a good deal of the northbound trade, and Schenectady, separated from Albany by many locks, was the obvious candidate as eastern terminus for the westbound trade of the state. With the rise of the railroads, these competitors became more hopeful of success: the city of Troy financed its own lines up to the spa towns of Ballston and Saratoga, and for a few years in the late 1830s looked likely to take that profitable business away from Albany's entrepreneurs.

But the pull of Albany would prove greater than the apparent advantages offered by neighboring locations. Its citizens' successes are mirrored in the pages of British travelers in America in the first half of the nineteenth century: Troy seldom figures as more than a day's excursion from the metropolis, and Schenectady rates only the odd line or two at the beginning of a western journey on the canal. The Troy-Saratoga line lost money, and Albany continued to dominate the holiday trade northward. The threatened line across the south of the state from the Hudson to Lake Erie eventually failed in a sorry mess of predatory financiers and frequent bankruptcies, and the introduction of the railroad worked to confirm the routing of the trade and travel of the state along the line of the canal—and that inevitably strengthened the position of Albany and furthered the rapid expansion of the city and its suburbs. Troy and Schenectady became, by the end of the period of fiercest rivalry bracketed by the travelers whose writings are reproduced here, less independent and more reliant on the city of Albany than they had been at the beginning of the century.

Albany's growth, though spectacular, differed from that of western cities like Rochester and Buffalo in two important regards. First, the city was an ancient foundation. The Dutch had set up their first trading post in the early seventeenth century, and the political and commercial importance of the place had been underlined during the wars with French and Indians that had concentrated military activity in the northern areas of the state. And, second, there existed as there did not in the case of other cities that mushroomed in the early nineteenth century, a portrait of the rural simplicity of life in the city—village, rather—before the commercial explosion of post-independence days. Mrs. Grant of Laggan's affectionate biography of Margaretta Schuyler, *Memoirs of an American Lady* (1808), drew a detailed portrait of life in Albany before the United States's independence. Writing without notes nearly fifty years after she had spent her childhood on the upper Hudson, Mrs. Grant recalled her earliest years with an accuracy that the great nineteenth-century antiquarian of Albany, Joel Munsell, seldom caviled with. A remarkable feat of memory, the book fixed with great exactitude the earlier years of the city for British readers. It also had its effects on American authors, among them Cooper in his *Satanstoe* and Paulding's *Dutchman's Fireside*.

Mrs. Grant's "Sketches of Manners and Scenes in America, as They Existed Previous to the Revolution" provided an index to the changes in Albany that travelers could not themselves have observed. But all visitors were impressed with the mingling of old and new in the city, whether they knew Mrs. Grant's work or not. Several travelers were charmed by what was, in America, unusual evidence of antiquity, especially in Albany's Dutch houses and irregular town plan. Most, however, felt more comfortable with the clean lines of its modern buildings, and their notes on the Dutch quarters leave little doubt about their preferences.

"Should the canal to Lake Erie be completed," wrote Henry Bradshaw Fearon in 1817, "this must become a first-rate town; it is, even at present, a place of extensive business." Between 1820 and 1830 the population doubled to nearly twenty-five thousand, and Fearon's prediction was triumphantly fulfilled. Yet Albany's very size rendered it difficult to portray. No traveler of the nineteenth century could equal Mrs. Grant's portrait of an entire community. Rather, they gave partial accounts, shaped by circumstance and their own interests. William Dalton and John M. Duncan give the outward lineaments of commercial expansion in the 1820s. I. Finch describes political life in the city. Andrew Reed is more interested in the city's public buildings and fascinated by the experiment in the education of girls at the Female Academy, and James Silk Buckingham describes, in typically encyclopedic detail, the city's appearance and public celebrations.

Albany was not only the center of travel in the northern states, but also a more local center for the attractions of eastern upstate New York. Tourists used the city as a base for visits to the spas, the Shaker colonies at Niskayuna and New Lebanon, and for longer trips to south and west, to Cooperstown and through Delaware County. All accounts bear witness to the importance of the city of Albany.

TWO VIEWS OF ALBANY, 1818 AND 1819

The canal would bring a great infusion of wealth to Albany after 1825, stimulating massive reconstruction in the city. In these two accounts, however, much of old Albany is still recognizable, waiting impatiently for the transforming completion of the great western enterprise.

William Dalton was a Cumberland farmer who spent the summer of 1819 in North America and returned to England enthusiastic about the United States. His passion for detailed observation nevertheless acts as a corrective to the inflated claims of overzealous authors who were at the time promoting large-scale emigration from Britain. Accompanied by a fellow farmer, William Laverick of Morland, he took notes on the spot and claims to have received so many enquiries about the prospects for emigration that he published his jottings as originally written, at his own expense.

John M. Duncan's brief description of Albany was originally part of a letter written in October 1818. An educated Glaswegian and something of a Scottish patriot, Duncan was a man of decided tastes, which his book reflects. He opposed slavery, universal suffrage, and Roman Catholicism, and focused on the American character, and literary and religious matters in the United States, to correct—as he put it—misapprehensions common in Britain. His Travels were printed at Glasgow University Press in 1823, and although presented as letters they bear evidence of considerable rewriting after his return to Scotland.

A great number of steam vessels are continually upon the river. Many of them are of a very large size, and cut their way through the water with great facility. Accommodations are provided for passengers on board, as well for sleeping as eating. In a vessel of this description we sailed from New York to Albany in twenty-six hours. The fare, including bed and board, was seven dollars each.

There is a tax laid upon every passenger in these steam boats, which is appropriated to the canal fund. The aggregate sum received during the last year was about nineteen thousand dollars. The amount required of each passenger, from New York to Albany, is one dollar.

The sum of one hundred and sixty thousand dollars, taken from the income arising from sales at auction, was, last year, applied by the State Government, towards the furtherance of the grand design of opening an inland navigation from Lake Erie to Albany.

ALBANY. — This town, which is the seat of legislature for the State, is situated on the west side of the Hudson. Being a very old settlement, it will be readily imagined that the plan of the town is far from being uniform. The old town is composed of streets narrow and irregular; but those streets which have a more modern date, are laid out and built with more taste. Many of these buildings are covered with tin, which has some advantages over slate, tile, or shingles. I did not observe any appearance of rust. The houses are, for the most part, built of brick, and look well.

From William Dalton, *Travels in the United States of America, and Parts of Upper Canada* (Applesby: William Dalton, 1821), pp. 72–75.

The House of Assembly is a noble structure, standing upon an elevated situation at the head of State street.

Albany ale is almost as much famed in this country as London porter is throughout England. It is sold by the brewers for eight dollars, or thirty-six shillings per barrel; and retailed by the tavern and hotel keepers at the rate of sixteen dollars, or twice the cost price. I was sorry to learn, that, although from the low price of malt and other ingredients in brewing, the brewers must receive a considerable profit, yet, some of them have been in the habit of infusing noxious drugs into the liquor. What monstrous wickedness, thus to undermine the constitution and destroy the health of their fellow-creatures, by the use of these deleterious ingredients, for the sake of a paltry gain!

This town is well watered from springs at the distance of two or three miles from the city—the water being conveyed to every part of the city by means of cast iron pipes. This being the great mart where the trade of an extensive back country centres, houses and stores let very high. The great Western Canal from Lake Erie, as also the Northern one from Lake Champlain, will join the river near this place. I have been favoured with a sight of the surveyor's estimate, for both these undertakings, from which it appears that the aggregate length of the former is about 350 miles, and the estimated expence upwards of one million pounds sterling.

Albany was an early Dutch settlement and the streets are filled with Dutch names, of most difficult and cacophonous utterance. The town consisted originally of a single street, skirting the bank of the river, which takes a slight bend here; but it subsequently extended backwards very considerably, and some of the recent streets towards the north are spacious and well built, and as usual lined with poplars. In many places there is a singular mixture of poverty and splendour. A number of the old Dutch erections are still standing; small houses of red and yellow bricks, with the gable end to the street, having a door and window in the ground floor, a single window in the next, and above it the year of their erection embossed upon the surface in huge iron figures, and the whole surmounted with an iron weather-cock rusted upon the rod. There is an air of antiquity about these buildings, which is interesting in a country where antiquity is so rare. The modern erections exhibit the same tasteful style

From John M. Duncan, *Travels through Part of the United States and Canada in 1818 and 1819,* 2 vols. (Glasgow: Glasgow University Press, 1823), 1: 322–24.

Albany: view in Albany—house of the first Dutch governors, c. 1820. From
Jacques Milbert, *Itinéraire pittoresque* (Paris, 1828–29). Collection of McKinne
Library, Albany Institute of History and Art

which prevails in New York and Philadelphia. Two or three of the publi
buildings are of white marble; one of them is surmounted with a very nea
dome, but in another the effect of the marble wall is sadly disfigured b
the untasteful addition of a red tiled roof. The Capitol, or State Hous
has rather a neat portico, and a dome surmounted with a statue of Jus
tice; it stands at the upper end of a very steep but wide street, running a
right angles to the river. Near the Capitol is a very neat Academy with tw
wings, built of reddish coloured freestone.

Albany, notwithstanding its commercial and legislative advantage:
does not contain above twelve or thirteen thousand inhabitants; the prob
ability is, however, that a great increase of wealth and population wi
take place, when the great western canal is completed, which is to conne
Lake Erie with the Hudson, joining the latter in the neighbourhood c
this city.

ELECTING A GOVERNOR, 1824

Some travelers' recollections and accounts are difficult to date with any certainty. Take the Travels *of I. Finch. They were published in England just after the passage of the parliamentary Reform Act in 1832, at a time when the United States was much examined as an experiment in the popular control of government and held up as both a model and a terrible warning of what the reform might hold for England. A gentleman-scholar fascinated by geology, Finch does not date anything of his two years' residence in America. We can, however, be sure that he was in Albany in 1824, when he wrote this spirited account of the election of a governor of the state, for De Witt Clinton was reelected that year in a hotly contested gubernatorial contest. Finch's sense of the literary market in England of the early 1830s was sharp, and the passage is likely to have frightened many lukewarm supporters of a more democratically elected parliament.*

Albany, the capital of the state, is one hundred and fifty miles from New York. It is advantageously situated for commerce, at the head of sloop navigation, and at the termination of the Erie and Champlain canals. State Street is a fine broad avenue in the centre of the city, with the Capitol, on the brow of the hill, at one extremity. The other is blocked up with houses, or it would afford a fine view over the river and the surrounding country.

Albany exhibits marks of its Dutch founders. Many houses are built of small bricks, with their gable ends to the street. Some have been described in the history of Irving.[1] Van Tromp Street is named after the celebrated Dutch Admiral.

On the east bank of the river, one mile south of the city, is a mansion, erected forty years since, with loop holes and narrow windows, that it might, in case of necessity, be defended against the Indians. The rapid

From I. Finch, *Travels in the United States of America and Canada, Containing Some Account of Their Scientific Institutions. . .* (London: Longman, Rees, Orme, Brown, Green, and Longman, 1833), pp. 53–55, 59–60.

1. Washington Irving's *A History of New York, from the Beginning of the World to the End of the Dutch Dynasty . . . by Diedrich Knickerbocker* was first published in 1809 and was very popular among visitors to the state.

Albany: City of Albany, in the State of New York, 4 June 1819. Drawn by G. Kane.
New York State Museum, Albany

advance of civilization may be noticed by this fact. It shews, at that recent
period, it was necessary to guard against their incursions. At that time the
sloops were usually a fortnight in sailing to New York, and, to convey the
passengers on shore, had a large tree hollowed out into a canoe.

There are several cascades within a few miles of the city; to these I
was accompanied by my friend Dr. J____. The rapids of Norman Kill are
worthy a visit. A small river dashes over ledges of rock, and the stream is
confined by precipitous banks covered with forest trees.

To form a harbor for the immense number of canal boats which arrive at Albany, a pier has been constructed four thousand feet long, and
fifty feet wide. It is made of piles driven into the bed of the river, and filled
with earth. Warehouses are built on the top of the pier. When the canals
are open, this harbor presents a busy scene; hundreds of boats are collected, bringing the various productions of the West and North; iron, timber, and marble, from the territory near Lake Champlain; flour, wheat,
maize, flax-seed, gypsum, and the riches of the West. Emigrants come
here with their families to take a passage in boats for the western country.

The capitol is advantageously situated on the summit of the hill, and is built of red sandstone. It is one hundred and fifteen feet long, ninety feet deep, and fifty feet high, with a portico in front.

This building contains the halls of legislation. The chamber of representatives is a commodious room; each member has an arm-chair and a separate table. Here assemble the representatives of two millions of people of one semi-sovereign State of North America. Every thing relating to the laws and government, the system of education, and internal affairs, is regulated by the deputies who meet in this hall. . . .

I was at Albany in November, when the elections for Governor, Lieutenant-Governor, and other state-officers commence, and had an opportunity of seeing these popular elections. They take place by ballot, yet they produce as much excitement in the minds of the people as elections in England. The party who were in power had refused the people some right which they wished to exercise, and popular opinion began to vibrate in favor of the return of Mr. Clinton and his friends to power.[2] A committee of delegates from all parts of the state met in convention at Utica, and nominated Mr. Clinton as Governor, and great efforts were made to elect him. Through the state the two parties began to make preparations for the war. Committees of vigilance were appointed! The liberties of the people were declared to be in danger! Tyrants had assumed the seat of government, and denied the people their rights! On the opposite side, arguments equally valid were made use of. The newspapers were busily engaged.

In the Capitol, on one side the hall, assessors for a district were stationed. They wrote in a book the names of individuals coming to vote, and took the folded piece of paper which they brought, containing the names of candidates preferred for different offices. These papers were placed in a small box, which had an opening in the top. The sentiments of every individual seemed to be known, and the majority nearly ascertained. In some instances, bets to a large amount were made by the opposing candidates.

Placards, hand-bills, and the usual electioneering paraphernalia, were employed, but there was no violence or riot, no open house kept. The voters (nearly all the people have the right) were too numerous.

On one occasion, an obnoxious senator went into a committee-

2. De Witt Clinton (1769–1828), trained as a lawyer, was mayor of New York City for most of the years between 1802 and 1815. The leading supporter of a canal to join Lake Erie and the Hudson, he was governor from 1817 to 1822, recaptured the position in the 1824 election, and held it until his death.

room of the opposite party, but he retired almost immediately; otherwise, I heard an opinion expressed that he would have been ill-treated. This was the most violently contested election that had ever taken place in the state.

FEMALE EDUCATION IN THE 1830s

In 1831 the Congregational Union was founded in Britain, and in 1834 its officers decided to send two of their number, Andrew Reed and James Matheson, on a fraternal visit to the North American churches. This visit excited some considerable interest in England—indeed, it was rumored that the journey had a party-political purpose. So, though nervous about offending the sensibilities of their American hosts, the two delegates published an account of their travels as a series of undated letters.

James Matheson was responsible for the accounts of Canada and Pennsylvania, and for collecting materials for the statistical appendix to the second volume. New York State fell to Andrew Reed. Reed (1787–1862) had been ordained in 1811 and served in various London churches for the rest of his life. A writer of hymns and devotional works, he was an industrious philanthropist, working to establish several orphanages and asylums in the London area. Female education was a matter of some controversy in England at the time, and he leaves no doubt about his position on the matter.

After a visit to Utica, Reed returned to Albany and wrote a brief description of the city's public institutions. It is supplemented here by a later passage that gives the Female Academy's curriculum in some detail.

I had not yet seen much of this town, and there was much that challenged inspection. The principal buildings stand on the top of the hill, called the Capitol; from which a fine wide street runs down to the river, and the closer parts of the town. The Capitol, or State House, occupies the very summit of this hill, and has a noble appearance, from its dimensions and elevation. The City Hall is of white marble, and worthy to be its compan-

From Andrew Reed and James Matheson, *A Narrative of the Visit to the American Churches, by the Deputation from the Congregational Union of England & Wales,* 2 vols. (London: Jackson and Walford, 1835), 1: 345; 2: 234–39; 1: 345–49.

ion. The Institute and the Academy are here also; and are respectable foundations. They make, as a cluster of public structures, a grand spectacle; although they have nothing, as works of art, demanding separate encomium. The Orphan Asylum, in the vicinity, is well conducted. Besides these, there are two new erections, which, from their pretensions, may require notice. The one is the Female Academy.[1] It is a large and very handsome portico, of the Ionic order; and it is only to be lamented that, with the exception of the base of the columns and the steps, it is constructed of wood, and not of marble. The lights under the portico are objectionable; and a great deal is sacrificed within, for the sake of external ornament. As a school for female education, it is, however, very remarkable; the first of its kind in this country; and it will require further consideration. . . .

Of the female academies, for the ordinary period of education, there is perhaps none that so fully merits attention as the institution at Albany. It is in a flourishing condition, and has recently erected a noble edifice for its accommodation. This erection supplies sixteen apartments as class and lecture-rooms, and is faced by a beautiful portico of the Ionic order, copied from the temple on the *Ilissus.*

The Institution is divided into six departments, exclusive of the classes composed of those scholars from each of the higher departments, who are pursuing the study of the French and Spanish languages, natural history, chemistry, and botany.

In the Sixth Department, the rudiments of education are commenced. The books used are, Worcester's Primer of the English Language, Webster's Spelling Book, the Boston Class Book, Leavitt's Easy Lessons, the New Testament, Parley's Geography, Olney's Geography, Emerson's First Part, and Colburn's First Lessons through the sixth section. This department is furnished with Holbrook's apparatus for primary schools.

In the Fifth Department, regular instruction in writing commenced, Colburn's Lessons and Olney's Geography concluded, Smith's Intellectual and Practical Grammar, Irving's Catechisms of the History of various Nations, and Trimmer's Elements of Natural History. As an exercise in the definition and use of words, and the structure of language, the pupils are daily required to incorporate in sentences, to be written by them, words given to them by their teachers.

In the Fourth Department, the studies of the Fifth reviewed; the books used are, the Malte Brun Geography, by Goodrich, Worcester's General History and Chart, Shimeall's Scripture History and Biblical Lit-

1. The academy was started in 1821, and moved to its new, neoclassical premises at 40 North Pearl Street in 1834, the year of this visit.

erature and Chart. In this department, Colburn's Sequel commenced; exercises in composition in the journal and letter form.

In the Third Department, Colburn's Sequel and Worcester's General History concluded, and the other studies of the Fourth reviewed. The books used are, History of the United States, Ancient Geography, Goodrich's Histories of Greece and Rome. In this department, Blake's Natural Philosophy commenced, and composition continued in the journal, letter, and descriptive form.

In the Second Department, Goodrich's Histories of Greece and Rome, Ancient Geography, Blake's Natural Philosophy, concluded, and the other studies of the Third reviewed; Porter's Rhetorical Reader, Ancient and Modern Geography, with construction of Maps, Ryan's Astronomy, Robinson's History of England, Beck's Chemistry, Watts on the Mind, Newman's Rhetoric, Colburn's Algebra, and Smellie's Philosophy of Natural History, composition in written essays.

In the First Department, the studies of the Second and Third continued as exercises; Blair's Lectures on Rhetoric, Moral Philosophy, Alexander's Evidences of Christianity, Paley's Natural Theology, Arnott's Natural Philosophy, first and second volumes, Simpson's Euclid, Logic, Guy's Astronomy, Bigelow's Technology, Schlegel's History of Literature, Constitutional Law, Legendre's Geometry, select parts of the English Classics, Kames' Elements of Criticism, Butler's Analogy, first part, Payne's Elements of Mental and Moral Science, linear drawing. In this department, critical attention is paid to composition, in which there are frequent exercises.

In addition to the recitations in the books above specified, the scholars in each department are daily exercised in orthography, reading, parsing, and writing.

This course of instruction is administered by a principal and a male assistant, and eight female assistants. The French language is taught by a professor; and when sufficient classes can be formed, lectures are given in the winter terms, on experimental philosophy, in its various departments, by skilful professors. The institution is supplied with maps, charts, globes, a chemical and philosophical apparatus, and an extensive library.

There are two examinations in the year. At the close of the examination in February, the names of those who have distinguished themselves are announced; at the July examination, premiums are given, and gold medals are awarded to those who excel in mathematics and original composition. Besides this, those who have gone through the whole course with approbation, are eligible to receive a diploma bearing the seal of the institution. This is its highest honour; and it is sought by those, especially, who are qualifying to become teachers.

The charges for tuition are as follows: — For the sixth or lowest department, three dollars per quarter; for the fifth, four; for the fourth, five; for the third, six; for the second, seven; and for the first, eight. . . .

The method of communication between the teacher and the pupil here, as in other cases, which I have noticed, is chiefly by recitation. Great care is taken not to use the text-book as a thing to be stored away in the memory, but as a guide to direct inquiry and investigation. In the one case, the mind is called into vigorous and wholesome exercise; in the other, it is burdened with a weight that destroys its elasticity, and prevents its growth. Much as this simple principle commends itself to us in theory, it is seldom brought into practice. This is still the great deficiency in our schools. The ordinary teacher, as by far the easier task, will content himself with loading the memory; while the man who is truly qualified for his work, will seek to train and strengthen the superior faculties. It is due to America to say, that great watchfulness is employed against this evil, and that many examples are supplied of its having been overcome. Perhaps nothing will contribute more to this, with them and with us, than to erect the art of teaching into a *fourth profession,* and to begin the work of education systematically, with *teaching the teachers.*

I must finally observe, that this Institution, also, owes much of its success to its decidedly religious character. Religion, without sectarian and denominational distinctions, pervades its instructions. The analysis of natural science and revealed science, conduct to one conclusion; and they are made to illustrate and support each other. If this is profitable to just attainment in knowledge, as it saves us from distorted and half-formed conceptions of the sublimer subjects, it is yet more beneficial to character, as it gives sobriety to the mind, and elevates the spirit with devout affections.

I must not omit to say, that this admirable establishment is raised and supported by subscription; and it corresponds exceedingly, with the single difference of sex, to our modern Proprietary or Grammar School. Why should not our daughters, equally with our sons, possess the advantages which these institutions, when well conducted, so readily supply? . . .

The other erection is a church, for the use of Dr. Welch and his congregation.[2] It is a very ambitious affair. All the good and approved things, it is attempted to combine; there are portico, turret, and dome. They are all executed after the best models, and with expensive ornament.

2. Bartholomew T. Welch was pastor of Albany's First Particular Baptist Church from 1828 to 1834, and in the latter year became pastor of the church here referred to, Emmanuel Baptist, on the corner of Pearl Street and Maiden Lane. He remained there until 1848.

On entering beneath the portico, you are surprised to find yourself, not in a lofty church, but in a room with low ceiling, and every way plain appearance. The fact is, the church is still above you; and by this arrangement height is gained for the external elevation, and a good lecture and school-room are provided, for the uses of the congregation. I ascended to the church. It is well arranged and fitted; except that the Corinthian columns, which rise from floor to ceiling, interrupt the sight, and are made to carry, in their way, the galleries. Dr. Welch is a Baptist; and one inconvenience in having the church over the room is, that he could not sink a baptistry in the floor. To meet this difficulty, a large oval tub, like a brewer's vat, is provided; it is placed on rollers and slides, and is drawn out from beneath the pulpit when it is wanted. It stands three or four feet high; and must, therefore, expose the persons to be baptized. Apart from this inconvenience, I know of none other, except it be that it deprives the worthy and popular minister of one argument from scriptural expressions, on which his brethren have been accustomed to lay great stress. It can no longer be said, that they go down into the water, and come up out of the water; for the fact is, they reverse the order, and go up into the water, and come down from the water. How far this may affect the validity, is a question which must be left with the hypercritics to determine.

The evening of the day, which had been thus devoted to the inspection of objects illustrative of the state of art, letters, and religion, was spent in interesting conversations at Dr. Sprague's. Chancellor Walworth, Professor Fowler, and other friends, took part in them, much to my advantage.[3] The revivals of that vicinity, and the wants of the West, were mostly the subjects before us. The Chancellor had, especially, good means of knowing the state of the West; and he candidly admitted the exigencies, as I was disposed to refer to them; but his deliberate opinion was, that the remedy was to be found in the voluntary principle, and not in any supposed provision made by the State.

On the morning of the 26th, I was to start with the coach at two o'clock. But, instead of coming at two, it came at one; and when this was complained of, the reply was, "That it was best to be before time." With too much kindness, Dr. Sprague arose to see me start fairly. We were not certain of meeting again, and, in fact, have not met since that night.

We cleared the town; crossed the bridge; and got out into the open country. The moon was sailing through the clouds, and by her occasional

3. William Buel Sprague (1795–1876) was pastor of Albany's Second Presbyterian Church from 1829 until 1869. New York State's last chancellor, the jurist and temperance supporter Reuben Hyde Walworth (1788–1867) took up the chancellorship in 1828 and resided in Albany until 1833, when he returned to his permanent home in Saratoga Springs.

lights was revealing to us a wild and hilly prospect. We made an ascent of a stiff hill; and came up with the Hartford stage, which was halting in the road. The driver had just ascertained that the boot had been robbed; and they were waiting to challenge us to the pursuit and rescue. The young man whose property was missing, whined piteously, and entreated help— "He had lost a large trunk, with thirty dollars in it, besides other valuables."

There was little need of this, not very heroic, pleading. Our party was strong, and in high spirits; there was something chivalrous in the deed; and they were ready for the chase. They put to the test the safety of our own luggage; agreed on the persons who should take charge of the teams; and set forward on the search. Still the effort had a very hopeless appearance about it. The misty moonlight lay on the road and its green margin, and made itself felt; but beyond this, all was wild forest, on whose shadows it could make no impression, and where a hundred robbers, with all their booty, might find speedy and effectual cover. The force divided itself into two parties, and decided on the tracks to be taken. Each one armed himself with stick, or otherwise, as he best could; for they did not know the strength of the foe. A dog fell in with the party to which our driver was attached; and he was wise enough to let it lead. It led them to the spot where lay the black trunk; and the discovery was announced to the other pursuers by the cry, which shot up amongst the trees, "Hurrah! the trunk is found." It appeared, that the robber, or robbers, had not been able to run with it far, and were proceeding to rifle it of its contents, when they must have been alarmed. The straps were cut off, but they had not yet been able to force the lock, so that all was safe. It also appeared, that the faithful dog, which had been the chief agent in finding the trunk, had first, by his barking, given notice of the robbery. The driver, on looking back to the dog, saw some moving shadows in the distance; and this sight may be supposed to have maimed his courage, for he certainly took but a small share in the general hue and cry. This dog would afterwards follow our coach and driver, as if for our protection. We could not induce it to go back; and it really went till we changed both, a distance of twelve miles. Of course the animal was in high favour with us all.

THE FOURTH OF JULY, 1838

Lectures were a popular form of entertainment in the nineteenth century, and many British travelers paid for their journeys by public speaking.

*Among the more renowned was James Silk Buckingham (1786–1855), who
lectured in various parts of the United States in the late 1830s. He had
much to speak about. Having gone to sea at the age of ten, he had fetched
up in India after the Napoleonic wars and founded a newspaper in Cal-
cutta so critical of the British East India Company that the paper was suppressed in 1823. The action eventually brought an annual pension to
Buckingham in partial compensation.*

*He returned to England and started several short-lived periodicals in
the 1820s, helping finance the ventures with lectures and books about his
travels. He was elected Member for Sheffield in the first reformed Parliament of 1832, and lobbied for the abolition of flogging in the British
armed services and an end to involuntary impressment into the navy. Giving up his seat in 1837, he spent four years in America speaking of his
Asian adventures and his support for the temperance cause. He was in
Albany, giving an illustrated lecture series on Egypt, in July of 1838, and
he writes of the city in great detail in one of the six volumes that resulted
from his stay in America.*

The plan of arrangement and subdivision is not so regular as many of the
American cities, but, like New York and Baltimore, while its older parts
are remarkably irregular, all its more modern laying out is as symmetrical
as could be desired. The principal street, which ascends from the banks of
the river and terminates at the foot of the Capitol on the hill, is a noble
avenue of at least 120 feet in breadth; Market Street and Pearl Street, by
which this is intersected at right angles, as these streets run nearly parallel
to the river, are also as fine streets as can be desired, of ample breadth,
from 80 to 100 feet, shaded on each side by rows of trees, and containing
many spacious and excellent mansions, interspersed with places of worship and public buildings, which produce a most agreeable effect.

Here and there are some striking contrasts, to impress on the spectator the difference which a century has made in the style of building and
scale of domestic comfort. The house we occupied at the south-east corner of Pearl and Steuben Streets, was a most commodious and delightful
mansion; it had formerly been the residence of the late governor, De Witt
Clinton, and was equal in size and accommodation to some of the best
houses in Baker Street, Harley Street, or other similar streets in the north-

From James Silk Buckingham, *America, Historical, Statistic, and Descriptive,* 3 vols. (London: Fisher, Son, and Co., 1841), 2: 284–87, 319, 336–40.

west of London. Next door to us was the residence of Governor Marcy, the present governor of the State;[1] and next to him was a new mansion, belonging to the president of the Albany Bank, Mr. W. Olcott,[2] as well-finished and fine a building as could be seen in any part of the world — indeed a sumptuous abode; while on the opposite, or north side of the street, were, in addition to the noble private dwellings, the two projecting Ionic porticos of the Female Academy and the Baptist church, which, with the graceful dome and turret of the latter, made a most beautiful architectural picture, which even an inhabitant of Rome, or Venice, or Genoa, would admire.

In contrast with all this, however, there stood at the north-east corner of Pearl and Steuben Streets, and right opposite the house we dwelt in, a Dutch burgher's residence, bearing the date of 1732; its yellow and ill-cemented bricks, its small windows and doors, its low body, and immensely disproportioned sloping roof, covered with tiles of all shapes and fashions, shewing what description of city Albany was likely to have been a century ago, and enabling one to judge of the amazing advance in opulence, taste, and comfort, which had been made since that humble dwelling had been first reared; in this respect the occasional presence of such relics, as land-marks, or indexes of the progress of time, and corresponding progress of improvement, is useful, and nowhere more so than in this country.

In the laying out of the new or upper part of the city, care has been taken to appropriate some portion of the space to public squares, for the recreation and health of the population, and public baths are spoken of as being likely to be undertaken by the city authorities.

The shops, or stores, as they are here universally called, are not equal to those of any of the larger cities we had visited, except Washington, which are decidedly inferior to those of Albany; but there are well-furnished warehouses here of almost everything needed, and an air of great activity and bustle prevails in the principal business streets.

The hotels are not many in number, but they are on a large scale, and have the reputation of being among the most comfortable in the country. Of the boarding-houses we heard also a very favourable ac-

1. William Learned Marcy (1786–1857), a Troy lawyer, was a U.S. senator from 1831 to 1833, giving up the seat to become governor of the state of New York through 1839. He was later Polk's secretary of war, and Pierce's secretary of state.

2. Albany's third bank, the Mechanics & Farmers Bank of Albany, opened in July 1811. Thomas Worth Olcott (1795–1880) worked there from its opening, became cashier in 1817 and president in 1836; he held the presidency until his death. He was well-known for his philanthropies in the Albany area.

count; and if they at all resembled the one in which we had the good fortune to be placed, they must be of the best description, as we had found
nothing so much like a comfortable English home, as the house of Mrs.
Lockwood, at 59, Pearl Street, where we remained for several weeks, and
enjoyed ample accommodation in rooms, good fare, and, above all, great
kindness and courtesy, and genteel and agreeable society. There is a large
Temperance Hotel in North Market Street, well furnished, supplied with
baths, and conducted, as we had heard from competent and impartial authorities, in a manner to afford great satisfaction to all who frequented
it. . . .

Of the other public buildings, the Capitol, or Legislative Hall, is one
of the most prominent. It stands on the summit of the hill, or highest part
of the city of Albany, and terminates the upward vista of State Street,
from the river, as the Albany Academy terminates the vista of Steuben
Street, each having their foundations at an elevation of 130 feet above the
Hudson. It is a fine building of stone, 115 feet in front, 90 feet in depth,
and 50 feet in height, independently of the small tower arising from the
centre, on the summit of which stands a figure of Justice. It has a base-
ment of 10 feet and two stories above that. The east front looking down
State Street, towards the river, has an Ionic portico of 4 pillars, about 33
feet in height; and in the interior are the two halls of legislation, for the
Senate and the Assembly, with the Supreme court of justice, and the court
of Chancery for the State, the State library consisting of 30,000 volumes,
and other rooms for committees and public business. The various rooms
are well proportioned, and well adapted to their respective purposes; they
are adorned with full-length portraits of Washington, of the several governors of the State, in succession, of the several chancellors of the State
also, with portraits and busts of other public characters of America. . . .

During our stay in Albany, we witnessed, for the first time, the celebration of the great National Festivity of America — the Anniversary of
the Declaration of Independence, on the 4th of July, now observed for the
62nd time; and we were much gratified by what we saw. The day was extremely fine — all business appeared to be suspended; and every one was
devoted to the enjoyment of holiday. The day-break was announced by a
discharge of cannon; and at sunrise, a salute of 13 guns was fired, in honour of the 13 original States that united in the Declaration of Independence. This was followed by the ringing of the bells of all the churches; so
that as early as five o'clock, the whole city was awake, and in motion. At
ten o'clock, the procession (formed to march through the town, on their
way to the first reformed Dutch church, where the "exercises," as all proceedings of public meetings are here called, were to take place,) was put in

Albany: view of Albany, n.d. (late 1830s?). Engraved by D. G. Thompson, published by Walker and White of Boston. Collection of McKinney Library, Albany Institute of History and Art

motion; and as they passed before our window in Pearl Street, we saw the whole to great advantage. The procession was under the direction of the adjutant-general of the State and the marshal of the day, assisted by several military officers, and moved in the following order:

MILITARY ESCORT.
Captain Strain's Albany Republican Artillery.
Captain Brown's Albany Union Guards.
MILITARY AND CIVIC ASSOCIATIONS.
Officers of the United States Army and Navy.
Albany Military Association.
Orator and Reader.
Revolutionary Officers and Soldiers, in carriages.
The Reverend the Clergy.
Executive of the State.
PHILADELPHIA STATE FENCIBLES.
Albany Burgesses Corps
The Common Council, preceded by its officers.

Sheriff and his officers.
Heads of the departments of the State, Chancellor, Judges of the
United States, State and County Courts, preceded
by their Marshals.
Fire Department, and the several Engine Companies with their
Engines, Hook and Ladder, and Axe Companies under
the direction of the Chief Engineer.
The Van Rensselaer Guards.
St. Andrew's Society.
Union Benevolent Society of Journeymen Tailors.
Albany Mechanics' Benefit Society.
Hibernian Provident Society.
Saddle and Harness Makers' Society.
St. Patrick's Benevolent Society.
Citizens and Strangers.

The military had really a fine appearance, being well dressed, well equipped, and well disciplined; the bands of music, of which there were several, were all good, and one very superior; the various companies and societies, all habited in some peculiar costume, or distinguished by some peculiar badge, looked remarkably well; and the populace, who thronged the foot-pavement on each side of the street, while the procession filled the centre, were as well dressed, as orderly, and as evidently interested in the proceedings of the day, as the best friend of the republic could desire. What we missed was, the waving of handkerchiefs from the windows and balconies, and the shouts and cheers of the multitude, which usually accompany such processions in England. But the Americans are more decorous than enthusiastic; and the staid and grave manners derived from the Dutch at Albany, make them quite as grave and silent on all public occasions, as the Quaker population of Philadelphia.

The part of the procession which touched us most, and made unbidden tears, not of joy or sorrow, but of mere exuberance of sympathy and feeling, start involuntarily into our eyes, was the sight of the veteran heroes of the revolution, as they passed us in the open carriages that contained them. As sixty-two years have passed away since the Declaration of Independence, the number of those who actually fought in the war of the revolution is now very small, and they are, of course, every year diminishing; so that in a few years more they will all have descended to the tomb. The veterans we saw were all above 80 years of age, and the oldest of them was 96. The hoary locks which were visible on each, with the associations which their years and services awakened, impressed us more powerfully than anything we had yet witnessed in the country; and it was evident, from the demeanour and bearing of all parties, young and old, toward these veterans as they passed, that one universal sentiment of veneration and respect for their age and character, pervaded all classes.

In the church, which was crowded in every part, the exercises consisted of music by the choir, prayer by the pastor, the reading of the Declaration of Independence by one of the citizens, and an oration in honour of the day by another — all of which were well performed; and on the procession passing from the church, it marched to the City Hall, and after a discharge of vollies dispersed.

In the afternoon, a second public procession was formed by the members of the Young Man's Association, a body combined for mutual instruction; and this, while it was less military, was more literary — in keeping with the character of the institution. They marched from their rooms in the Knickerbocker Hall to the second Presbyterian church, in regular order; and, in addition to the usual exercises of the day, similar to those performed in the morning, there were three original odes, all written expressly for the occasion by ladies of the city, one by a pupil of the Female Academy, and each highly creditable to the talents of their writers; with a longer poem, by a gentleman of Albany, and member of the association.

In the evening, the public places of amusement were all open, and illuminations and fire-works were exhibited at different quarters of the city. There was also a great public dinner held in one of the domed edifices, about 500 yards from our dwelling, from whence the cheers and huzzas came so loud and so frequent over the toasts that were drank, as to excite some apprehension for the perfect sobriety of the guests. There were, indeed, some instances of intemperance visible in the streets, but they did not amount to half a dozen, and were among the humblest class of labourers; so that the general sobriety of the day was one of its most remarkable and most pleasing features.

The day was closed by a delightful serenade of music opposite the house of the governor, W. L. Marcy, which, as it adjoined our own residence, we enjoyed in perfection. The night was delicious, after the warmth of the day; and the moon, now just about the full, was really brilliant. The busy hum of the streets was hushed; for though there were still hundreds of well-dressed persons, of both sexes, taking their evening walks beneath the trees that here, as at Philadelphia and most other American cities, line the pavement on either side, yet the sound of their footsteps could scarcely be heard. The band was of first-rate excellence: we understood that it came up from Philadelphia with the State Fencibles, that it was under the training of a coloured man, named Frank Johnson, who was an able musician, and who, having recently been in Europe, had come back greatly improved.[3] The only military bands I ever remember to have heard superior to it were the royal band that attends at the Palace of St. James's in London, and the band of the National Guards at Paris. The music, too, was as well chosen as it was well executed; and our only regret was when it ceased, which was not, however, till nearly midnight. . . .

Albany is singularly deficient in the number of its benevolent institutions, compared with the other cities of America, or with the extent of its own population, wealth, and resources. The only one of interest or importance is the Orphan Asylum, which I went to visit, with one of the directors, and with which I was much pleased. The building is a large brick edifice on the western edge of the town, advantageously situated for the health and comfort of its inmates. The edifice cost about 20,000 dollars, which was raised by private subscription; a few individuals contributing half of the sum required, in payments of 2,500 dollars or 500l. sterling each; and the rest being readily obtained from the inhabitants generally.

The building is enclosed with a spacious and excellent garden of fruits, vegetables, and flowers, which the orphans cultivate themselves: and about five acres of ground afford them pasture for cows, and spacious and airy play-grounds.

Though called an orphan asylum, the directors have found it advisable to take in destitute little children, who had one parent living, but that parent unable to provide for its offspring, as in the case of destitute widows; and sometimes, where both parents were alive, but where the father being a drunkard, and the mother scarcely able to maintain herself, the little children were really as badly off as if both father and mother had been in the grave. I was assured by the director, Mr. Wood, that in an investigation which he deemed it his duty to make, previously to preparing one of the last annual reports, he had found that in fully nineteen cases out of every twenty, the little children, whether orphans or otherwise, were destitute and helpless, entirely because their fathers, or mothers, or both, had been persons of intemperate habits, and expended what they ought to have bestowed on their children in intoxicating drink.

3. Johnson was employed for many years by John Clarke, who made his fortune bottling and selling spring water. "The first music furnished at the hotels was in 1822. The band, composed of colored men and led by Frank Johnson, first played at 'Congress Hall,' until the completion of the 'United States,' when they played at each hotel on alternate evenings" (William L. Stone, *Reminiscences of Saratoga and Ballston* [New York: Virtue and Yerston, 1875], p. 295).

There are at present about 100 children in the Asylum, from 3 to 10 years of age. At their entry, if there be any persons who have a claim to them by relationship or otherwise, the consent of such person is obtained to the giving up the child wholly to the direction of the Asylum till it shall be 21 years of age. The child is then provided in food, raiment, and lodging, and receives a plain, but religious, education. Their diet is wholly vegetable; and this is found, by some years' experience, to be not only sufficiently nutritious to ensure all the required strength, but superior to animal diet in its being less likely to engender diseases, the average health of the children, notwithstanding the destitute condition in which many of them are taken in, being greater than the average condition of any similar number not so fed. They work in the garden with great cheerfulness, cultivating their own food; and this again, while it is a pleasurable and even instructive recreation, is found to be highly favourable to their health.

LEBANON SPRINGS AND THE SHAKERS IN 1835

It is reasonable to suppose that when Mother Ann Lee came to America in 1774 with adherents of her United Society of Believers, she had no intention of founding a major tourist attraction. But the creed of the sect differed wildly from the better-known forms of nonconformism, and expressed itself in a social organization and modes of worship that attracted visitors from all over North America and Europe. Motivated by curiosity about the sect's beliefs, prurient interest in men and women living together in a celibate community, and a wish to be entertained by the Shakers' unusual ways of praising God, they turned out hundreds of pages about the society's eccentricities. Few were sympathetic. By the 1830s the Shakers were publishing pamphlets to rebut the more outrageous libels and prefacing their services, still, remarkably, open to the public, with requests that tourists maintain a sober demeanor and ignore what they had read in popular accounts. Travelers seldom responded to these requests, and by the time of Dickens's journey in America access to the services had been severely restricted.

The first small settlement was at Niskeyuna (Watervliet), eight miles northwest from Albany. As the society grew, more settlements were established: New Lebanon in New York (1787); others in Massachusetts, Connecticut, New Hampshire, and Maine in the late eighteenth century;

*and in Ohio and Kentucky, and briefly in Indiana, in the early nineteenth
century.*

*The Watervliet colony was much visited as Albany grew in impor-
tance, but the New Lebanon foundation was best known. A couple of
miles from the tourist spa of Lebanon Springs, and close to the turnpikes
from Pittsfield and Stockbridge to Albany— the main road links between
New England and New York— the community suffered innumerable visitors. Few described the physical appearance of the settlement, but James
Stuart published this brief celebration in his* Three Years in North
America.

> They have at this settlement about 3000 acres of land. Their
> buildings are very clean-looking both without and within, a
> little detached from the road, as well as from each other, and
> extend for about a mile. They are large, plain, and handsome,
> — almost all painted of a yellowish colour. Not a weed or nui-
> sance of any kind is to be seen in their fields, gardens, or even
> in the adjoining road through their property. Their wood is
> put up with the greatest regularity with solid pillars of stone as
> gate-posts. Their orchards are large, and in excellent order,
> and their agricultural operations well managed. They manu-
> facture and sell brushes, boxes, pails, baskets, ladies' reti-
> cules, and a great variety of domestic utensils. Their garden
> seeds and vegetable medicines are celebrated all over the Union,
> — their gardens being on a great scale. Their cyder is excellent.
> The females are also employed in domestic manufactures and
> house-work, and the community fed and clothed almost en-
> tirely by its own productions. Not being burdened with the
> care of children, they are more at liberty than other communi-
> ties to follow their occupations without interruption. (1: 292)

*Under the pen name of A. Thomasen, Andrew Bell wrote a book
about his year in North America (August 1835–August 1836), which was
published in 1838. A businessman from Southampton, he claims to have
been cured of enthusiastic republicanism in 1830, when he was based in
Paris at the time of the uprisings. He traveled in America to convalesce
from an unspecified illness and, not surprisingly, one of his first stops
was the health resort of Lebanon Springs whose mineral waters were, if
not healing, at least a reasonable excuse for the fashionable classes to
mingle in the summer. Bell took the obligatory excursion to New Lebanon, but differs from most authors in writing of the Shakers with some
sympathy.*

The watering-place, called New Lebanon Springs, is built on the top of a hill, of gentle ascent. It is composed of a bathing-house, and three very extensive and stately taverns, forming a kind of square; its conspicuous position upon a hill, like "a city that cannot be hid," at a distance, with the hundred shifting lights in the windows, gave it the appearance of some illuminated palace in a theatrical scene; a comparison that was still further helped by the sounds of music and revelry which fell upon the ear as we approached it. Having taken up my quarters at one of the taverns, I found myself in the midst of the gayest company I had yet mixed with in America. . . . Although not of the gayest turn of mind myself, I have always been, like Goldsmith's Doctor Primrose, an admirer of happy faces;[1] and here there was a freedom of intercourse, a forgetfulness of the cares of life, an oblivion of its distinctions, all reigning about this charming spot, which it was quite delightful to meet with, and what I hardly expected to find, and indeed never did find afterward, in any part of America. Numbers of the young ladies—some with their parents, but mostly with their sweethearts—tired with much dancing in the concert-room, were walking about the grounds, pleasantly laid out garden-fashion, in the centre area of the buildings; the *stoup* or colonnade in front of the taverns had rows of chairs for gentlemen; and there sat the latter smoking, discussing lightsomely their own affairs or those of the nation, and all the world enjoying itself in its own way. But the tell-tale moonlight, which shone bright over all, showed me lady arms twined round favoured necks, with a most loving simplicity that thought no ill. These pairs moved around jauntily, keeping time in their steps to the cadence of imaginary music, the instruments having now ceased. It grew late, but no one seemed to think of going to rest: how could they, and leave such a bright shining moon behind! Although I have been, in my time, rather scurvily treated by many individuals of my species, there *have been* moments when my heart has swelled within me with such an expansion of love to human kind, that I thought I could lodge the whole race within its core. . . .

In moments of pain and sorrow, in the desolation of a dejected soul, in the dreariness of enforced solitude, when I wish to expel from my mind the gloomy sensations of the intolerable present by pictures of the agreeable past, I shall always recall to mind the evening I passed at Lebanon Springs.

From Andrew Bell ("A Thomasen"), *Men and Things in America; Being the Experience of a Year's Residence in the United States*. . . (London: W. Smith, 1838), pp. 74–75, 76–82, 86–92.

    1. Dr. Primrose is the hero of Oliver Goldsmith's *The Vicar of Wakefield* (1766).

Early next morning, which was Sunday, I got up to have a look at the healing waters. I found twenty or thirty people assembled around them, and drinking them by large tumblers-full, being used both inwardly and outwardly. It is the most remarkable water I have ever seen for clearness. The bottom of the reservoir was lined with a shining silvery grey-coloured deposite; and the fluid over it so transparent, that at a few feet distance it was difficult to believe there could be water there at all. Thin wreaths of smoke curled lightly over the reservoir's mouth. This hot spring issues from a rock, with a flow of eighteen barrels a minute. Part of the water is carried, by means of pipes, into the baths hard by. . . .

Having breakfasted early at the tavern, along with some twenty persons, mostly gentlemen — few of the ladies being visible as yet — I set out to visit the Shakers. After a circuitous walk of three miles, I found myself in front of their meeting house. It is a plain square building, having the exterior of a large riding-house. It was not yet opened. Opposite to it, the high road passing between, is the Trustees' house — a substantially-built and very neat structure, two stories high; such a place as would be fit for the residence of an English gentleman of moderate fortune. This building, with the meeting-house, school-house, &c. stands on rising ground, which still continues to ascend, till it ends in a woody ridge. The descending ground, whereon stands the meeting-house, ends in a hollow, inclosing various mills and work-shops advantageously placed about a stream which there runs, so as to make its water-power available. As for the dwellings of the brethren, owing to the undulating surface of the land, scarce one is visible from the spot I have been trying to describe; they are scattered up and down in all directions on the different farms. Having no one to point out the property to me, or give me any authentic information about the society, I inquired of one of the first brothers I met whether the establishment could be seen that day; he answered me briefly, but civilly, that Sunday was an inconvenient day, but that if I were only "curious to see their worship," the meeting house would be opened in an hour or two. I told him that was not all I wanted; that I had come from afar, and wished to get as much information as they were willing to give. After some slight hesitation, he knocked at the door of the head-quarters, and it was opened by "a sister," an elderly female, who showed me up to "the Elder." This was a middle-aged man, shrewd-looking and intelligent, with an intellectual forehead and penetrating eye. He seemed a perfect man of the world, and was of ready speech, having certainly nothing of the enthusiast in looks, manners, or conversation. He asked me what I wanted with him. I made an apology for coming on such a day, when, as I had just heard, it was not usual for visitors to be received; but that I had come from abroad, was pressed for time, as I was obliged to hasten back to New York, &c. He told me it was not possible for him to show me the working part of the establishment, nor the grounds, because it was with them a day of absolute rest, and therefore he had no one to send with me; but he would willingly shew me the government house; which he thereupon did, and took me through the different rooms himself, with unceremonious civility. They were all well and substantially, though plainly furnished, and particularly neat and clean—the whole a model of order and comfort. The *pierre de touche* of a house is its kitchen; and none in London could exceed theirs in neatness of equipment. If the great business of life be to live well, in one sense of these words no means or appliances are wanting in the premises set aside for "the elders and trustees of the people called Shaking Quakers." One apartment, which he called "the store," was full of articles, of light manufacture, for sale to visitors or others, mostly the handiwork of the sisters, such as baskets, cradles, and the like, with packets and samples of various kinds of seeds and grains, plants, bundles of healing herbs, &c. He assured me, these were in great request in most parts of the country around, and their sale added considerably to the general funds; also, that the general produce of their fields and dairies had a higher value in the market than that of other producers. Next to the store, he showed me the laboratory. He told me that more than one of the "brothers" had studied medicine; and that they had everything "within themselves," even to a printing house.

We now returned to the sitting room, and he seemed to be preparing to leave me; but I had a similar desire to that of Voltaire, who, in his Travels in England, relates, that he asked Thomas White of London, a leading Quaker, to whom he was introduced, "to be good enough to instruct him in his religion." I expressed to my Shaker, though in less direct terms, a similar wish. He asked me, fixing his keen eyes on mine, if ever I had heard anything remarkable about them in my own country, before. I said I had not, excepting some slight accounts I had read in books of tourists, who all treated the subject in a strain of levity that had induced me to put little trust in them. He said that his duties would prevent him, for the present, from gratifying my desire; but that it was a pity I was so urgent, as I was welcome to call next day, or whenever it suited me, and that then he, or some other to whom he would mention my desire, would give me every reasonable explanation. "In the meantime," said he, directing my attention to a heavy octavo volume lying on the table, "there is a book which will tell thee more about our people than I can. And here again is a little work, lately sent forth by us, in our own defence, which will explain some things that concern us; should thou never find time to read it, it will be as a remembrance to thee — of my brethren I was going to say, but they are thine also;" so saying, he put into my hand a small pamphlet of 36 pages 12mo.[2] "To-day," said he, "thou mayst see, if thou wilt, a kind of worship which will be altogether new to thee. The hour of meeting will soon arrive, and so I must leave thee; but take thy seat at that window, and thou mayst turn the interval to profit by perusing the volume I have shewn thee." So saying, he left me. . . .

As the hour of service approached, a flock of visitors began to arrive, some on foot, but mostly in carriages. No less than three stages came, full of ladies and gentlemen, from Lebanon Springs alone. Presently came "brothers and sisters" in quick succession: they were mostly conveyed in well-built spring carts, and all dressed in the same sober uniform; which is even plainer than that of the Quakers, and as spotlessly clean. The men wore old-fashioned square-cut fustian frock coats; plain fronted shirts, without collars; some few with ample cravats, but mostly without. The women wore a dress of light greyish fawn-coloured stuff, fashioned in such a way as to hide as much as possible the contour of the body, and make all the sisters appear of one shape. They wore very high-heeled shoes, which added considerably to the height of their persons; and, being generally lean, and destitute of any projections to break their straight poplar-tree outline, gave most of them, when they stood up, the appearance of the ghosts of giantesses. Most of their complexions were pale, and their looks universally downcast and melancholy. At first they took their places on long forms ranged under the walls to the right; over their heads was a long row of pegs for bonnets; their head pieces were of a shape like that of our coal scoops, with retrenched handles; the material they were made of was apparently some cheap cotton fabric, and its colour a slaty grey. Similarly ranged, on the opposite side to them, sat the brethren, each under the shadow, not of his own fig-tree, but of an immense broad-brimmed hat of plaited straw; and a useful article this is, too, in summer. The position and look they assumed was the same as that of the sisters; and the hands of all were disposed in a convenient fashion for what is called *thumb twaddling.*

The visitors had entered by side doors in front of the building — the ladies by one door, the gentlemen by another; the same separation of sexes being observed for the audience as for the performers. The latter sat sidewards to the rows of the sisters, the former were similarly placed as to

2. The title of this pamphlet is given elsewhere as *A brief Exposition of the established Principles and Regulations of the United Society of Believers called Shakers* (New Lebanon: Calvin Green and Seth Y. Wells, 15 March 1830).

the brethren; and we were ranged on seats sloping down from the entry-wall for a short way into the room. Behind the sisters was their door of entry; the brethren entered from behind also, but the door of the latter led into a side-room, like a vestry: thus were all parties kept separate. There were about one hundred and fifty men, and, as near as may be, the same number of women. The spectators were full two hundred, occupying but a small space.

After the doors were shut, a dead stillness prevailed among the members for ten or fifteen minutes, and the silence was maintained unbroken by us also. All at once we were startled by a man's rising up with a sudden jerk; the others got on their legs in an instant; and, after taking off hats, hanging them up, and stripping themselves to their shirts, they huddled the chairs together, and drew up in a long line. A similar operation was going on among the sisters—omitting the stripping; they unbonnetted, however, and taking off their tiny shawls, stood up opposite to the men. These confronting lines were not parallel, but rather angular, so as to increase their length, the open part of the angle being that nearest to us. No two lines were ever more admirably *dressed* by any drill-serjeant. Midway between the ranks, stood a select band of women, about a dozen or so, upon whom, as on a pivot, the whole machinery of the evolutions that followed seemed to turn. They always sung (or screamed) the loudest and gesticulated the most energetically. They were like the *fuglemen* to a regiment when it is exercised. But let us take things in their order.

The two parties stood as immovable as a long avenue of statues, with eyes fixed on the ground, for full five minutes; at the end of that time symptoms of life began to manifest themselves by a kind of spasmodic projecting and retracting of some of the sisters' toes, which presently spread along the whole female line, and then communicated itself to the men by a quick infection; to this was soon added an astounding yell,[3] the starting-note of a kind of ranting hymn, uttered by the strongest voice of the centre band, which was immediately caught up by all; and off they set, in a kind of singing gallopade. The same words were, no doubt, sung by every one; but the confusion of so many voices, some not keeping ex-

3. Made the more astounding by the Shakers' consideration of the building's acoustics. As Charles Daubeny reports, "The church was a large oblong building, perfectly plain within and without, and remarkable only for its neatness, rivalling in that respect the Moravian establishment at Hernhutt [sic]. It had a vaulted roof, underneath which, at a little distance below it, was suspended a large wooden sounding board, extending about half way from the centre of the room to either end, as a means of assisting their voices in singing" (*Journal of a Tour Through the United States, and in Canada, Made During the Years 1837-1838* [Oxford: Charles Daubeny, 1843], p. 18).

act time, made it difficult to hear them connectedly. They rang the changes, however, very often on the following lines —

> "In the day of doom will Jesus come
> To save my soul alive!
> To save my soul alive!"

Their style of singing, I am almost ashamed to say, made me think directly of Signor Corri, (for even in the most sacred places will profane thoughts now and then intrude). This singer, while in England, one day passing near a meeting-house of Ranters, while voicing an uproarious hymn, put his hands in his sensitive Italian ears, and asked, with a look of dismay, "Vat deese peoples vere dooin." Being told they were singing the praises of God, he rejoined, "Den dey must tink he haf ver' bad ear."[4]

The hymn, or whatever it were, of the Shakers, was "a joyful noise" to the letter. All this while the brothers and sisters were moving about, sometimes in circles, at other times in ellipses; one while the brothers stood still and let the sisters whirl round them; otherwhiles the reverse; but however the figure changed, there was never any commingling of sexes. Both had their arms drawn close to their bodies, leaving the hands sticking out in a strange manner; and with these last, like a turtle's fins, they kept *flapping* time to the quick measure of their song. Meantime, loudest and most active in all this were the centre band of women. Many of them were quite hoarse before it was concluded. There they stood, like the axis of a wheel, while round them moved the wide circumference of this "periodical fit of distraction," as douce old David Deans would say.[5] At last, with every appearance of fatigue and lassitude, again they sat down, and a dead silence reigned for fifteen minutes or so. Then the Spirit moved a man to get up and speak. He was evidently a "weak brother." His rambling unintelligible discourse united the two essentials of bad oratory, being at once extravagant and dull. It was really what old Colonel Crockett would have called a strain of "almighty twaddle." When he had ceased, after a reasonable pause another got up. This was a speaker altogether of a different stamp; but his discourse was much more addressed to us than to his own people. He intimated, among other things, while deprecating the contempt of the world for his community,

---

4. Domenico Corri (1766–1825) was born in Rome, settled in Edinburgh in 1771, and moved to London in 1787. He was a singer and composer, and a music-publisher in later life.

5. Davie Deans appears in Scott's *The Heart of Midlothian* (1818).

that it contained in its body some who had been well considered by that world they had renounced for ever; it was not because the world despised *them* that they left a distinguished place in its ranks: it was because they despised *it,* on account of its vanity, its nothingness, its total insufficiency, with all its allurements, to satisfy a reasonable soul. So long as he confined himself to this part of his subject, he spoke with easy fluency and great feeling. I strongly suspected, indeed, that he alluded, in much of what he said on this head, to himself; but when he came to treat of the peculiar notions of the Shakers, there was a sad falling off: — he sank at once into downright rigmarole [which Bell summarizes].

After having conveyed this kilderkin of meaning in a tun of words, he suddenly stopped, and sat down; then there was a silence again for a quarter of an hour. The "Spirit" moving no one else to speak, the affair closed as it had begun, only to another tune which was of a slower measure; but carefully kept time to, with the same wagging of *fins* as before: the figures also were a little different, and of course having a less dizzying effect on the spectator's head. No bible, or psalter-book, indeed no book of any kind, was used, nor prayers offered up; all was either extempore or learned by heart; howbeit their evolutions must have been well practised, for they were as perfect as those of dancing on a stage. When this second vocal gallopade was finished, the doors were thrown open, and the meeting broke up. The sisters immediately departed; the majority of them got into spring-carts, and in these were driven home by one or other of the brethren. Those of the latter who remained, dispersed into little groups, probably discussing the merits of the speakers; and I, observing that they shunned contact with "the world" to which I belonged, and having no hope of further edification or amusement, took a first and last farewell of the Shakers.

THROUGH SCHOHARIE AND DELAWARE COUNTIES IN 1825

Travelers' motives for visiting particular places vary widely: geologists, farmers, actors, and lawyers had different interests and satisfied their curiosity in different parts of the country. But some journeys were made for reasons that were entirely personal. I. Finch's walk through Schoharie and Delaware counties was such a journey.

Finch was distantly related to the chemist Joseph Priestley. Born in 1723 and long a dissenting minister in the north of England, Priestley was

a voluminous writer of theological works as well as conductor of the ex-
periments for which he is now remembered on electricity, the chemical na-
ture of combustion, and the discovery of oxygen. He had emigrated to the
United States in 1794 and settled in Northumberland, Pennsylvania,
where he died in 1804. He was buried in the Quaker burying-ground there.
Finch, who was in Albany at the beginning of 1825, decided to visit his re-
lation's grave.

If the motive for his visit was personal, Finch's journey can only be
described as irremediably eccentric. There was no direct route to North-
umberland from Albany: it required taking the Hudson steamer to New
York City, sailing to Philadelphia, and then traveling overland by stage-
coach. Finch, deciding that he preferred the direct route, set out in the
middle of winter—and walked. Delayed by deep snow drifts and bitter
cold, and frequently getting lost, he managed eventually to complete the
journey; and as a by-product left one of the very few accounts of Scho-
harie and Delaware counties by a British traveler.

I had a relation reposing near the Susquehanna, and I had not yet paid a
visit to his tomb, although his name had often introduced me to agreeable
society and to valued friends. In many a gay and crowded party, I had re-
proached myself for not having performed this sacred duty. I examined
the map, and found the distance was near two hundred and fifty miles,
and there was no distinct road between the Delaware and Susquehanna;
but I took a short sketch of the route, and determined,

"Viam inveniam, aut faciam."[1]

I proposed to walk, and the chief difficulty was the season of the
year. It was winter, and the ground was covered with snow. But, when we
wish to accomplish any object, a few obstacles are no great impediment.
Besides, I was accustomed to take a great deal of exercise; enjoy the beauties of the country, and have often walked in a snow-storm in England
merely to observe the beauty of the landscape, and the gay appearance of

From I. Finch, *Travels in the United States of America and Canada, Containing Some Ac-*
count of their Scientific Institutions . . . (London: Longman, Rees, Orme, Brown, Green,
and Longman, 1833), pp. 295–306.
    1. "I found the right road, or rather I made a road for myself."

the forest. I promised myself that if I was successful in my present visit, I would make another pilgrimage at a gayer season of the year, when the flowers were in bloom, the birds were singing, and all nature wore a gay and animated aspect.

It was the 22nd of February, 1825, that I commenced my solitary pilgrimage from the city of Albany; it was a dark and cloudy day, like the November of England. At six o'clock in the evening I arrived at Rennselaerville, a pleasant village, near the borders of a small stream, and on the declivity of a hill. The mountains of Catskill are seen to the southwest. The distance was twenty-three miles, and I felt very little fatigue.

Feb. 23. The landlord informed me that a farmer was proceeding in his sleigh near to Waterville, where I intended to go, and would be happy to have my company. Although this broke in upon my resolution, I could not well refuse the offer. My companion wished to make a small detour to visit a friend, and we arrived towards noon at Middleburgh, and stopped two hours at the hotel. The unexampled success of the New York Canal had spread a rage for canals through the State; and in this small town, surrounded by mountains, and nearly cut off from all communication with their fellow-citizens, the inhabitants had caught the reigning fashion. During our stay there was nothing talked of but the subject of internal navigation, and we left them arranging the time when they should meet the canal committees from the neighboring towns. I was afterwards informed that a route for a canal was surveyed in this part of the country, but found to be totally impracticable.

Two miles south of the town is an eminence where, in ancient times, a band of Indians are said to have formed an ambush; after waiting for a favorable opportunity, they sallied down upon the peaceful inhabitants, and, killing a great number, carried the rest into captivity.[2]

At a short distance from the town, we arrived at the Valley of Scoharie, where a river of the same name flows toward the north. The hills on each side were covered with a profusion of forest trees; the birch, cedar, walnut, and sumach, grow luxuriantly. The river was sometimes hid from our view by the forest, or covered with ice; at other times it rushed impetuously over its rocky bed. The field and the forest, the hill and the valley, were all covered with snow; I wrote my name on the snow in the valley as a memorial of my journey, and if a few summers' suns have not melted it

2. Captivity and Indian-raid stories abound in the area, which was on the front line during much of the Revolutionary War. In 1780, Sir William Johnson had, as a typical example, led a force of 800 through the area, unsuccessfully attacking the Middle Fort near Middleburg.

away, it is there still to be seen. We had to go some distance to cross the river where the ice was sufficiently firm to bear our sleigh. At seven o'clock in the evening we arrived at a small house where a tavern had been formerly kept.

We found the court of King Caucus was to be held there. In the States of North America, all the officers, from those which refer to the government of a town to the Governors of States, are chosen by Caucus. The two parties meet at separate inns, and canvas the merits of the various candidates. They are put in nomination, and whoever has the majority of votes is supported by the whole party. It is similar to the associations which take place previous to the public meetings in England, where resolutions are prepared before they are submitted to the general voice. The inhabitants of the valley were assembled to choose their county officers. The room was desolate, with not a single article of furniture; and, after waiting half an hour, we proceeded onwards.

Our road now led through woods of fir and pine, and the contrast between the dark gloom of the forest and the snow with which it was covered was very striking. The road was narrow, up a steep ascent; we heard the noise of a mountain torrent on our left, but the night was dark, and we could not distinguish the stream. My guide had previously taken the sleigh-bells from the horse, that we might move silently through the forest. He dreaded to encounter the Hermits of Scoharie, men who, with an axe as their sole companion, penetrate into these forests to cut down the pine timber. He said, that, being in want of every necessary of life, they sometimes stopped travellers on the road. We passed two hermitages, but were fortunate in not meeting with the owners.

After travelling several miles through the forest, we began to emerge from its gloom. The moon had now arisen, and shed her brilliant light over the landscape. . . .

The night was intensely cold, but I remember with pleasure my sleigh-ride in the Valley of Scoharie.

At eleven o'clock at night we arrived at a small inn. My guide departed to his farm in the neighborhood, and, after taking some refreshment, I retired to rest. The distance travelled this day was probably thirty miles.

Feb. 24. On inquiry, I found that I was nine miles from Waterville. The snow was deep, and for two miles I walked through a forest where the path was not very distinctly marked, and arrived at the main road. After proceeding three miles further, I perceived on the left a small pond, the source of the river Delaware. I soon arrived at Waterville, the highest settlement on the river, where there are several saw-mills and a few stores. Great activity is displayed in cutting down lumber in the forest, and preparing it for market. A few miles beyond the town I observed a farm-house by the side of the road, and wishing to make some inquiries, I called, and found the proprietor at home. He immediately had refreshments brought out, and insisted on my staying to partake of them.

He had been confined a long time to the house by an attack of the gout, or some other disorder, and had time to reflect on the political condition of his country. I was quite surprised at his mode of viewing the subject. He said, "In most countries they are content to have one despot; but here there are two tyrants to whom I am obliged to submit — the President of the United States, and the Governor of the State of New York. I voted against both of them, yet they are put in authority over me. And yet they call this a free country! When my party were in power, they did not give me any office. They talk of making a canal down this valley; but the first man who comes on my farm to take levels, I will shoot him." This individual had a large farm, and was surrounded by the comforts of life. When he made these and numerous other speeches of the same kind, his eyes sparkled with delight, and he quite forgot his sufferings from disease. I remained so long listening to his speeches that I did not arrive at Delhi till some time after dark. The road for the last few miles was very bad, the snow having partially thawed; the distance I had travelled this day was twenty-four miles.

Delhi is a flourishing town, and contains an excellent hotel, where I obtained every attention that I desired. The business transacted is chiefly in preparing lumber, and there are a few stores. The church, school-house, and court-room are situated at the side of an open square. The houses are painted.

Feb. 25. Setting out rather late in the morning, I pursued my journey. Great part of the distance was through woods, but there were some spots of cultivated ground. In a few miles, the valley enlarged, and, seeing a house, finely situated on an eminence, I called there to obtain a glass of water. I was highly gratified with my visit, although it was only for a few minutes. It was the neatest house I have seen in America; every thing was arranged with the most scrupulous exactness. The proprietor had a farm of several hundred acres of woodland and cultivated ground, and the house commanded a fine view. The ladies were engaged in spinning flax. The father was representative for his county, and was at Albany, attending the meeting of the Legislature, but he was expected home in a few days to attend to the business of the farm.[3] Altogether, it presented a charming rural scene. I have often thought of the neat farm-house in the Valley of Delhi, and the picture of happiness which it seemed to present.

3. The Delaware County representatives at Albany in 1825 were, according to *Dela-*

Early in the afternoon, I arrived at Walton, a distance of only four-teen miles.

The road for nearly four miles pursued the course of the river. The banks were precipitous and clothed with wood; and in the middle of winter, the scenery was wild and romantic. But I had now to encounter a very formidable obstacle, of which I had been informed at Walton; this was a steep hill, nearly five miles across, covered with a forest, and not a single house to enliven the view. The road was covered with ice, and was in many places so steep and slippery that it was difficult to ascend. When I had proceeded near a mile, I was joined by a traveller on horseback; but, after accompanying me some distance, he continued his journey. I began for once to be tired of the monotony of the forest; even the tulip-trees had lost their charm. The road in descending the mountain was exceedingly slippery and dangerous, and I was rejoiced when I had passed this ice-covered hill. I arrived at night at Port Deposit, having travelled a distance of twenty-three miles.

Feb. 27. Sunday. I remained the whole day at this small town; it snowed incessantly. The inhabitants of Port Deposit gain a subsistence by engaging in the lumber trade. They proceed to the forest in summer, cut down the lofty pine trees, and saw them to a certain length; when the snow falls in winter, the timber is drawn by oxen and horses to the saw-mills, and cut into boards. In spring, they are collected in rafts, each of which contains thirty thousand boards; these are floated to a distance in the river, and when the stream becomes wider, two are joined together. The double rafts are guided by four men, one of them has greater wages, and is called the pilot; he has the principal command.

If they escape the perils of the flood, and are not stranded on some of the rocks or shoals with which the river abounds, they arrive in a few days at Philadelphia. The state of the market varies; sometimes the sale is rapid, at other periods they have to wait a long time before they can dispose of their cargo. When it is sold, they return home on foot.

The country round Port Deposit is covered with wood; the oak and pine are cut, the rest of the forest is left standing. When the proprietors reside near their land, the persons who cut lumber are obliged, though very unwillingly, to purchase it, and sometimes pay fifty dollars per acre. Every year they are obliged to penetrate deeper into the forest.

Deer abound. The wild elk is sometimes caught in the districts to the

---

ware County, New York, History of the Century 1797–1897, General Erastus Root, the post-master at Delhi, and William Townsend (d. 1849), whose farm spread over much of the village of Walton. His large family included four girls.

north. Bears and wolves are numerous; the panthers find a safe retreat in the interminable woods.

The distance between the Delaware and Unadilla, in this part of their course, is not more than fifteen miles. The guide whom I had on the following day said, that in the first settlement of the country, provisions were scarce, and they sometimes went to the Unadilla to procure fish, which were caught in great quantities.

On one occasion, his family were destitute of food; he went on foot to the Unadilla, and procured as many fish as he could carry. On returning home through the forest, he heard a noise, and looking back, saw six wolves following his steps, attracted by the smell of the fish. They came near. The struggle in his mind was now severe, between his dread of being attacked by the wolves, and his fear of seeing his wife and children starving at home. He persevered, and carried his provisions safe; the wolves followed him the whole distance to his cottage, but did not attack him.

Feb. 28. I had a guide as far as Staruccaville; beyond this I lost my way in the forest.

A BRIEF TRIP TO OTSEGO COUNTY IN 1836

Charles Augustus Murray, having sampled the hospitality of Albany society, traveled westward on his mare Polly to Otsego County. Having stayed a few days at Hyde Hall, he headed south to Cooperstown and met James Fenimore Cooper there. Cooper had returned to take up permanent residence in the village his father had founded after spending the years from 1826 to 1833 in Europe with his family.

Cooper's popularity as a best-selling novelist was already in decline in the mid 1830s; this, and the fact that he resided in Cooperstown, not the easiest place to reach, saved him from some of the importunities that his more famous and accessible contemporaries suffered from autograph hunters and worse. Still, several accounts of him survive in the literature of travel, though the passages concerned mostly say more about their authors than about the American novelist. Joseph John Gurney, a Quaker visitor a few years after Murray, had an introduction to Cooper through the English novelist Amelia Opie and left a brief portrait of his host at Cooperstown. The tinge of disapproval in the following passage stems from Cooper's frivolity in writing fiction and from his not being affected by the revivals that were sweeping upstate New York at the time (and

which fascinated Gurney). "On our return to the hotel, I found our friend
Fenimore Cooper in his white jacket, ready to row me in his little boat,
that I might examine the beauties of the lake to the greatest advantage.
. . . Although his great talents have been employed in a direction which I
can by no means approve, I ought to acknowledge, that his conversation
was interesting and instructive. He abounds in the knowledge of men and
things, and expressed many sentiments with which I could concur" *(*A
Journey in North America, p. 294*). Murray is a far more tactful writer:
typically he neither names Cooper directly nor reports the substance of
the conversation.*

From Albany I proceeded on horseback to Lake Otsego, a distance of
fifty-four miles, which I easily performed on my active nag, in less time
than the coach, which started at the same hour, although it had three or
four relays of horses, so deep and muddy were the roads. Indeed, I have
no hesitation in saying, that it was far less fatiguing to ride those fifty
miles than to have performed them in the stage.

Otsego is a beautiful sequestered lake, and all the neighbourhood is
classic ground, being the scene of one of the American novelist's best
tales, and at the same time that of his own residence. At the upper end of
the lake stands Hyde Hall, the seat of the late G. C. Esq.;[1] an English gentleman who settled in this country and built here a house more resembling
the good English 'squire mansions than any which I have seen elsewhere.
Here I remained several days, upon a visit to his widow Mrs. C. and
others of his family, and must use the tautology common to every candid
traveller in America, when I say that I was most hospitably and kindly
received.

The house, which is a plain, Grecian, stone building of large dimensions, contains some very handsome rooms, and commands a splendid
view of the lakes and the surrounding hills and woods;[2] while in the dis-

From Charles Augustus Murray, *Travels in North America During the Years 1834, 1835, and
1836. . . ,* 2 vols. (New York: Harper and Brothers, 1839), 2: 234–35.

  1. Hyde Hall was built 1813–1815 by George Clarke, a descendant of the lieutenant-
governor of the colony from 1736 to 1743 of the same name. The governor had married
Anne Hyde in 1705, whence the name of the property. Hyde Hall's builder died in 1835.

  2. Tyrone Power had been a guest the previous year, and says of Hyde Hall that it "is
built upon a natural terrace, part of a fine hill that juts out into the lake, and creates a little
bay that laves its south side, and forms a safe harbour for the boats of the family" *(Impressions of America,* 1: 367).

tance, over the water, the neat white houses and spires of Cooper's-town emerge from the green and gently sloping shores. Among the inmates of the house, was a daughter of our hostess; she had been married two years, and been a mother one, yet she had all the youthful animation, glee, and beauty of sixteen. In such company, fishing, rowing, walking, and riding, made the time pass so quickly, that I was obliged also to remind myself that I was a traveller, and not a sojourner. On Sunday, I went down to Cooper's-town, where I heard a sensible discourse, and had the pleasure of dining and spending the afternoon with the Walter Scott of the Ocean.[3] His house, both in size and appearance, looks like the parent of the thriving village in the centre of which it stands. Before it is a circular lawn, now the scene of several pleasure-garden improvements; beyond which the lake, with its wooded and verdant promontories, its sloping banks, and the bold headlands which are at its upper extremity, forms a most agreeable landscape; it is, however, already described by the highly gifted possessor in his tale of "The Pioneers," many of the characters of which are family portraits. Its heroine was drawn from a very near relative, the memory of whose beauty and graces, both mental and personal, is still fresh in the neighbourhood.[4]

3. In his own day Cooper's fame rested as much on his sea novels, starting with *The Pilot* (1823), as on the work for which he is known now, the Leatherstocking Saga.

4. Elizabeth Temple, the heroine of *The Pioneers* (1823), was thought by many a portrait of Cooper's sister Hannah, who was killed in a riding accident in 1800 at the age of twenty-three. Cooper in late life denied the claim, notably in his preface to a new edition of the novel published in 1849.

The Spas and the Champlain Valley

EIGHTEENTH-CENTURY MEDICINE did not affect the vast majority of the population, which relied for healing on a popular pharmacopoeia. Medicine was a science for the relatively rich, but, crude and inexact, it dealt adequately with few ailments more complicated than simple fractures. For the amorphous bulk of undifferentiated discomfort, it prescribed three main treatments: opium-based pain-killers, blood letting, and massive drafts of mineral waters. The efficacy of these treatments is questionable, but the social effect, especially of taking mineral waters, is undeniable. To take the waters at a spa became simultaneously an attempt to alleviate suffering and a conspicuous demonstration of wealth.

Bath was the preeminent health resort of eighteenth-century England. During its summer seasons the old congregated annually to repair the ravages of the winter's excesses in town, believing, or at least hoping, the waters would relieve arthritis, gout, venereal disease, dyspepsia, and a hundred other complaints. Socially they flaunted their wealth, often of recent acquisition, and sought (sometimes to buy) suitable marriage partners for their children. The young who accompanied their parents created their own showy, fashionable subworld, which soon supplanted the medical reasons for attendance. By the turn of the century, the apogee of conspicuous consumption, dandyism, was flourishing, and Bath was its summer stage.

Through the 1770s the cream of colonial society joined their metropolitan cousins at Bath and the other spas—indeed, the sugar planters of the West Indies were among the wealthiest and showiest of the spas' customers. The colonial presence, however, was severely curtailed by American independence and the Napoleonic blockade. More local health resorts began to develop and to develop in their own ways. Thus by the early nineteenth century sea bathing, under royal patronage, had begun to supplant taking the waters as the chief medicinal and social diversion of Britain's summer months. But in North America the spa continued to reign supreme. As Andrew Reed observed in his *Narrative of a Visit to the American Churches* of the early thirties: "The people here all run from the sea in the summer; while with us [British] they are all ready to run into it" (1: 318).

Chief among these later-flowering resorts were Saratoga Springs and Ballston Spa. French, Indian, and later British incursions from the north had retarded commercial exploitation of the mineral springs of Saratoga County, and it was not until after the War of 1812 that their full-scale development began. The new, rapid transportation—steamers on the Hudson, and railroads a little later on—made Saratoga more accessible both to southerners escaping the summer heat, and to the rich of the northern cities, where summer was the cholera season. Eventually a regular circuit of resorts was established; and the greatest among them was Saratoga Springs, a mecca for some of the rich, several of the famous, and large numbers of those who aspired to wealth or fame.

British travelers flocked to the watering places in eager pursuit of that elusive and mythical creature, the "American Character." They found much to divert them. The manners of the Americans on vacation astonished them, and many entertaining pages record the speed with which Americans ate, the freedom of conduct afforded young and unattached women, and the unanimity with which their parents' conversations turned on the supremacy of the almighty dollar. But other accounts of the spas were written by authors who missed the height of the intense, short season. They record the emptiness of the spas between the migrations of the gaudy flocks of the fashionable.

The reported charms of Saratoga in the summer vary directly with the intimacy of the writer with American social circles. Thomas Hamilton's *Men and Manners in America* reveals he knew relatively few people; he summarized his feelings briefly in this way: "If Saratoga was dull, Ballston was stupid" (2: 193). Few of the better-connected travelers agreed with him. Most found the villages dull only when the fashionable caravanserai had departed for the year. In the high season the British met old acquaintances and formed new ones, joining in most of the attractions that the resorts offered. Charles Joseph Latrobe, after spending two summers at the springs, summarizes the events of a typical day thus:

Well, you may ask, how do the people spend their time? — Much as other honest idle people do. The excitement of the morning chiefly consisted in the bustle consequent upon the departure of a host of guests to Ballston Springs, Schenectady, or Albany, by the Rail-road, about ten o'clock. Then followed a listless time, during which the gentlemen amused themselves by various excursions, or slunk away to smoke, or to the billiard-table, or the reading-room; while the ladies whiled it away in the drawing-room, in their chambers, with books from the circulating library, or in visiting. The approach of the dinner hour, which, if I mistake not, was three in the afternoon, and the return of the cars on the Rail-road, set the blood and the flagging spirits of all in motion. . . . The toils of the toilet being at an end, for a quarter of an hour before dinner the drawing-rooms, and the back and front piazzas of the hotels, swarmed with a resuscitated crowd, like an ant-hill into which a mischievous boy, or an equally mischievous professor of natural history, has thrust a stick.

The meal was followed by an informal processional as people digested the food they had just gulped down in the massive public dining-rooms, and the evenings were taken up by "balls, cotillion parties, occasional concerts given by wandering minstrels," and whist, although cards were not generally considered to be fashionable (*The Rambler in North America,* 2: 129. 30, 133).

Excursions in the vicinity included visits to Ballston and, for fishermen, Lake Saratoga and its neighboring ponds. A popular patriotic outing for Americans, and a melancholy one for transplanted Englishmen, was the drive to Stillwater, scene of Burgoyne's capitulation in 1777. The romantic charms of Lake George drew many tourists, while slightly farther afield were the ruins of Forts Ticonderoga and William Henry, and the main route to Lower Canada by the Lake Champlain steamers.

So strong an attraction did Saratoga become that it altered the typical tourist itinerary. The first traveler's account in this section dates from before the great popularity of the resorts: Lieutenant Francis Hall took the direct route from the upper Hudson to Quebec, via Troy and Whitehall, ignoring Saratoga Springs entirely. But for tourists in the twenties and thirties the spas were an important stop on their travels through New York. James Silk Buckingham stayed for a while near Ballston and left a detailed account of the lesser resort. Beaufoy and Alexander Mackay spent time in Saratoga Springs, and both portray society there in lively prose. James Stuart's account approved so greatly of things American that it provoked several responses, among them Richard Weston's sour minority report about life near Lake George. Harriet Martineau, however, greatly enjoyed Saratoga society and her excursion to Lake George.

By contrast there is virtually nothing written about the Adirondacks before the 1850s, and camping there would not become popular until after the Civil War. Similarly, British authors neglect the farming communities directly south of the Canadian border. Potsdam and Massena go unmentioned, and while Ogdensburg is occasionally glanced at, it is only from the St. Lawrence River or the Canadian bank. Only the irrepressible Charles Murray, who hired a horse and cart at Ogdensburg and crossed the North Country in order to avoid cholera-ravaged Montreal, left any description of the area; and he summarizes his impressions in a few lugubrious lines.

> In the course of this long journey, the villages were "like angel visits, few and far between;" the roads execrable, being made upon the anti-mac-adam corduroy system. The miles of gloomy silent forest, apparently interminable — the dull monotony of this bosky desert — its loneliness unrelieved by the appearance of any living creature, save now and then the shrill cry of the woodpecker, and the hissing whisper of the catydid, produced a corresponding effect upon our spirits. A group of shepherds, collected round a wolf, which they had just slain as an expiatory sacrifice to appease the manes of eight sheep, devoured by him the previous night, formed the only banquet in which our appetite for interest or incident was permitted to indulge. We heard indeed of bears, deer, &c. but saw none. (*Travels in North America*, 1: 71)

This antipastoral vision of the North Country sharply contrasts the idyllic impressions that most British travelers create of life in the resorts of Saratoga County.

A NORTHERN TRIP IN THE WINTER OF 1816

The War of 1812 dammed the flow of British visitors to North America for a short while, but the prewar trickle grew to a steady stream as peace in the New World coincided with the cessation of hostilities in Europe.

Francis Hall, a young lieutenant in the 14th Light Dragoons, was among the earliest of those who took advantage of newly settled conditions to travel in America. He arrived in New York in March 1816 and spent eleven months examining conditions (and, from the frequent quotations in his published account, reading copiously among earlier visitors). During his visit he spent some considerable time in a New York State damaged by the war and just beginning to recover from its incursions.

Hall did not follow the normal practice of his later compatriots: he spent the early part of the winter in the northern states rather than migrating south as soon as the weather turned cold. He left a rare glimpse of traveling in the Champlain Valley at the end of 1816, a glimpse the more interesting because at this early date Saratoga goes unmentioned, and Troy assumes an importance as a transportation terminus that it was soon to lose to a resurgent Albany.

The realization of Hall's comment on Troy—"every mark of growing opulence"—would be postponed forty years in British accounts by Albany's more spectacular attractions. For Troy, though occasionally noted for its ladies' academy, would become important as a manufacturing and industrial center at a time when British travelers were becoming more interested in standard tourist fare than in investigating economic growth. In the 1830s, it is true, the actress Fanny Kemble would find an attraction in Troy, but it was an attraction that very few of her fellow travelers would recognize. "The situation of the warehouses, on the side near the river of the main street of Troy," she wrote in her Journal, *"is exceedingly pretty. They are, for the most part, large, long rooms, opening to the street at the one end; and on the other, looking down from a considerable height, upon the Hudson" (2: 234–35). In one such store she was entertained by a china-store operator and local booster while waiting for the ferry to Albany.*

By the mid-forties Troy's industries were beginning to gain attention as more of Britain's mercantile middle classes took advantage of rapid transatlantic crossings to meet their American counterparts. Archibald Prentice's Tour in the United States *is a typical early example of this different interest. He was a fervent anti-Corn Law Leaguer in Britain, edited the Manchester* Times, *and came to the United States to recuperate from his political activities. In his comments on Troy the intense, practical curiosity of the emigrant-writer and the pleasure-seeking of the tourist coalesce. He records nothing of the appearance of the place: true excitement for him vests in public policy. "Troy is at the extremity of the steam navigation of the Hudson, and it is consequently a great* depôt *for the fertile back country with which it communicates by railway and canal. It has also the advantage of a considerable amount of water power. Mr. Marshall possesses a fall of two hundred and forty feet. His extensive factories for spinning, weaving, and calico printing, illustrate the mischiefs inflicted by a government which acts in ignorance or defiance of the true principles of political economy . . ." (p. 98). Troy becomes in this account an example of the effects of a government's meddling through tariffs and artificial monopolies with the operation of market forces and the ideal conditions of free trade.*

Such messages about political economy were not there for the reading when Francis Hall made his trip. His is a more personal narrative, where the recent past — the British defeat at Plattsburgh — weighs far more heavily than any economic concern.

Troy is little short of a mile in length, and bears every mark of growing opulence. There is a large barrow-formed mount, at the end of the town, on the road side, which, though evidently a natural rock, might represent the tomb of Ilus to this new Ilium, were Yankey imaginations disposed to run classically riot.[1] The road runs pleasantly on the banks of the Hudson, which here form a long stripe of flat ground, evidently an alluvion, about a mile in breadth, beyond which the hills again rise, intersecting the country in a N. W. direction. Betwixt Pittstown and Cambridge we crossed the Hoosick river, and continued our way through a wild and mountainous country, whose remoter heights were now fading in evening mists. From Pittstown we had quitted the course of the Hudson, and moving in a N. E. direction, were falling in with the various chains of hills which spring laterally from the great N. E. chain of the West Point mountains. Salem is beautifully embosomed amid these ramifications, which seem to divide the low country into a number of separate basins, each watered by its own sequestered stream. Masses of slaty rock are every where scattered through the country. Land, we were informed, was worth about 20*l.* per acre; a considerable sum, where it is so plentiful. The Americans, who are never deficient when improvement is in view, have introduced the use of gypsum, as the most transportable, as well as the most profitable, manure. A farmer here, with whom, as is usual in the States, we fell into conversation, informed us that the average quantity employed was three

From Francis Hall, *Travels in Canada, and the United States, in 1816 and 1817* (London: Longman, Hurst, Rees, Orme, and Brown, 1818), pp. 43-52.
    1. Ilus was the legendary founder of Ilium (Troy) and grandfather of King Priam.

pecks per acre, united with the seed: that it was of great service to clover; and well employed on all sandy or gravelly soils, adding a curious remark, if correct, that it produces no effect on land within 30 miles of the sea.

Granville is situated in one of these mountain basins, and is but a few miles from the foot of the Green and Bald mountains, which form the continuation of the great chain. The streams in this neighbourhood no longer fall into the Hudson, but make a northerly course to Lake Champlain. At Granville we quitted the main north road, to go to Whitehall, and take the benefit of sleighs, across the lake. I observed a quantity of red clay-slate in this neighbourhood, resembling the cliffs of the St. Lawrence near Quebec. The aspect of the country remained much the same, only growing more wild and wintry as we proceeded. The snow which had hitherto been partial, now began to impede the progress of our waggon, which had been moving at the rate of three and a half miles per hour. We were frequently obliged to alight, and walk down steep hills, thickly encrusted with ice and snow. A fine bear had preceded us, as we discovered by his large round foot prints, but he was not complaisant enough to show himself from some craggy knoll, and welcome us to his solitude. A small ground squirrel was the only specimen of bird or beast we encountered. The valley closes in as you approach Whitehall, until its lofty barriers barely leave space sufficient for the site of the village, and the course of a small river, called Wood-creek, which rushes into the lake, with a small cascade; its right bank rises perpendicularly several hundred feet: strata of dark grey lime-stone, disposed at regular parallels, exhibit an appearance of masonry so perfect as to require a second glance to convince one a wall is not built up from the bed of the stream. The heights on the opposite side of the valley are equally bold, and marked with the same character; their summits are every where darkened with forests of oak, pine, and cedar; large detached masses of granite are scattered generally through the valley, and among the houses of the village, which, like several others on our road, very much resembled a large timber-yard, from the quantity of wood cutting up and scattered about for purposes of building: indeed it is impossible to travel through the States without taking part with the unfortunate trees, who, unable like their persecuted fellows of the soil, the Indians, to make good a retreat, are exposed to every form and species of destruction Yankey convenience or dexterity can invent; felling, burning, rooting up, tearing down, lopping, and chopping, are all employed with most unrelenting severity. We passed through many forests whose leafless trunks. blackened with fire, rose above the underwood, like lonely columns, while their flat-wreathed roots lay scattered about, not unlike the capitals of Egyptian architecture. I believe some

traveller has observed that there are no large trees in America, an observation not very wide of truth, to judge from what may be seen from the
high road; a few steps however into any of the woods, shew that they have
abounded in very fine timber, numerous remains of which are every where
left standing; but the extreme prodigality with which the finest timber
trees have been employed, being often piled together to make fences, and
so left to rot, has begun to produce a comparative scarcity, especially near
large towns, which has considerably increased the value of the property of
woodland.

At Whitehall we embarked in sleighs on Lake Champlain; the afternoon was bright and mild, and well disposed us to enjoy the pleasing
change from our snail-paced waggon to the smooth rapidity of a sleigh,
gliding at the rate of nine miles an hour. The first object our driver was
happy to point out to us, was several of our own flotilla, anchored near
the town, sad "trophies of the fight." The head of the lake called, "the
Narrows," does not exceed the breadth of a small river; the sides rise in
lofty cliffs, whose grey strata sometimes assume the regular direction of
the mason's level, sometimes form an angle more or less acute with the
horizon, and sometimes, particularly in projecting points, seem almost
vertical to it. Our driver pointed out a curious fissure in the left bank,
called the "devil's pulpit;" it is in about the centre of the cliff, and seems
broken with great regularity, much in this figure ∇ .

Tyconderoga point stands out in an attitude of defiance to those
who ascend the lake, but its martial terrors are now extinguished, or
marked only by the crumbling remains of field works, and the ruin of an
old fortified barrack. Lake George unites with Lake Champlain, at the
foot of this mountain point, by a narrow stream, on the right bank of
which, rises Mount Defiance, and on the opposite side of Lake Champlain, Mount Independence; names which bespeak their military fame in
days of old, but now, like retired country gentlemen, they are content to
raise oak and pine woods, instead of frowning batteries. At Shoreham,
nearly opposite to Crown Point, we found good accommodation for the
night, at Mr. Larenburg's tavern, and set off the next morning before
breakfast; but we had soon cause to repent of thus committing ourselves
fasting to the mercy of the elements. The lake now began to widen, and
the shores to sink in the same proportion; the keen blasts of the north,
sweeping over its frozen expanse, pierced us with needles of ice; the thermometer was 22° below zero; buffalo hides, bear skins, caps, shawls and
handkerchiefs were vainly employed against a degree of cold so much beyond our habits. Our guide, alone of the party, his chin and eye-lashes
gemmed and powdered with the drifting snow, boldly set his face and

horses in the teeth of the storm. Sometimes a crack in the ice would compel us to wait, while he went forward to explore it with his axe, (without which, the American sleigh-drivers seldom travel,) when, having ascertained its breadth, and the foothold on either side, he would drive his horses at speed, and clear the fissure, with its snow ridge, at a flying leap; a sensation we found agreeable enough, but not so agreeable as a good inn and dinner at Burlington. Burlington is a beautiful little town, rising from the edge of the lake; the principal buildings are disposed in a neat square; on a hill above the town stands the college, a plain brick building, the greater part of which is unoccupied, and seemingly unfinished.

We crossed the next morning to Plattsburg, curious to view the theatre of our misfortunes;[2] it is a flourishing little town, situated principally on the left bank of the Saranac, a little river, which, falling into the lake, makes, with an adjacent island, and Cumberland Point, a convenient bay, across which the American flotilla lay anchored, to receive our attack; the untoward issue of which, decided the retreat of Sir George Prevost's army. . . .[3]

The fortifications are on the right bank of the Saranac; the American commandant obligingly conducted us through them; they consist of two square forts palisadoed, but with neither out-works, nor covered way. This officer informed us, that they had not even their gates hung when our army first arrived before them. Our retreat surprised them as much as it did many of our own people; it must however be observed, that though little or no doubt existed, that the works, if attacked, would have been carried, the object of the expedition fell to the ground with the loss of the flotilla, by means of which alone, the transport of stores and provisions could have been secured. The fight must have been for honour only, and Sir George Prevost certainly took the boldest part, when he declined it.

"Travelling after all," says Madame de Stael, "is but a melancholy pleasure;" an observation doubly true, if applied to travelling over an uniform surface of ice, in very cold weather. Curiosity freezes under such circumstances, and the only prospect which rouses attention is the inn, or village, which is to afford the comforts of food and fire. I observed,

2. On September 11, 1814, Thomas Macdonough's American fleet defeated the British, thereby foiling a joint naval and land-borne assault on Plattsburgh. The attack of the military forces under Sir George Prevost by land was abandoned despite its likely success as a result of the battle on the lake.

3. Sir George Prevost (1767–1816) became governor-general of Canada in 1811. During the War of 1812 his caution led to defeat in the two engagements at which he commanded: Sackets Harbor and Plattsburgh.

however, that the shores of the lake gradually sunk down to the level of the water, while the mountain ridges fell off to the right and left, leaving a broad and nearly level expanse of wood and water. Traces of cultivation diminished as we approached the frontier; a few solitary houses, commonly the resort of smugglers, were scattered on the shore, embosomed in forests of a most uninviting aspect. Betwixt Champlain and Isle aux Noix, travellers take leave of America, and enter on the Canadian territory.

TEMPERANCE IN THE BALLSTON AREA, 1838

After experiencing the Fourth of July in Albany and noting how few drunks were to be seen, James Silk Buckingham traveled to Ballston Center. There he stayed with an American adherent of one of his pet causes: temperance. His host, Edward Cornelius Delavan (1793–1871) had, ironically, first become rich in the wine trade. Turning against strong drink, he augmented his fortune in the late 1820s by speculating in Albany real estate while becoming increasingly involved in the temperance movement. Together with Eliphalet Nott, president of Union College, he had founded the state temperance society in Schenectady, and by 1830 he was campaigning full time for the temperance cause. A good public speaker and resourceful publicist, Delavan was well known among British travelers for his Temperance House hotel in Albany, often known simply as "Delavan's," where many took rooms during their visits to the state's capital.

In the farming district in and around this spot, Ballston Centre, where, from the influence exerted by Mr. Delavan, and the spread of the temperance publications, the practice of total abstinence from all that can intoxicate is nearly universal, the health and longevity of the population is greater than in any part of the country; the deaths do not reach two per cent. per annum, varying between one and six-tenths and one and eight-tenths; the ages extend to eighty and ninety ordinarily; and, by the latest

From James Silk Buckingham, *America, Historical, Statistic, and Descriptive*, 3 vols. (London: Fisher, Son, and Co., 1841), 2: 418–21, 424–25.

examination of the labouring people, it was ascertained that there was only one person in 1152 receiving pecuniary relief as being unable to subsist himself.

On Mr. Delavan's own farm, there was scarcely a labourer who had not money placed out at interest: his coachman, cook, and house-servants had several hundred dollars each, accumulating in the saving's bank; and additions made to this from the surplus of their wages every year. The gardener and farm-servants were in the same prosperous condition, and had, moreover, small plots of land of which they were the owners. Throughout the whole of this district, the farmers, to a man, refuse to sell their grain for distillation, or for malting; while all the produce of their orchards, which is considerable, is devoted to the fattening of cattle, instead of the making of cider: and besides the great moral good thus effected in withholding the supplies of these materials for conversion into intoxicating drinks, they happily find themselves benefited rather than injured, in a pecuniary sense, by their present appropriation.

The Sabbath we passed at Ballston Centre offered a beautiful illustration of the effects of liberal institutions and temperate habits on the condition of domestics, and the relative position of masters and servants. Though there are no parish churches, in the sense in which we understand that term in England, there are sufficient places of worship for all who desire to attend them, including Presbyterian, Episcopalian, Methodist, and Baptist, which are the four most numerous denominations of Christians here. These churches (for all places of worship are so called, and the term chapel is never used)[1] are placed at convenient distances, and generally with reference to centrality among the worshippers frequenting them; but while they are not more than half a mile from some of the farm-houses, they are six and seven miles from others.

No distance and no weather, however, prevents a general good attendance, as every family has one or more vehicles, open or covered, and abundance of horses, by which the whole family, servants, and all, are easily conveyed to the church. Those who live near, return from the morning service to dinner at half-past twelve, and go to church again at one; but those who live at a distance generally bring a cold dinner with them; and in the interval between the morning and afternoon service, partake of it on the grass, in the neighbouring grounds if the weather be fine; or at the nearest inn or house of accommodation, if the weather is bad. Some of the waggons bring 20 and 30 persons of the same farm to church, for

1. In English usage, "chapel" is reserved for the place of worship of nonconformist denominations, "church" for those of the Church of England.

Ballston Springs, 1838. By William Henry Bartlett, from N. P. Willis, *American Scenery* (London, 1837–40). New York State Museum, Albany

none remain at home, and all are on a perfect footing of equality in the enjoyment of their privileges for that day.

From Mr. Delavan's residence, which in England would be called a "country seat," rather than a farmhouse, as it has all the elegancies of a gentleman's abode, and its occupier is a man of large fortune, the vehicle which conveyed the family to church was called "the Steam-boat," from its great length, though drawn on four wheels, and by a pair of horses. In it were seats for sixteen persons; and in the same vehicle, the family and guests, or visitors, and all the servants, without distinction, drove to church in the forenoon — returned to a cold dinner at half-past twelve — repaired again to church in the afternoon — and all the house-servants and farm-labourers, after tea, which was taken at four, set out on foot to walk to the Sunday-school, and attend evening worship again after this. Amidst this devotion of their whole attention to religious duties, and complete freedom from labour of all kinds, there was no gloom, no discomfort, and no appearance of weariness, but as much of cheerful enjoyment visible in the countenances and conduct of all, as could result only from the occupation being such as both the will and the heart approved. Without the slightest wish to prevent the freest exercise of individual opinion as to the observance of the Sabbath, I could not but wish that the mingling of the devout, the healthy, and the cheerful, which I witnessed on the first Sunday that I had passed among the rural population of America, could be substituted for the idle, dissipated, and intemperate manner in which it is too often passed by the rural, as well as by the civic population of my native land. . . .

Ballston is an incorporated village, under a board of trustees, elected annually by the inhabitants, who are about 1,200 in number. The courthouse for the county of Saratoga is also here; and there are three churches, several large hotels, and a weekly newspaper published in the village. There are several springs; the principal of which are the original Ballston Spa, the Washington spring, the Sans Souci spring, Louis spring, and the Park spring. The waters of all these do not differ much from each other, their principal ingredients being muriate of soda, carbonate of soda, carbonate of lime, carbonate of magnesia, and carbonate of iron. The two principal hotels will accommodate about 400 persons, and there are many private boarding-houses for invalids. The environs of Ballston furnish many agreeable rides, and the river Kyaderosseras affords excellent fishing for trout.

TWO VIEWS OF SARATOGA, 1820s AND 1840s

"Riding, driving, playing at bowls, and drinking the very nasty, but, I believe, very valuable waters, were the pastimes of the day," recalls George Drought Warburton in his Hochelaga *(2: 23). But Saratoga Springs offered far more than this to dozens of British travelers: it was the stage on which "The American" could be observed on vacation.*

The village itself was relatively small. Life focused around enormous hotels, each named for a spring—the Congress, the Pavilion, the Union, the United States—but even in the thirties Saratoga left Andrew Reed with the strong impression that it had just emerged from the forest.

The Americans who passed the summer there seemed to the more hypercritical English socialites as though they, too, had just come down from the trees. For it was at Saratoga Springs that the full range of differ-

*ences in national manners became apparent, and there that they were
chronicled in detail. The manners of the observers are now quite as interesting as those of the observed were at the time. The British of the early
nineteenth century were confident that their own customs and behavior
defined the norms of civilized life. Travelers' reactions to American manners show how roughly these suppositions were buffeted by American social life. The tone of published descriptions varies hugely, from haughty
indifference through shocked distaste to quasilibelous caricature—
agreeing only in the strength with which tourists held to their opinions.*

*Saratoga out of season was a ghost town, haunted by the promise of
absent society. "A British Subject," whom Allan Nevins identifies with
the name of Beaufoy, missed the high season during his travels in the mid-
twenties. His Saratoga is a neutral place of empty buildings and anticipation, one of the few not shaped by the reaction of the writer to the summer crush of people.*

*By extreme contrast is a passage from twenty years later, Alexander
Mackay's account from his* Western World. *Born in Scotland and a Toronto journalist for several years in his youth, Mackay (1808-1852) was
sent by the London* Morning Chronicle *to report on the Oregon border
disputes in Congress. He traveled widely, sampling public opinion on the
matter, and his investigations resulted in a splendid book long cited as the
best account of the United States by a Briton. In his description of high
season at the spa it is the vast number of people and the unself-conscious
exhibition of their manners that dominate. The buildings and the town's
appearance recede in importance as Mackay pursues his detailed vision of
the widely reported American characteristic of doing everything in a hurry
—even relaxing.*

Out of Season in the Late 1820s

Saratoga is laid out in one long wide street, which has a most cheerful appearance; for though all the houses, with one single exception, are built of
wood, yet, being neatly painted, and having columns and verandas, overgrown with woodbine, clematis, &c., the whole town is pleasing and gay.
Besides several dozen boarding and lodging-houses, inns, &c., there are
three hotels on the most extensive scale, each having accommodation for
nearly three hundred visitors, in addition to baths and billiard tables. The

From Beaufoy, *Tour through Parts of the United States and Canada. By a British Subject*
(London: Longman, Rees, Orme, Brown, and Green, 1828), pp. 135-36.

furniture and fitting up is handsome, the tables well supplied, and wines, with all other luxuries, may be had on calling for.

The proprietors of these hotels take it by turns to give nightly balls,[1] with good bands of music stationed in the gardens; and they enforce such excellent regulations, by turning any person out of the three houses, who misconducts himself in either, that, although the company consists of all classes, very few quarrels take place.

The season this year is uncommonly backward, by reason of the cold weather in May, and therefore I have not seen Saratoga in all its glory of crowds and fashion; which I lament exceedingly, because families from every part of the Union, even from New Orleans, three thousand miles off, are said to frequent its healing waters.

The roads about this neighbourhood are sandy, the country poor but undulating; and among the many agreeable rides, is that to the charming little lake of Saratoga, where an unexpected scene of rich farms and pastoral beauty is displayed. A few miles further, is the neat village of Ballston, with some large handsome hotels for visitors to the springs of that place. The soil about there is richer, and has evidently been much longer under cultivation; but the houses are often unpainted, and have not that clean, comfortable appearance of the newer settlements to the west. One reason given me was, that the occupiers were generally tenants instead of owners, the farms in that quarter being very extensive. The hire of a labourer, they told me, was fifteen shillings a-week, besides meals.

Another excursion, and very naturally a favourite one with the American public, is to the remains of Fort Edward, and thence to Bemiss Heights, where, on October 17, 1777, General Burgoyne and a British army of 6000 men, were compelled to surrender to General Gates. A road from thence runs along the side of the Hudson to Waterford, a fine village, and so on to the Cohoes Falls, and Albany.

High Season in the 1840s

Saratoga has lately been losing caste, but it is still to a considerable extent, a place of fashionable resort. For a time the "select" had it all to themselves, but by-and-by "everybody" began to resort to it, and on

From Alexander Mackay, *The Western World; or, Travels in the United States in 1846-7. . . ,* 2d ed., 2 vols. (Philadelphia: Lea and Blanchard, 1849), 2: 213–16.

1. Warburton reports that these popular entertainments were known as "hops" (*Hochelaga,* 2: 23).

Saratoga Springs: view of the village, c. 1820. From Jacques Milbert, *Itinéraire pittoresque* (Paris, 1828–29). New York State Museum, Albany

"everybody" making his appearance the "select" began to drop off, and what was once very genteel is now running the risk of becoming exceedingly vulgar. The waters are held in considerable repute as medicinal; but of the vast crowds who flock annually to Saratoga, but a small proportion are invalids. The town is very elegant, the main street being enormously wide, and shaded by trees. The hotels are on a very great scale, and so are their charges. At this, however, one cannot repine, seeing that it is everybody's business to make hay when the sun shines. It scarcely shines for three months for the hotel-keepers of Saratoga, the crowds of flying visitors going as rapidly as they come with the season. For nine months of the year Saratoga is dull to a degree—duller, if possible, even than Washington during the recess of Congress. Suddenly the doors are opened—the shutters are flung back from the windows—curling wreaths of smoke rise from the long smokeless chimneys—and the hotels seem suddenly to break the spell that bound them to a protracted torpidity. A day or two afterwards, a few visitors arrive, like the first summer birds. But long ere this, from the most distant parts of the Union people have been in motion for "the Springs," and scarcely a week elapses ere the long-deserted town is full of bustle and animation, and ringing with gaiety. A better spot can scarcely be selected for witnessing the different races and castes which constitute the heterogeneous population of the Union, and the different styles of beauty which its different latitudes produce. . . .

The huge pile constituting the hotel covered three sides of a large quadrangle, the fourth side being formed by a high wall. The whole enclosed a fine green, on a portion of which bowls could very well be played. The three sides occupied by the building were shaded by a colonnade, to protect the guests from the hot sun. This part of the establishment was generally appropriated by them, where they lounged on benches and rocking chairs, and smoked and drank both before and after dinner. The meal just mentioned was the "grand climacteric" in the events of each day. A few families who visit Saratoga dine in their private apartments, but the vast majority dine in public; and they get but a partial view of Saratoga life, who do not scramble for a seat at the *table d'hôte.*

In the chief hotel the dining-room is of prodigious dimensions. It is, in fact, two enormous rooms thrown into one, in the form of an L. Three rows of tables take the sweep of it from end to end. It can thus accommodate at least 600 guests. The windows of both sections of the dining-room looked into the quadrangle, and my friend and I observed that several of the loungers in the colonnade every now and then cast anxious glances within as the tables were being laid for dinner. It soon occurred to us that there might be some difficulty in getting seats, a point on which we sought to set our minds at rest, so that we might be prepared, if necessary, for the crush. But we could effect no entrance into the dining-room to make inquiry, every approach to it being locked. At last, however, we caught in the colonnade a tall black waiter, dressed from top to toe in snow-white livery [whom they bribe to reserve chairs for them at dinner]. . . .

The doors were still locked, but by-and-by we perceived parties of ladies and gentlemen entering the dining-room by those connecting it with the private apartments, and taking their seats at table. The *ignóbile vulgus,* in the interior colonnade, were kept out until the ladies and those accompanying them were all seated. Then came the noisy jingle of the long wished-for bell. Back flew every door, and in rushed, helter skelter, the eager crowd. We took our post at the door nearest the chairs set apart for us, on which we pounced as soon as we were pushed in, and were thus secure in the possession of places from which we could command a look of both arms of the dining-room. It was some time ere all were seated; and in the *hurry scurry* of entering it actually seemed as if some were leaping in at the windows. It was not because they were famished that they thus pressed upon each other, but because each of them wished to secure the

best available seat. It was amusing to witness, as they got in, the envious
glances which they cast round the room, and then darted off in dozens for
the nearest vacant chairs. At length all were seated, and the confusion
subsided, but only to give rise to a new hubbub. No sooner was the signal
made for a general assault upon the edibles, which were plentifully
served, than such a clatter of dishes and a noise of knives and forks arose,
mingled with a chorus of human voices, some commanding, others sup-
plicating the waiters, as I had never heard before. In one room were
nearly 600 people eating at once, and most of them talking at the same
time. The numerous waiters were flitting to and fro like rockets, sometimes tumbling over each other, and frequently coming in very awkward
collision. Every now and then a discord would be thrown into the har-
mony by way of a smash of crockery or crystal. The din and confusion
were so terrific as utterly to indispose me to dine; I could thus devote the
greater portion of my time to looking around me. The scene was truly a
curious one. There were many ladies present, but the great bulk of the
company consisted of the other sex. The ladies were in full dress, the *table
d'hôte* at Saratoga being on a totally different footing from that at other
hotels. In about twenty minutes the hall looked somewhat like the deck of
a ship after action. The survivors of the dinner still remained at table,
either sipping wine or talking together, but the rest had disappeared as if
they had been carried out wounded or dead. Their fate was soon revealed
to us; for, on emerging shortly afterwards into the interior colonnade, we
found them almost to a man seated in arm-chairs or rocking-chairs, some
chewing, but the great bulk smoking. Before dinner they risked their
necks to secure seats at table; after it their anxiety was to secure them on
the colonnade. Hence their sudden disappearance from table.

SARATOGA COUNTY IN THE FALL OF 1828

*James Stuart, born in Scotland in 1775, spent three years in North Amer-
ica between 1828 and 1831, and his detailed, favorable account of the
United States, its people, and its institutions provoked controversy in
Britain, in which he participated with some zest. Stuart was no stranger to
public attention. A keen Whig, he and his politics had earlier been the
objects of numerous anonymous attacks in the columns of the more conservative Scottish newspapers. The most extreme and scurrilous article
appeared in the Glasgow Sentinel, and Stuart, having discovered the iden-*

tity of his assailant, Sir Alexander Boswell, killed him in a duel in 1822. He was arrested for wilful murder; the trial was one of the major causes célèbres of the twenties; and the jury acquitted him of the charge.

Stuart left Scotland after flirting with bankruptcy in 1828. In 1831 he returned to make his home in London, where he assumed the editorship of the Courier, *published his approving opinions of the United States, and defended them against all comers. He received political appointments in the late 1830s and died in 1849.*

Stuart was a professional writer and controversialist with strong interests in agriculture and emigration. He made his way to Saratoga in the fall of 1828 and stayed in the area for several months, perhaps because lodgings were cheap and easily procured after the bulk of the guests had left the spas to head south, or back to the cities, for the autumn and winter.

The great hotels were about to close. Intending to remain for some time here, we went to one of the lesser houses open for visitors during the whole year, and afterwards to a private boarding-house. The gentleman who had accompanied us from Britain left us to our regret on his return, a few days after we reached this village. It consists of one fine broad street, fringed with trees, on the sides of which are so many large and splendid hotels, that it appeared to me that there was more extensive accommodation for company here than at Harrowgate.[1] Fifteen hundred people have been known to arrive in a week. They come from all parts of the states, even from New Orleans, at the distance of between 2000 and 3000 miles, to avoid the heat and unhealthy weather, which prevail in the southern part of the states during the end of the summer, and to enjoy the very wholesome and pleasant mineral waters of Saratoga. . . .

The taste [of the waters] is very agreeable; and the briskness of the water at the fountain delightful. Three or four pint tumblers are generally taken in the morning before breakfast. We also, as most people do, use it at meals from choice, although it is never so good as at the fountain, before there is any escape of gas. The people resident in the village and its neighbourhood, within six or eight miles of the place, have it carried to

From James Stuart, *Three Years in North America,* 2 vols. (Edinburgh: Robert Cadell, 1833), 1: 190, 192–200, 171–77, 179.

1. The Yorkshire spa of Harrogate was popular in the eighteenth century, but its main development dates from about 1820.

their houses, preferring it very much to ordinary spring water. The quantity of gas is such, that a very nice sort of breakfast bread is baked with Congress water, instead of yeast. So large a quantity of it is bottled, and sent all over the states, that the proprietors, Messrs Lynch and Clarke, are said to be making a fortune of it.[2] Even the American packet ships are supplied with it in abundance; but there is a very considerable loss of the gas in bottling, which renders the taste insipid, and the least loss of gas occasions a precipitation of iron, which gives the water a muddy appearance. Seltzer water in the bottled state is as pleasant as Congress water, except at the fountain.

The use of the water is chiefly recommended in bilious, dyspeptic, and calculous complaints, for diseases of the skin, and for chronic rheumatism; but the great bulk of the people who resort to these celebrated springs, many of them regularly once a-year, come for amusement, and for the preservation, rather than the recovery, of health, at a period of the year, when the violence of the heat renders a visit to a high and comparatively a cold country very desirable. I have found the use of the water and the baths so beneficial for a trifling complaint, for which I had last year tried the water at Harrowgate, that we resolved to remain here and at Ballston springs for a couple of months. The gay people had almost disappeared before we arrived. The invalids seemed to live very sparingly, — hardly tasting any liquid but the water, and tea, which here, and at other places where we have been, we sometimes observed ladies take at dinner. Many of those invalids are quite able to take exercise in the open air, and would, if I am not much mistaken, derive as much benefit from it, if taken in moderation, as from the use of the water; but they seem to confine themselves to a five or ten minute walk in the morning, when they go to the fountain, and to a drive in an open carriage for an hour, or an hour and a-half. When they meet us walking several miles for exercise, and the pleasure of being in the open air, they, whether acquainted with us or not, frequently stop their vehicles, and very civilly offer us a ride with them, and can hardly believe us serious, when we, in declining to avail ourselves of their kindly meant offer, tell them that we prefer to walk. There are few more striking points of difference between this country and Britain, than in the numbers of the people who ride and walk on the public roads. It ab-

---

2. Bottled Saratoga water was extremely popular through the United States and on American vessels. John Clarke, a Yorkshire immigrant, had bought the farm on which the Congress Spring was situated in 1826. By his death in 1846 he owned substantial amounts of land in the vicinity, having made a fortune from the sale of bottled water. A brief description appears in William Stone's *Reminiscences of Saratoga and Ballston* (New York: Virtue and Yorston, 1875), Chap. 28.

solutely seems disgraceful to be seen walking; and, though there are no fine equipages here, every one rides in his gig, dearborn, or open carriage of some description or other. This circumstance no doubt proves the easy circumstances of the mass of the people, as well as the value of time to a mechanic, or labourer, whose wages may be from one to two dollars a-day, and can better afford to pay for a conveyance, and spend less time, than to walk, and spend more. Still I am persuaded that our habits in this respect are far more favourable for health; and that dyspepsia, a very general complaint in New York State, and in this country, is in no inconsiderable degree owing to the people supposing, that enough of exercise can be had in carriages and waggons, especially by persons almost always partaking of animal food largely three times a-day, who hardly ever walk a mile, or mount on horseback.

There are four great hotels. Congress Hall, the largest, is 200 feet long, with two immense wings. The United States Hotel contains as much accommodation. This is the hotel to which the Ex-king Joseph Bonaparte resorts when he pays an annual visit to the springs.[3] He now associates at the public table as an American citizen, which he did not do at first on coming to this country. There are of course public reading-rooms, library, and ball-rooms, and a newspaper press. Backgammon boards, and draft or checquer-boards, as they are called here, are in the bar-rooms generally all over the country, and the bar-keeper not unfrequently playing at checquers with the people, who appear as respectable as any in the house. Backgammon is not so often played here. Cards seldom seen.

We have here, and in the whole of our excursion hitherto, been much less annoyed with musquitoes than we expected. The common fly has been far more troublesome. And in the canal boat, and twice or thrice in hotels, we have had to submit to be tortured by bugs.

Apples are very abundant in this neighbourhood, sold at 3d. Sterling per bushel. We see large quantities of them dried by exposure to the sun, first pared, and cut in quarters, and then laid in any convenient situation, frequently on the house tops. Peaches are dried in the same way. Apple sauce is made of the apples thus prepared, which is used with roast beef and many other dishes, without any mixture of sugar.

The whole appearance of the place is cheerful,—the population residing in the village between 2000 and 3000. There are four or five churches,

3. Napoleon Bonaparte's elder brother Joseph (1768-1844) was king of Spain from 1808 until 1813; he came to the United States in 1815, and was much visited by British tourists in Philadelphia, at his summer mansion in Bordentown, New Jersey, and at Saratoga. After 1832 he spent only two years in America (1837-1839), and died in Italy.

Saratoga Springs: colonnade of Congress Hall, 1837. By William Henry Bartlett from N. P. Willis, *American Scenery* (London, 1837–40). Collection of McKinney Library, Albany Institute of History and Art

with spires covered with tin glittering through the trees, Presbyterian, Baptist, Methodist, and Universalist; the two first rather handsome houses of some size. There was not public worship regularly in all the churches, the crowded season being over; but two of the churches at least were open every Sunday; the sermons good plain discourses, but there was no eminent preacher when we were here. In the Methodist and Universalist churches, the males occupy the pews on the one side of the church, and the females on the other. This practice we afterwards found not to be unusual in the Methodist churches in the United States. The Methodists generally kneel at prayer, and stand while singing, but the practice varies in different churches. Ladles are common, as they used to be in Scotland, handed about by the church officers or deacons for offerings of money, previous to the last prayers; the singing good, usually accompanied by instrumental music, and but few of the congregation joining. Everywhere there is a band of singers. The deacons and congregation very attentive in giving seats to strangers. There is never any whispering nor speaking in the church before the clergyman comes in. Few people of colour in the churches, and such of them as are there assemble in a corner separate from the rest of the people. Such of the inhabitants as do not go to church, seem to be under no restrictions. They shoot or work, or amuse themselves as they choose. We saw a house get a thorough repair on two Sundays, but this is not usual. . . .

In the beginning of October, the mornings became frosty, and the ice occasionally of some thickness, but the sun had great influence in the middle of the day, so that Fahrenheit's thermometer generally rose in the course of the day to 70°, sometimes to 78°. And during the whole month we had a cloudless sky and pure atmosphere, — finer weather than I ever before witnessed at this season. The leaves of the trees began to change their colours soon after the month commenced, and acquired at different periods colours of such beauty and brilliancy, as are not to be seen with us. The maple became of a fine scarlet, — the hiccory and walnut as yellow as a crocus, — and the sumach of a deep red. The appearance of a forest at this season is altogether superior in magnificence, beauty, and clearness of tint, to any similar scene in other countries. During this tract of charming autumn weather, which is called by the Americans the Indian summer, we made various excursions to the neighbouring country. There is not any object to be compared to York Minster, or Fountain's Abbey, or to many noble parks within reach of the multitude, who annually resort to Harrowgate for their health or amusement; but the neighbourhood of Lake George, — and the Hudson and its falls, — of Saratoga Lake, — and Ballston Lake, — offers many temptations to those who take pleasure in the beauties of nature. Saratoga Lake, about five miles from the springs, is a fine sheet of water, where there is good fishing, and where pleasure-boats can be had. There is also a fishing pond conveniently situated, only two miles from the springs, the proprietor of which, Mr Barhyte, of German extraction, makes strangers very welcome to enjoy the sport.[4] Although he has a considerable property, not of trifling value, we found the first time that we called in the evening to see the place, that he was at work with the necessary implements, mending his shoes. I positively at first took him for a shoemaker, but he received us so hospitably, that I soon was convinced of the mistake I had so nearly committed. Every one in this country is taught to do much more for himself than with us. I have never met an American, who, when put to it, could not use the needle well. Mr Barhyte set down cyder, and peach-brandy, and forced us to partake, before he would show us his grounds. The pond is not of great extent, but the scenery about it, though on a small scale, is sweet. It pleased Joseph Bonaparte so much, that Mr Barhyte told us, he would have been very glad to acquire it as a retired situation for himself on his annual visit to the springs; but Mr Barhyte was not inclined to sell. King Joseph got the first lesson to fish from Mr Barhyte, in which, however, he says, he is by no means a proficient. . . .

[In Warren County] The country is sandy and stony, but there are fine hills in the distance, and the prospect of the lake, surrounded by mountains, very beautiful, in descending from higher grounds on Caldwell [Lake George], the village, or rather county town, at the southwestern edge of the lake. Caldwell has been but recently built, but it contains public buildings of all kinds, — a jail, being the county town of the county of Warren, — a newspaper, — and a great and charmingly situated hotel for strangers coming to see the lake or to fish. Having arrived at Caldwell, we hired a small boat to take us out on the lake, and directed our charioteer to have the carriage ready for us as soon as a signal, which we arranged, should appear from our boat. The lake very much resembles the lakes of Westmoreland, and some of the Scotch lakes. Hilly country (mountainous it is called here, though none of it is above 1500 feet high,) surrounds the lake on all sides. The shores are finely broken, and the lake

4. Jacobus Barhydt (c. 1754–1844) was an early settler of Saratoga; his lake was a favorite resort and fishing place, especially between 1820 and 1835. Something of a local character, he figures in a number of the legends recorded in Stone's *Reminiscences*. Joseph Bonaparte offered him $20,000 for the property; his response is reputed to have been, "If it's worth that to you, it's worth that to me" (Stone, *Reminiscences,* pp. 158–59). His property eventually became the Yaddo art colony.

itself sprinkled with a great number of beautiful islands, on one of which, where we landed, there is a tea-house. The waters of the lake are deep, and most transparent; and fish, especially red trout, is excellent, and most abundant. The lake is about thirty-six miles long, of very various breadth, nowhere exceeding four miles. . . .

Caldwell itself stands so nearly on the site of the ruins of the British Fort William Henry,[5] that the batteries erected to attack it [in 1759] cross the street of the present village.

SARATOGA AND WARREN COUNTIES IN THE MID-1830s

James Stuart's Three Years *was attacked in periodicals and in books, but nowhere with such deep, bitter animation as in Richard Weston's* Visit. *Weston, an Edinburgh bookseller and occasional publisher, claims to have been so impressed by Stuart's glowing account of life in the United States, which he read soon after his wife's death, that he turned over the running of his business to his son and set out to examine prospects for himself.*

There can have been few more unlikely candidates for American citizenship. Weston comes across from his narrative as the archetype of the unreconstructed Scot: pugnacious, bristling with national pride, wholly inflexible in manners and customs, sharp-tempered, and disputatious. He crossed the Atlantic in steerage and hated both the company and the experience. He was quoted what he considered outrageous prices by boarding-house owners in New York City, and he returned to the quayside to find a group of thieves in the process of stealing his luggage. The first half of the book is a litany of America's dishonesties, cheatings, and vulgarities, punctuated only by Weston's disgust with the country, the people, and all the writers — especially Stuart — who had ever mentioned the possibility of emigration. The second half recounts his long stay with (long-suffering) relatives in upstate New York, a time which he appears grudgingly to have enjoyed. He also made a brief tour through western New York, the high point of which is his refusal to acknowledge anything beautiful or re-

---

5. Fort William Henry was constructed in the fall of 1756 by General (later Sir) William Johnson. George Munroe surrendered the garrison to Montcalm on August 9, 1757. His troops were massacred by Montcalm's Indian forces (described in Cooper's *Last of the Mohicans*) and the fort was destroyed the following day.

*markable about Niagara Falls. Returning to Scotland, he produced an
acerbic commentary based on the copious notes he took continually while
on his travels.*

*In this excerpt he dismisses Saratoga in a few lines. He appears unan-
nounced at a niece's house near Glens Falls and makes his way to his
nephew's lumbering business near Luzerne, in Warren County. He ends by
contradicting Stuart's brief, amiable description of Caldwell, now the village
of Lake George.*

Went on to Saratoga Springs. The American fashionables come in great
numbers here to drink the waters, which are said to be very salutary to invalids. Saw the use of rocking-chairs. I heard some noise in a house as if it
was a school, and tapped at the door, which the teacher opened. I told
him I was from Britain, and had used the liberty to come in, to observe his
method of teaching. He desired me to sit down, and calling up a class, put
some questions to them in spelling. I observed they did not spell as we do,
and asked the teacher whose dictionary he used. He replied, giving me an
American snake-like stare, Webster's; I said Johnson's was much used
with us; "Johnson!" said he in a triumphant manner, "he could not spell;
indeed you have no good dictionary in England." This was too much of a
good thing. . . .

Went on towards Fort-Miller in a heavy rain, the sandy soil giving
way under my feet. The country, being undulating and wooded, did not
permit me to see far. I went, as I thought, in a northerly direction, where I
knew Fort-Miller lay; the shadows of evening were fast approaching, and
I knew that to lie down in the rain would finish me. I was angry with myself for taking so much toil, angry with Mr Stuart and others for writing
so fluently about America. . . .

I however at last came to a house a little off the road, and groping
for the gate, found it and opened it. No sooner was I in, than it shut of its
own accord. A large dog came up and smelt at me; I patted his head and
spoke to him; he snarled none, nor growled. This I considered a good
omen, and went up to the door and tapped; the familiar American answer
was given, "Come in." I opened the door; a lady was sitting at a table with
two daughters sewing, and an elderly gentleman reading the bible. I ac-

From Richard Weston, *A Visit to the United States and Canada in 1833; with the View of
Settling in America.* . . (Edinburgh: Richard Weston and Sons, 1836), pp. 146–47, 148–65,
172–73.

costed them, telling how I was going to Fort Miller, and repeating the rest of my story, adding that I was faint and weary, that I required lodging, and had money to pay for what I got. The lady, as well as the rest of the family, kept staring in my direction; they were in the light, (the light being between them and me) and as I was outside of the door, they could not see me. The lady said, "Come in, that we may see what you are like." I accordingly stepped in and walked up to the table, the dog by my side, my cloak dripping with the rain lying on my left arm, a bundle fastened round my neck, and my umbrella in my hand; I was drenched to the skin. She put some interrogatories to me, which I answered, then rising, relieved me of my cloak and bundle, and umbrella, bidding me throw off my coat, and ordered a dumb lad by signs to get some wood to lay on the fire. She then brought me a dry shirt and a great-coat of her husband's to put on. She said that her family had joined the Temperance Society, and had no spirits in the house, but she would soon have a cup of tea prepared for me. The dumb lad kept heaping wood on the fire, and I got into a glow of heat; had tea, felt much relieved, and was truly thankful that I had fallen in with such a matron.

The master of the house was from Ireland, had been about thirty years in this country, had purchased about eighty acres of land, and was in comfortable circumstances. His lady was born in America, but her parents had been likewise from Ireland. . . . This kind and sensible person's name was Brisbane. His son was a surgeon, and kept the post-office at Schuylerville. We had family worship that evening, and I suppose it was performed every evening. The books were brought in, and a psalm read and sung with patriarchal reverence. At the conclusion, he asked me if I was sufficiently recovered to read a chapter in the bible; I felt myself quite well, and answered yes. He pointed the chapter out to me, and I read it; we then all fell on our knees, while he prayed in a humble and fervent manner, making allusion to my destitute and forlorn condition. My heart was melted within me to find such sympathy, when I had so recently experienced none at all.

We separated for the night, the lady shewing me into a room, where the bed on which I lay was as soft as if I was floating on water; the crickets and the grasshoppers made a cheerful chorus, gently lulling me asleep, and I dreamt I was at home.

Breakfast was on the table before I awakened next morning. When I made my appearance in the kitchen, the family asked how I felt; I replied quite well, and that I would now pursue my journey. The lady said this was Sunday (by this time I had lost all reckoning, and knew not whether it was Sunday or Saturday) and that I had better stay a week or two to refresh myself; my board would cost nothing, and, as they were going to the church at Schuylerville, she wished me to go along with them, for her son, the doctor, would be so glad to see me, as he was always speaking about the medical classes in Edinburgh. I consented; we had family worship after breakfast, and were driven in a waggon to church. The church had been formerly built of wood, but was lately burnt down, and rebuilt of stone, with columns at the door made of brick and plastered over, for the Americans are fond of ornament. Waggons drawn by horses or steers, gigs, coaches, and saddle-horses, conveyed the different members of the congregation. General Schuyler's coach was pointed out to me; his arms were tastefully painted, for the aristocracy in America are quite as proud as those in Britain.

The church, which was small, had galleries only the breadth of a single seat on three sides. There was a pulpit, but no precentor's desk. The two side galleries were entirely empty; but the one opposite the minister was occupied by a numerous band of singers, male and female, who sang four tunes to cheerful or plaintive airs, which, as they were something like those I had heard at Hope Park Chapel, Edinburgh, brought vividly to my mind's eye the many well-known countenances I was in the habit of seeing there. But alas! I was far from Hope Park, and none of the faces I saw here resembled any of my townsmen.

After we came out of the church, being in conversation with some people at the door, whom Mr and Mrs Brisbane introduced to me, I observed close to the church a man busy at work with a horse yoked to a machine formed like a rake, and used for the purpose of raking hay. The teeth of this machine were more than twelve times longer than those of our hand-rakes, and swept along the ground in a horizontal direction. When a sufficient quantity of hay had accumulated, the man with a lever handle darted the teeth nearest the horse to the ground, by which means the rake turned, and, there being two sets of teeth, the hay was left on the field. The horse never stopped, but continued to drag along the machine, which ran upon two wheels; and the hay was gathered into straight lines.

There was within view a beautiful Gothic wooden building with towers, columns, and ornaments, used as an Episcopal place of worship. . . .

By break of day the family were all up; by sunrise they had breakfast; family worship was gone through, and the wanderer far from his home mentioned, and the Almighty solicited to protect him, and carry him safe home. I lay some time after I awoke, that they might think me still sleeping; and when I came out of my room, said I would now proceed on my journey. "You will take breakfast first," said the lady; "we breakfast much earlier in America than you do in Britain, I guess." I asked what I was to pay; "Nothing," said she, and at the same time offered me a clean shirt, telling me that there was no time to wash mine for me. I thanked her for her kind offer, but said that I had plenty of shirts in my trunk, which would be waiting for me at Whitehall. These kind people, not content with all they had done for me, beseeched me, if I ever got to Montreal, to write them, and to direct my letter to their son, the postmaster, whose letters went free, or, if I should become unwell, to return to their house, and make it my home. With many blessings and good wishes on their part, and much sorrow on mine, I parted from them. — And I did write them as directed before I left America. . . .

I went and visited a cotton spinning-mill, nearly opposite to General Schuyler's house; it was built with stone, — (General Schuyler's was built of wood, and gaudy, white painted). Saw the manager; he told me cotton-spinning did not succeed so well with the Americans as with us; the want of capital and the unsteady government were the cause, there being so many different interests. The territory was too large to have only one legislature; it would be better, he said, if the Union were broken up, and the territory divided into smaller states; even the high protecting duties levied by the government were of no avail. From the danger of the wooden fires, women could not wear cotton dresses; and owing to the alternate excessive heat and cold, the men, as well as the women, had to wear worsted stuff, which everyone manufactures for himself from the raw material the best way he can. There was a good fall of water; hours of labour from five in the morning till seven at night; breakfast taken before beginning to work, dinner at twelve, supper after seven; wages from nine to twelve dollars per month; but they were paying the hands off — indeed I saw this mill advertised for sale shortly afterwards. . . .

Returned to Fort-Edward, and thence to Fort-Ann, where, however, no vestiges of a fort are to be seen. At this place there was a muster of militia, some on foot, and some on horseback; saw them go through some evolutions, which they performed very well, the drums and fifes playing Yankee-Doodle and Hail Columbia, the only two national airs.

Observing some men pulling out stumps of trees with a stump-machine, I went and saw the process. Two steers dragged the machine from stump to stump. A trench was dug around them, the roots branching from them being cut with an axe. A chain was passed below and fastened, and a horse yoked to a rope which was wound round a thing shaped like a drum. As the horse pulled, this put in motion three sets of wheels and pinions, which increased the power to a great rate. The chain that was fastened to the stump went round a drum also, and as the stump was raised, the remaining roots were cut away. These roots make good

fences; but the ground is not much improved by their removal, as they
run along the surface and are easily blown over. The machine was a clumsy
piece of workmanship — the wheels and axles might have answered the ca
of Juggernaut. . . .

Arrived at Sandy-hill, a person having learnt my name asked if I wa
any relation to Judge Weston; I said I did not know, but that I had som
relations in America whom I had not yet found, enquiring at the same
time where this judge resided. He pointed to a brick house, and said tha
was his residence. I went towards it and rung the bell, which was an
swered by a hired help (there are no servants in America) to whom I pre
sented a card with my name written on it. The judge, she said, was in the
garden, and if I would open the wicket-gate at the end of the house,
would find him there. I did so, and having accordingly gone up to him
and handed my card, I enquired whether he was any relation of mine, and
if he knew my late brother, where his widow resided, and how her family
were. He answered, that he was no relation of mine, that he had been
born in America, that he knew my late brother well, that his widow wa
dead, that the family were dispersed, and that he had lost sight of them al
except James Douglas Weston, whom there was no mistaking, as he wa
making dollars; that he had married into a rich family in Lucerne, and
that I would have no difficulty finding him. . . .

I took my way to Glens-falls, having crossed the Hudson again on a
bridge of wood, which was only for foot passengers. There are severa
dams across the Hudson to raise the water to feed the canal; that at Fort
Miller is said to raise it forty feet; they are built of wood. Trees are laid
across the bed of the river, then these are crossed by trees laid first short
lengths, then longer and longer, as the dam is raised. These crossings form
an inclined plane with the river, at an angle of about forty-five degrees.
As the water is raised, the sand accumulating on the upper ends of the
trees makes them more secure; besides, they are strongly pinned, and are
very durable.

Having come to Glens-falls, I observed several very powerful mills
some for grinding corn, a very large one for sawing timber, and one for
cutting limestone, which is plentiful in this neighbourhood, into slabs, a
we cut our marble for tomb-stones and other ornamental purposes. Saw
several lime-kilns; they burn the lime with wood; when brought to a cer
tain heat, the kiln is allowed to cool down, and the limestone, if good
falls into lime — if it does not fall, it is cast away. Here, it is generally ver
good, being as white as chalk, and after being sifted, is put into barrel
for exportation.

I observed several men making charcoal from wood for the use o smiths. The operation is somewhat similar to that of making the same article from coal, and requires considerable skill; a large quantity is piled up, covered with sand, and then set fire to.

Having left Glens-falls, I ascended the Queensberry Mountains; some stragglers whom I passed seemed to have a notion who I was, and when I enquired about Mr Wilkie, who is married to a niece of mine, their conjectures were confirmed. Some of these immense forests had at one time been on fire; the tall stems of some of the trees, rising high above the younger and greener wood, having been long laid bare with the blast, appeared like white marble columns. When I got to the top of the hills, I sat down, and having the valley of the Hudson before me, fancied I might with a good glass have seen as far as Albany. Few houses were in sight, but those that were, being painted white, had a marble-like appearance. The house in which my brother died was pointed out to me from this spot; it was a frame-house of the better order. By the attentions shewn to me everywhere, I suspected that the news of my being in the neighbourhood had preceded me.

Having again enquired for Mr Wilkie's house, I was directed to the proper place. Four outside steps led into the house, which was a frame one, with several broken panes in the windows. The room I was shewn into had a stove in the centre; there was a woman mopping the floor, and as I stood with my bundle over my shoulder, my cloak hanging on my arm, and my umbrella in my hand, she stared at me very keenly, and I at her. I accosted her in this manner: "Are you Mary Weston?" "Yes," said she. "Then I am your uncle." "What!" she exclaimed, "Richard from Scotland?" "Yes," I replied. Immediately she flew and relieved me of my cloak, bundle, and umbrella, and as I felt myself lame from walking, and faint and exhausted, she brought me water to wash myself, gave me a clean shirt, and bathed my feet, putting clean stockings on me, and, as she had no spirits in the house, said she would make me a dish of tea. She then took a tin trumpet and blew several strong blasts to bring her husband from the woods. She apologized for having no sugar, but I was a philosopher by this time, and could take tea without it. I asked her if she had any maple trees; and she answered that she had, but that it was so troublesome to make sugar, that what they really needed they purchased. I thought on Chambers' Information for the People; that number of his on America has been the ruin of several to my certain knowledge.[1]

---

1. Robert and William Chambers, both prolific writers, were Edinburgh booksellers (and hence commercial rivals of Weston's) in the 1820s and founded their publishing company with the appearance of *Chamber's Edinburgh Journal* in 1832. Their *Information for*

[Weston, refreshed, walks into the woods to meet his niece's hus band.] He led me over his farm, which consisted of about one hundre and twenty acres; he had sheep, of hogs I suppose he had a hundred, sev eral cows, three horses, two steers, and a number of geese and barn-yar fowls; shewed me his rye, his Indian corn, and his buck wheat. Two of h fields were as stoney as the paved streets of Edinburgh, scanty grass grow ing up between the stones, as I have seen in some of the less frequente streets, particularly George's square and Buccleuch place. All the ligl sandy particles that had once covered the stones had been washed awa nor would it have been possible from their number to clear these fields c them. Hogs with frames on their necks were in the one field, and sheep i the other; they were both railed in with worm-fences. In the remainir fields, which had not been so long cleared, the soil was somewhat deepe though partaking of the same ingredients; these stones, however, togeth with the trees and stumps, are useful in preventing the soil from beir washed away.

Next day, my relative drove me in his two-horse waggon across tl country to Whitehall, where I had a view of part of Lake Champlain; tl canal enters it here. The houses in this place, as every where else, are bui of wood, though stone and lime abound in the neighbourhood. I am cor vinced the Americans build houses only for themselves, not for their de scendants. I spent the remainder of this day in examining the country; it really a wild and miserable place.

[Mr. Wilkie takes Weston to his nephew James's house in "the mour tains of Lucerne."] We now reached my nephew James's house; it wa built about three feet from the ground, with stone and lime, not like tl other houses; it stood on the east side of a rising ground, and was tw stories high on the east side, and one on the west, the upper storey beir of wood, and painted brown; a small board that surrounded the wir dows, in imitation of our curb-stones, was painted white. "We will not g into the house," said Mr Wilkie, "as it is likely he will be at the upper sav mill; for James is the boy for the dollars, no mistake." Accordingly w went thither and found him; he was a tall strong fellow, about six fe high, and was working among boards in boots, trowsers, and a red flar nel shirt, his head bare; his features reminded me of my late brother. Ha ing been introduced, he shook me affectionately by the hand, and looke at me steadfastly, scrutinizing me from head to foot, and repeating tl

---

the People, a cheap, popular series, first appeared in 1833. William Chambers would wri his own account of an American tour in 1854, under the title Things as They Are America.

look often, as if he were guessing I was not the person I pretended to be. He now dropped working, and put on a ragged waistcoat above his shirt, his clothes being all homespun, and led me to the house. I was introduced to his lady, also dressed in home manufacture; she was below the middle stature, but neat and clean. Her father and mother came in, the former a tall man above six feet high, and the latter a fat bouncing woman. My nephew went into the buttery, a closet off the kitchen, and brought out a bottle of spirits and a tumbler, poured some out and drank it, then, crossing his hands, put the bottle into my right hand, and the tumbler into my left, and bade me help myself, for I was now in a free country. I had learned this method before, as it is very common for the Americans to drink standing, so I poured out a little and drank it, crossing my arms as he had done, and then returned the bottle and tumbler. He next handed it round to all the company in the same manner, when my welcome to the free country of America was drunk by all present.

A hired female help went out of the kitchen with a tin trumpet, and gave several loud blasts as the signal for dinner. A large table covered with a cloth was set in the middle of the floor; butcher meat, pork, potatoes, butter, honey, and sauce, or what we would call jam and jelly, were placed upon it; tea was likewise prepared, and cyder set down, as if a large party was to dine. It was about twelve noon. The hired helps, male and female, of whom there were about twenty, came in, and washed their hands. My niece took the head of the table; two young children, one on each side, sat next her; then, on the right, her husband, next to him myself, and then Mr Wilkie, the eldest son next him. The hired helps of the male sex sat on the right side according to seniority, and the females on the left, each having a knife and fork. All the company, including the domestics, helped themselves to what they pleased. The lady poured out a cup of tea for me, and sweetened it with sugar; both of my entertainers occasionally pressing me to help myself, as it was their custom, though contrary to ours. The whole scene made me think I had been put back four hundred years at least; I considered the lady the feudal head, the guests the members of the family; and the hired helps the vassals and retainers. Indeed, there are vassals in America, though there are no servants; and I soon discovered that my niece could make her hired female helps obey her as well as if they had been servants; so could my nephew—no murmuring, else they are paid off at a month's or even a week's end; and they make sure of getting others to fill their places readily. . . .

Next morning, he drove me to Caldwell [Lake George]. As this is one of the places of note in Mr Stuart's Three Years, I mean to be more particular with it than with some others I have described. The prison and court-house are built of wood; there is also a handsome wooden church. The town contains just twenty houses of wood, white-washed, and one of stone; it lies on the west side of Lake George, a beautiful expanse of water, studded with upwards of three hundred islands, both banks being covered with wood of a stunted growth, and many of the surrounding hills with wild fern. One of the hills near the town goes by the name of Rattle-snake Hill, from several rattle-snakes' dens being upon it; and I saw some people who kept the rattles of those they had killed as trophies. The Americans say that the waters of Lake George are the purest in the world, and that they have even been imported to Europe, and used in religious houses as holy water.

I happened to go to the court-house to hear some cases tried. In the passage is a space staked off with wooden spars, where the prisoners about to be tried are confined, in order that they may see and be seen by others; it put me in mind of a hen's-crib. You ascend a wide stair, and enter a large well lighted hall having some square pews like what are to be seen in our old churches, some seats like those in our modern churches, and also common forms or benches. Though the hall was very large, there were few people assembled. The statutes at large were placed so as any one might lift a volume and examine it; I myself did so, and no person interrupted me. One of the pews opposite the bench was filled with lawyers, who were sitting in every variety of posture, some having their feet higher than their mouth, and rocking as if they were on a hobby-horse, others with their feet on a square table in the centre.

The jury were sworn by kissing the book, and took their seats; they had neither pens nor paper. The first case was that of a person for stealing wood; witnesses were called, who gave their evidence in good English, but interlarded continually with "I guess it was so," never giving a direct answer, another very common phrase being, "I want to know." There were many other cases, one fellow for horse-stealing—he got the state prison; another for fire-raising, setting fire to a wood—this is a very common offence, and severely punished—not proven; another for shooting a deer—he was fined in twenty dollars—as these animals are getting scarce, the penalty for shooting them is high, and yet it is continually asserted at home that there are no game-laws in America.

Sometimes a witness did not appear when called, and an officer being despatched for him, he would generally be found playing at the game of ten-pins. Originally nine pins only were used; but the New York legislature passed a law to prohibit it on account of its gambling nature. The people, however, were too knowing to be done in this manner, and therefore added a tenth pin, which it would have required a new act to suppress.

I visited the ruins of Fort George and Fort William Henry; and my heart warmed when I saw brick of British manufacture. The American bricks are entirely red from the greater admixture of sand; but the British brick is blue in the heart from the clay preponderating. These forts, which lie very low, had originally been bomb-proof, having a covered way from the forts to the lake to bring in water.

A TOURIST PARTY AT LAKE GEORGE IN THE MID-1830s

A visit to Lake George was, among landscape amateurs, one of the more lasting souvenirs of a tour in North America. So it would prove for Harriet Martineau. Martineau (1802–1876), brought up in a nonconforming household in Norwich, was an unlikely literary giant and, if anything, a less likely tourist. By 1834 she had scored resounding success with a series of novels that appeared under the unappetizing title of Illustrations of Political Economy. *The volumes were written with astonishing speed; renderings of economics in fictional form, they sold with a rapidity yet more astonishing.*

Exhausted by her labors, Martineau decided on a tour of America as a restorative. She set sail with a companion, Louisa Jeffrey, in 1834, and her tour saw her triumphing over handicaps that would have stopped most people of the time. Martineau was a declared abolitionist at a time when abolitionists in the South and West risked, at best, tar and feathers. She lacked the senses of taste and smell—though this may have been an advantage. It probably saved her from several of the less pleasant aspects of traveling in the 1830s. And she had been profoundly deaf since her late teens. She was most easily recognized by her ear trumpet, a companion as constant as the quiet Miss Jeffrey.

On her return to England in 1836, she received offers from many publishers for a work on America. The London firm of Saunders and Otley won the bidding war. The result, Society in America, *a confusing mixture of reflections on political economy and passages from her travel journals, was quite successful and much read. But fortunately for later generations, Saunders and Otley prevailed on her to produce a more personal and livelier account of her travels, based on the letters and journals that she had written during her three years in North America. The* Retrospect of Western Travel *was published in 1838. From it comes this detailed account of her party's enjoyment of the most popular longer excursion from Saratoga Springs—a visit to Lake George.*

It was about noon on the 12th of May when we alighted shivering from
the rail-car at Saratoga. We hastened to the Adelphi; and there found the
author of Major Jack Downing's Letters,[1] and two other gentlemen, reading the newspapers round a stove. We had but little time to spare; and as
soon as we had warmed ourselves, and ascertained the dinner hour, we set
forth to view the place, and taste the Congress Water. There is nothing to
be seen but large white frame-houses, with handsome piazzas, festooned
with creepers, — (at this time only the sapless remains of the garlands of
the last season). These houses and the wooden temple over the principal
spring are all that is to be seen, — at least by the bodily eye. The imagination may amuse itself with conjuring up the place as it was less than half a
century ago, when these springs bubbled up amidst the brush of the forest,
— their qualities being discovered by the path through the woods worn by
the deer in their resort to it. In those days, the only edifices were a single
log-hut and a bear-pound; a space enclosed with four high walls, with an
extremely narrow entrance, where it was hoped that bears might get in
during the dark hours, and be unable to find their way out again. Times
are much changed now. There are no bears at Saratoga but a two-legged
species from Europe, dropping in, one or two in a season, among the gentry at the Springs.

The process of bottling the Congress Water was in full activity when
we took our first draught of it. Though the utmost celerity is used, the
water loses much of its virtue and briskness by bottling. The man and boy
whom we saw filling and corking the bottles with a dexterity which only
practice can give, are able to dispatch a hundred dozen per day. There are
several other springs, shedding waters of various medicinal virtues: but
the Congress fountain is the only one from which the stranger would
drink as a matter of taste.

The water-works are just at hand, looking like a giant's shower-
bath. At the top of the eminence close by, there is a pleasure rail-road, — a
circular track, on which elderly children may take a ride round and round
in a self-moving chair; an amusement a step above the old merry-go-
round in gravity and scientific pretension. But for its vicinity to some
tracts of beautiful scenery, Saratoga must be a very dull place to persons

From Harriet Martineau, *Retrospect of Western Travel*, 3 vols. (London: Saunders and Otley, 1838), 3: 260–64, 266–69.
    1. "Major Jack Downing" was the pseudonym of two writers of humorous political
commentary in the form of letters. Seba Smith (1792–1868) wrote for the Portland, Maine,
Courier from 1830 to 1833; Charles Augustus Davis (1795–1868) continued the pseudonym
in the columns of the New York *Daily Advertiser* in 1833 and 1834. It is not clear which author Martineau met.

shaken out of their domestic habits, and deprived of their usual occupations: and the beauties of the scenery must be sought, Saratoga Lake lying three miles, Glen's Falls eighteen, and Lake George twenty-seven miles from the Springs.

At dinner, Mr. R., the gentleman of our party, announced to us that he had been able to engage a pretty double gig, with a pair of brisk ponies, for ourselves, and a light cart for our luggage. The day was very cold for an open carriage; but it was not improbable that, before twenty-four hours were over, we might be panting with heat: and it was well to be provided with a carriage in which we might most easily explore the lake scenery, if we should be favoured with fine weather.

The cart preceded us. On the road, a large white snake made a prodigious spring from the grass at the driver, who, being thus challenged, was not slow in entering into combat with the creature. He jumped down, and stoned it for some time with much diligence, before it would lie down so that he might drive over it. As we proceeded, the country became richer, and we had fine views of the heights which cluster round the infant Hudson, and of the Green Mountains of Vermont.

We were all astonished at the splendour of Glen's Falls. The full though narrow Hudson rushes along amidst enormous masses of rock, and leaps sixty feet down the chasms and precipices which occur in the passage, sweeping between dark banks of shelving rocks below, its current speckled with foam. The noise is so tremendous that I cannot conceive how people can fix their dwellings in the immediate neighbourhood. There is a long bridge over the roaring floods, which vibrates incessantly; and clusters of saw-mills deform the scene. There is stone-cutting as well as planking done at these mills. The fine black marble of the place is cut into slabs, and sent down to New York to be polished. It was the busiest scene that I saw near any water-power in America.

Lake George lies nine miles beyond Glen's Falls. We saw the lake while we were yet two miles from Caldwell, the pretty village at its southern extremity. It stretched blue among the mountains in the softening light; and we anticipated what our pleasures were to be, as we looked upon the framework of mountains in which this gem is set. We had just emerged from a long and severe winter; and it was many months since we had loitered about in the full enjoyment of open air and bright verdure, as we hoped to do here. This trip was to be a foretaste of a long summer and autumn of out-door delights.

The people at the inn were busy cleaning, in preparation for summer company: but they gave us a welcome, and lodged and tended us well. Our windows and piazza commanded a fine view of the lake, (here just a

Lake George: Caldwell (Lake George), 1838. By William Henry Bartlett, from
N. P. Willis, *American Scenery* (London, 1837–40). New York State Museum,
Albany

mile broad,) of the opposite mountains, and of the white beach which
sweeps round the southern extremity of the sheet of waters, — as transparent as the sea about the Bermudas.

As we had hoped, the next morning was sunny and warm. We employed it in exploring the ground about Fort William Henry, which stands
on an eminence a little way back from the water, and is now merely an insignificant heap of ruins. . . .

After wandering for some hours on the beach, and breaking our
way through the thick groves which skirt it, dwelling upon the exquisite
scene of the blue lake, with its tufted islands, shut in by mountains, we
wished to find some place where we might obtain an equally good distant
view, and yet enjoy the delights of the margin of the water. By climbing a
fence, we got to a green bank, whence we could reach a log in the water;
and here we basked, like a party of terrapins, till dinner-time. The foliage
of the opposite woods, on French Mountain, seemed to make great prog-

ress under the summer warmth of this day; and by the next morning, the soft green tinge was perceptible on them, which, after the dry hardness of winter, is almost as beautiful as the full leaf.

After dinner, we took a drive along the western bank of the lake. The road wound in and out, up and down on the mountainous barrier of the waters; for there was no beach or other level. One of the beauties of Lake George is that the mountains slope down to its very margin. Our stout ponies dragged us up the steep ascents, and rattled us down on the other side in charming style; and we were so enchanted with the succession of views of new promontories and islands, and new aspects of the opposite mountains, that we should have liked to proceed while any light was left, and to have taken our chance for getting back safely. But Mr. R. pointed to the sinking sun, and reminded us that it was Saturday evening. If the people at the inn were Yankees, they would make a point of all the work of the establishment ceasing at sunset, according to the Sabbath customs of New England; and we must allow the hostler a quarter of an hour to put up the ponies. So we unwillingly turned, and reached Caldwell just as the shutters of the stores were in the course of being put up, and the last rays of the sun were gushing out on either side the mountain in the rear of the village. At the Lake House, the painters were putting away their brushes, and the scrubbers emptying their pails; and by the time twilight drew on, the place was in a state of Sunday quietness. We had descried a church standing under the trees close by; and the girl who waited on us was asked what services there would be the next day. She told us that there was regular service during the summer season, when the place was full, but not at present: she added, "We have no regular preacher just now; but we have a man who can make a very smart prayer."

The next day was spent in exploring the eastern side of the lake for some distance, on foot; and in sitting on a deep grassy bank under the pines, with our feet overhanging the clear waters glancing in the sun. Here we read and talked for some hours of a delicious summer Sunday. I spent part of the afternoon alone at the fort, amidst a scene of the profoundest stillness. I could trace my companions as they wound their way at a great distance, along the little white beaches, and through the pine groves: the boat in the cove swayed at the end of its tether, when the wind sent a ripple across its bows: the shadows stole up the mountain sides; and an aged labourer sauntered along the beach, with his axe on his shoulder, crossed the wooden bridge over a brook which flows into the lake, and disappeared in the pine grove to the left. All else was still as midnight. My companions did not know where I was, and were not likely to look in the direction where I was sitting: so when they came within hail, — that is, when from mites they began to look as big as children, — I sang as loud as possible to catch their attention. I saw them speak to each other, stop, and gaze over the lake. They thought it was the singing of fishermen; and it was rather a disappointment when they found it was only one of ourselves.

The Erie Canal

THE NORMAL ITINERARY for those wanting to marvel at the falls of the Niagara in the eighteenth century had travelers approaching them from the west — from southern Ontario. The settlement and development of central and western New York State was delayed until military operations during the war of independence — notably the Clinton-Sullivan expedition — had destroyed the power of the Iroquois nations. But for many British writers the earliest settlements were not fit subject matter for commentary; nor did the British travel extensively in the area, for the massive influx of new settlers, mainly New Englanders, did not immediately improve overland transportation. Moreover, until after the War of 1812, there were relatively few travelers who wrote specifically for those considering emigration from Britain.

Conditions changed, and with extraordinary suddenness, in the latter half of the second decade. In Britain, military demobilization after the final defeat of Napoleon increased unemployment, and with it interest in emigration; in the United States, the peace of 1814 gave New York greater security from military incursions, while agricultural markets expanded with the growth of cities along the eastern seaboard and uninterrupted trade with Europe.

The key to agricultural prosperity for western New York was the construction of the Erie Canal, which, coincidentally, made the newer settlements more accessible to British travelers. After 1825 accounts of the state from the canal increased as rapidly as the area's population. John Howison traveled overland, from west to east, before the canal's completion, an unusual and quite difficult trip for the time. A mere decade later,

135

after the canal was fully in operation, dozens of travelers would be writing each year about heading west to Niagara Falls.

Shorter journeys in the wide lands west of Albany divide roughly into four sections. The first involves the longer-settled Mohawk Valley and terminates at about Utica; the second includes the cities of the northern feeder canals, especially Oswego and Watertown, that connected the Erie Canal with Lake Ontario and the lands of its eastern shores.

Journeys in the central and western sections of the canal tend to congregate around cities largely created by the remarkable increase in population and economic activity that the canal's construction sparked. Syracuse, famous for its salt industry, came to focus descriptions of the midstate section after the city's rapid growth in the thirties; before about 1840 it competed for attention with the attractive variety of canal towns, notably Auburn, Geneva, and Canandaigua. In the western portion, however, there was never any doubt about the preeminent city. Rochester's expansion — explosion, rather — after the War of 1812 rendered it unique. It dominated British reflections on the rise of the United States as a commercial and powerful force in the world.

A TOUR FROM ROCHESTER TO UTICA IN 1820

Of John Howison little is known. His Sketches of Upper Canada, *from which this extract is taken, was followed by three more books between 1825 and 1834, about foreign travel and Britain's colonies. A well-read gentleman, presumably of independent means, Howison spent 1818 and 1819 in Ontario, touring the colony and reflecting on the new settlements there. His account details the privations that came in the aftermath of the War of 1812, especially the draining of specie to the United States and the consequent adverse effects on business and development in Canada. A strong supporter of government assistance to immigrants, Howison was based at the Talbot Settlement for some eight months; yet his refined, romantic sensibility brings him to express mixed feelings about the frontier crudities of early Canadian society and the quality of Ontario's early immigrants.*

In June 1820, after thirty months in Canada, Howison crossed into the United States at Lewiston, New York, and reached New York City just in time for the celebrations of the Fourth of July. This extract covers his journey from Rochester to Utica, through an area in which the early sec-

tions of the canal were already open. The commercial frenzy of central and western New York State contrasts sharply with Howison's earlier descriptions of cash-short Upper Canada.

About mid-day I arrived at the village of Rochester, which is eighty-five miles distant from Lewiston, and lies upon the bank of the Gennesee river. It contains about three thousand inhabitants, and has the neatest appearance imaginable, almost all the houses being regularly built, and painted white. The streets, which are spacious, present a succession of well-furnished shops; and the bustle which continually pervades them gives the whole place an air of activity and commerce. This town was begun to be built only about five years ago, and its present magnitude and importance appear astonishing even to the people of the United States, among whom villages increase more rapidly than in any other part of the world. Rochester owes its prosperity chiefly to the fine water power which it commands. Besides the Gennesee river, there are many smaller streams in the immediate vicinity of the town, that are admirably adapted for driving machinery. Grist-mills, saw-mills, carding-machines, and manufactories, &c. are always in operation here; and I was shown a very ingenious and newly-invented apparatus for making nails, together with various other pieces of curious mechanism, which I had neither time nor inclination to inspect minutely.

In the afternoon I took a ramble through the village, and visited the Great Falls of the Gennesee river, which are close by it. Their pitch is eighty feet; yet, the quantity of water thrown over them being small, the effect is not very grand or imposing, particularly to one who has viewed the Niagara cataracts a few days before. They are unfortunately surrounded with machinery; for the rattling of mills, and the smoke of ironfounderies, of course, neither harmonize well with the wildness of uncultivated nature, nor give any additional interest to a scene where they are so manifestly out of place.

I next strolled about two miles out of town, that I might survey Clyde Bridge, or rather the ruins of it; for half of this magnificent structure fell several weeks before I arrived at Rochester. This bridge, which was built of wood, and consisted of a single arch, was thrown across the

From John Howison, *Sketches of Upper Canada, Domestic, Local, and Characteristic . . . and Some Recollections of the United States of America,* 2nd ed. (Edinburgh: Oliver and Boyd, 1822), pp. 299–307, 309–314, 316–20.

Gennesee river, for the purpose of opening a nearer route between Canandaguia and Lewiston. . . .

Clyde Bridge, when entire, formed a piece of architecture which was altogether unrivalled by any thing of a similar kind in Europe or America. The span of the arch was 352 feet, and the height of its summit above the surface of the river 196 feet. The bridge itself was 718 long and 30 wide; and though the whole structure contained more than 130,000 feet of timber, it was completed by twenty workmen in the space of nine months.

Next morning I proceeded to the village of Pittsford, and, while they were preparing breakfast for me, walked to the Grand Canal, which passes within a quarter of a mile of the place. Here I found about a dozen labourers actively employed in digging and embanking. The country being level, and the soil easily worked, they made rapid progress in the excavation: the parts of it that were completed measured forty feet wide, and four feet in depth. The workmen told me that they were boarded by the contractor, and received only half a dollar a-day, — a wage which shows how much the price of labour has declined in the populous parts of the United States. The commissioners for the Grand Canal divided the line into sections of one mile each; these were publicly contracted for, and the person, who made the lowest tender, had, of course, the preference. Many of the first contractors realized a great deal of money by the business; but there is now so much competition in the purchase of the sections, that the persons desirous of obtaining them are obliged to offer at the lowest rates possible.

About 12 o'clock we reached the village of Canandaguia, which is 29 miles from Rochester, and it is indeed difficult for description to do justice to its surpassing beauty and fascinating elegance. Canandaguia is about a mile long, and consists of one street, both sides of which are ornamented with a row of lovely poplar trees; behind these are the houses, placed at a little distance from each other, and generally having shrubbery and flower-plots before them. One usually connects the idea of poverty and meanness with that of a village; but Canandaguia presents an appearance very different from any thing of the kind, the worst habitations in it being extremely neat and clean, and the best highly elegant and tasteful. There is a beautiful church at one end of the street; and a handsome meeting-house, jail, county-room, academy, and hotel, adorn the other parts of the village, although its population does not exceed 1800 souls. It is situated upon a cultivated slope, at the bottom of which lies a lake, several miles in circumference, and encircled with pretty cottages and rich forests.

Fifteen miles beyond Canandaguia is Geneva, a village nearly as captivating in its aspect as the former. It too has a lake, I suppose as beautiful as its celebrated namesake in Europe, which Rousseau has immortalized. In passing through the United States, the traveller is particularly struck with the elegance and magnitude of the villages; and often feels inclined to ask where the labouring classes reside, as not a vestige of the meanness and penury, that generally characterize their inhabitants, is to be discovered. One would almost suppose Canandaguia and Geneva to have been built as places of summer resort, for persons of fortune and fashion; since so much taste, elegance, comfort, and neatness, are displayed in the design, appearance, and arrangement of the houses which compose them.

After we had passed through Geneva, I could not help looking back upon it with a tender regret. The lake, which stretched itself beneath the village in stillness and purity, had never reflected any but scenes of peace. The forests that waved around had never been invaded by any visitors more rude than the husbandman or wood-cutter; and the fields, then glowing with the richness of harvest, were annually permitted to ripen their crops, and to distribute plenty among a happy people. The village had, as yet, known but one generation of inhabitants; and nothing that composed the prospect had hitherto been witness to the oppressions, miseries, and iniquities of mankind, as is the case with almost every stone and bit of ground in Europe. All things were young, vigorous, bright, and hopeful. But how long was this delightful state of things to last? Would not revolutions of different kinds speedily disturb the calm that prevailed? Was it not to be feared that the troublous scenes of the old world would ultimately be reacted in the new, and make its people look back, with painful regret, to the outset of their history?

We next stopped at the village of Waterloo, eight miles beyond Geneva. It happened to be court-day here, and the place was so crowded with judges, lawyers, and farmers, that it had a very gay and animated appearance. The hotel at which I alighted particularly drew my attention, as it was three stories high, and built of brick. As I proposed to dine before we set out again, I communicated my intention to the landlord, who ushered me into the bar-room, which was very large and commodious, and full of *Yankey* loungers. There were fifteen or sixteen chairs in the apartment, but I could not procure one for my own accommodation, although five or six persons only were seated. — But each of these individuals occupied three or four chairs. He sat upon one, laid his legs upon another, whirled round a third, and, perhaps, chewed the paint from the back of a fourth. — However, those who had segars in their teeth, contented themselves with collecting the smoke in their mouths, and blowing it out in volumes when any one passed. None of them offered to resign me a chair; but I suppose the clouds of tobacco vapour, which filled the room, prevented them from observing that I wanted one.

Fortunately, the landlord soon announced that dinner was ready, and showed me into an elegant room, fifty-six feet long.

Four miles beyond Waterloo is Cayuga Lake, which we crossed by means of a wooden bridge, one mile and a furlong in length. The supporters of the bridge rest upon the bottom of the lake all the way through, the average depth of water being six feet. The bridge is wide enough to admit a carriage, and likewise foot-passengers; and the whole structure is so strong and well knit together, that, notwithstanding its vast extent, scarcely any tremour is perceptible when a heavy-loaded waggon passes over it. When viewed from one extremity, it appears gradually and beautifully to converge into a narrow point at the other, and at last eludes the eye in the minuteness of its termination.

About six in the evening we arrived at the village of Auburn, and I abandoned the stage there, intending to go to Utica by way of the Grand Canal. Having seen my portmanteau disposed of, I entered the tavern, and desired that water might be sent into a room. "Water!" exclaimed the landlord, "why, here's water and towels enough in the bar—I guess all the gentlemen washes there." I surveyed the bar from curiosity, and found things in such a state, that I would rather have worn the coat of dust I had received while in the stage, than attempted ablution in it. However, after some parley and hesitation, my apparently unheard-of request was granted, and soon afterwards they rung a bell to announce that tea was ready. I immediately obeyed the summons; and, on entering the public room, found eighteen or twenty people already seated at a table, which was abundantly furnished with beef-steaks, ham, fowls, preserved fruit, cake, cheese, &c. The hostess, who was rather pretty, stood at one end of the table, and poured out tea, gracefully enough, to those who called for it, and occasionally joined in the conversation, with the same ease as if she had been one of the guests. Most of the people were respectable enough in appearance. . . .

In the morning I strolled through the town of Auburn, and found it even more extensive and respectable than I had anticipated. It contains spacious streets, excellent houses, plenty of shops, and about 3000 inhabitants; and, moreover, appears to be a place of considerable trade. There are two churches in it, one of which is extremely pretty in its architecture; and I cannot but allude to the attention which the Americans invariably bestow upon buildings for religious worship. No place in the State of New York, that has any pretensions to the name of a village, is destitute of a respectable church and regularly ordained clergyman. This circumstance is highly creditable to the Americans, and ought to refute the notion so commonly entertained, that they are not a religious people; for it is not very probable, that individuals would furnish means for the erection of churches, if they had no object in view but national policy, or the enjoyment of human applause. Auburn is particularly interesting to the traveller, from its being the site of the second penitentiary erected in the State of New York.[1] This building is extensive, strong, and of a gloomy appearance, being composed of dark-coloured stone, and surrounded with a very high and thick wall. The town also contains a court-house, bank, printing-office, extensive book-store, &c. and even a soda-water shop. This last appendage of luxury is to be found in most American villages; which, I believe, in general comprise a greater number of comforts and conveniences within their limits, than places of double their magnitude and population in Great Britain.

Next day being Sunday, I went to the State's prison, that I might hear divine service performed before the criminals. The public are freely admitted on these occasions, and when I reached the gate in the wall that surrounds the building, I found eighty or ninety people waiting for entrance. I was a good deal astonished at this circumstance, as it was impossible to suppose them all strangers; and I thought it argued a degree of depravity in the inhabitants of Auburn, to make a practice of idly viewing the children of guilt, and the outcasts of society. In a little time, the female part of the crowd was admitted, and soon after the males. We ascended many flights of stairs, and traversed several dreary passages, along which soldiers were posted with fixed bayonets, before we reached the place of public worship, which lies next the roof of the building. I had scarcely seated myself, when the clanking of fetters struck my ear, and, as the criminals soon began to enter the apartment, I was wholly occupied, for some time, in scanning their countenances as they passed. They were all dressed in the same garb, and looked as if they lived well, and met with gentle treatment. Their number amounted to about two hundred, and I observed eighteen or twenty blacks among them. When they had seated themselves on the benches assigned them, the clergyman gave out a psalm, which was sung in the worst style possible, and then proceeded with the service in the usual manner. It was indeed shocking to hear their fetters clank, during the singing of hymns, and in the midst of prayers. The sermon was an indifferent one; but I must confess I paid but little attention to it, being chiefly employed in examining the faces of the crimi-

1. The first being Sing Sing.

nals, and endeavouring, by physiognomical means, to ascertain who were the most hardened and depraved among them. A majority of the countenances had a stupid expression, but a few bore the marks of strong passions and mental atrocity; and, I believe, a detailed inspection might have enabled me to discover in the features of all, an index to their respective characters. I should have been glad to have put to the test the systems of Spurzheim and Lavater, by applying their principles to the subjects then before me.[2] It is in jails, penitentiaries, and mad-houses alone, that physiognomy can be studied with advantage and effect. The common multitude pass so quietly through their term of existence, and are so seldom the victims of strong and constant passions, that their countenances, partaking of the character of their lives, afford comparatively little scope for the observations of the physiognomist. . . .

Next morning, there was a large party at my hostess's breakfast table, in consequence of its being court-day. Judges, lawyers, clients, pursuers, and defendants, all associated together good-humouredly, and without ceremony, and seemed to vie with each other in the use of the knife and fork. The judges had no useless pride. They assumed none of the airs of the bench while at table, as they and the lawyers treated each other with equal degrees of respect. I must confess, however, that I could not approve of their manners, which were slovenly and clownish, and unlike those of people of education, or knowledge of the world.

After breakfast, my host drove me in his wagon to a place called Weed's Port, upon the bank of the Grand Canal, eight miles from Auburn; and here he left me to wait till the trackboat made its appearance. I walked for some time along the canal; but at last becoming tired, I went into a small shop on the way-side, which contained a few dozen candlesticks, several snuff-boxes, and some pieces of ribbon, &c. The owner stood behind the counter, and I merely bid him good morning, and seated myself; for the Americans have a very slight opinion of a man who uses any ceremony towards them. After some time, he took down a bottle and dusty glass, and asked me if I would drink some bitters, but this I declined. "Well now," said he, "I swear you're from the old country, 'squire." I told him that I was. "I guessed as much," returned he, and having given me a very significant look, he cautiously put the cork in the bottle, and returned it to its place. There was a long pause. "Belike, 'squire,"

2. Both suggested direct relationships between observable physical characteristics and psychological traits. Johann Christoph Spurzheim (1776–1832), a German phrenologist, popularized theories regarding the topology of the cranium; Johann Kaspar Lavater (1741–1801), a Swiss philosopher and theologian, was best known for his heavily illustrated *Essays on Physiognomy* (1775–1778), translated into English in 1797, which included a chapter by Goethe.

said he again, "as you a'nt in drinking trim, you may have a mind to read a bit. Here's my brother's Treatise on the Trinity." He accordingly presented me with a small volume, which I read until the canal-boat came up.

On going aboard the boat, I found its accommodations of a much meaner description than I expected. It was about thirty feet long, had a small cabin fore and aft, and was drawn by two horses, at the rate of nearly four miles an hour. The water in the canal was four feet deep, and tolerably transparent, but I could not perceive that it had any current. . . .

The canal-boat stopped at a small village called Syracuse, a little after sunset. All the passengers slept on board; and in the morning, at dawn, the horses were again yoked. We travelled the whole day without interruption, and reached Utica about nine at night.

Utica is ninety-six miles from Auburn, and is a very extensive and flourishing village, containing, I suppose, five thousand inhabitants, with many spacious streets and excellent buildings. — The canal passes through the middle of it (though the water had only been admitted within one mile of the town at the time I was there); and this advantage must hereafter render Utica a place of no small commercial importance.

Next day I visited a cotton-manufactory, three miles from the village. The machinery, which is very beautiful, and occupies four flats of a large building, is moved entirely by water. There are about eighty persons employed: these consist chiefly of women and children, who have a much more healthful and happy look than any work-people I ever saw in British manufactories. Many of the females were reading the Bible, and others sat sewing, during the intervals of leisure which their respective occupations afforded them. One woman could attend two looms; and each of these, on an average, made twenty-five yards of cotton a-day. Their wages were one *cent* per yard, part of which was paid in goods; and they provided themselves with board. The children received 14s. New York currency (7s. 7d. sterling) per week, and worked twelve hours every day. Cotton stuff was sold at the factory at 16 *cents* per yard (8½d. sterling); the superintendent of which informed me that the concern proved very profitable, and that he found no difficulty whatever in getting labourers, or, as he delicately termed them, *helps,* upon the terms already mentioned.

I quitted Utica at two in the morning, in the mail-coach. In America, the comfort of a stage-passenger is much more attended to than in Britain. He is not obliged to walk through dark, and perhaps dirty streets, to the mail-office, and to seek for people to convey his baggage there in the middle of the night; as the coach calls at his residence, if within the limits of the town, and takes him comfortably up. I had five fellow-passengers; but it continued so dark, and they were so silent for a considerable time, that I neither could see their faces nor ascertain what sort of characters they were: but I afterwards found that they were a lawyer from the state of Ohio, a young lady who appeared to be his niece, a stout jolly Irishman, a simpleton from Lower Canada, and another person, whose character I could not discover. — At five o-clock we stopped and had breakfast, which was a very good one, but much too early to be acceptable to me.

The country, a little way beyond Utica, is in a high state of cultivation, and the different farms which compose the prospect present aspects equally various and beautiful. The road winds, for a considerable way, along the Mohawk river; and, in consequence of this, much delightful scenery meets the eye of a traveller. Lofty cliffs, covered with trees, tower on one side of the stream, and are vividly reflected in its tranquil waters; in the midst of which, clusters of romantic rocky islands raise their verdant heads, and add indescribable variety to the scene. Nothing can be more wild than the appearance of the Mohawk, the sides of it being bordered with immense fragments of brown rock, which have fallen from the cliffs above, and darkly overshadow the waters. The fields around are level and extensive, and, when we passed, were covered with crops, the different colours of which formed an immense variegated carpet, enlivened with pretty villas, nurseries, flocks of cattle, and cottages.

THE MOHAWK VALLEY

The fertile farmlands of the Mohawk Valley west of Schenectady were settled in the mid- and late eighteenth century by immigrants mainly of Dutch and German stock. Subject to frequent raids during the Revolution, the villages that they founded recovered rapidly after independence, retaining the national characteristics of their settlers longer than Albany and the Dutch river towns of the Hudson Valley. The coming of the canal, which closely followed the course of the lower Mohawk River, brought travelers through the area in large numbers for the first time. But, oddly, few authors recorded its Germanic flavor.

There are several reasons for this omission. No tourist spent considerable time in the Mohawk Valley; the newer western lands interested them more, and Niagara Falls acted as a great magnet pulling them across the state. Villages with names like Rotterdam, Amsterdam, and Frankfort were noted, if at all, from the decks of the canal packets. James Stuart's brief comments from his Three Years in North America *are more de-*

tailed than most. "The country through which we passed has been long settled, — originally peopled by the Dutch — the present proprietors speaking both Dutch and English; farm-houses good, with orchards loaded with fruit, and every appearance of comfort and plenty. The outsides of many of the houses painted of different colours; white, green, mulberry brown. Great part of the canal is close to the river. . ." (1: 68).

Indeed, the canal packets themselves provoked much more comment than the surrounding countryside: they were a form of travel foreign to middle- and upper-class Britons, in which tourists were forced to rub shoulders with all classes of Americans. And the longer-settled, cleared farmland of the Mohawk Valley was prohibitively expensive for the audience that emigrant writers aimed at. They also hurried west, drawn not so much by the promise of sublime experience as by the prospect of cheap, available land.

A CANAL JOURNEY IN 1834

Many locks separated Albany and Schenectady, and thus the latter town served as the embarkation point for the canal's west-bound traffic. Utica, some eighty miles further west, was typically the first break in the British passenger's journey. The dozens of accounts of travel on the canal that made it into print are represented here by David Wilkie's description of a journey he took in the early summer of 1834. Wilkie, a red-headed Scot, spent six months in New York and Ontario, checking the prospects for those considering emigration from Britain. Several writers were discomposed by the crush on the packets: Andrew Reed suffered through the boisterous antics of a group of working men traveling to a mechanics' convention in Utica, and Harriet Martineau had to put up with a dozen or more Presbyterian clergymen. Wilkie is one of the few travelers not to complain vociferously about crowded conditions on the canal packets.

Bidding adieu to Schenactady, we went on board the canal packet about to start for the west. The evening was delightful, and we enjoyed the scenery, so altogether new to us, with a high relish. The boat shot along,

From David Wilkie, *Sketches of a Summer Trip to New York and the Canadas* (Edinburgh: Sherwood, Gilbert, and Piper, 1837), pp. 78–86.

slowly it is true, but with the motion enough to render the evening air cool and refreshing. We were within sight of the stream of the Mohawk, which in some places crept along under the overhanging foliage like a silvery serpent enjoying the shade, and at others it was seen dashing over rocks, in the form of little cascades, which gave a pleasing variety to the landscape. Abundance of verdant plains and green haughs[1] spread out on each side of the river, as well as many sandy and unproductive spots. But the latter we were willing to let slip from memory, in summing up the catalogue of beauties scattered along our path; for we felt in a mood to be pleased with every thing and every body in our survey of the New World. As the god of day soon drew in his beams from the face of nature, and the river blackened into a huge dark chasm, we proceeded to take a peep inwardly, — not of ourselves, good reader, — but of our cabin accommodation. There was a goodly company on board, considering the size of our vessel — about thirty gentlemen, and half as many ladies. Four steps broad and twenty-one feet long was the capacity of the gentlemen's sleeping and dining cabin, and here, a score and a half of us had to be stowed away.

When we descended from deck between eight and nine o'clock, being the retiring hour, we found all the sleeping apparatus displayed in full form. On each side of the long narrow space were hung three tiers of canvas-bottomed frames, hardly broad enough to allow the occupant to stretch himself on his back, and three lengthwise, in all, affording accommodation for eighteen, and our surplus number had to betake themselves to the more humble couch afforded by the floor. Our berths were allotted to us by precedence as the names were placed in the way-bill. When each cognomen was sung out by the captain, the individual doffed boots, coats, and vest, and hoisted himself into his place; a process which afforded us a good fund for amusement, as those who were blessed with any thing like rotundity of person felt considerable difficulty in getting fairly into the narrow recess, which afforded but a very threadbare portion of elbow room. I contrived with little difficulty to crawl into my lair, and although enjoying less room, I believe, than if I had been a mummy in one of the Pyramids, I passed a very unconscious and refreshing night. By peep of day I crept from my shelf with all the caution of a snail from its shell, for with undue haste my nose might have run foul of some obtruding stern quarters, or my toes saluted the gaping mouths of the prostrate snorers. I got safely on deck, however, and after performing the refreshing process of ablution, made use of my newly opened eyes to the greatest advantage in my power.

After passing many pretty and romantic villages on the banks of the

1. "Haugh" is Scots dialect for a meadow.

Little Falls: Little Falls on the Mohawk, 1839. By William Henry Bartlett, from N. P. Willis, *American Scenery* (London, 1837–40). Collection of McKinney Library, Albany Institute of History and Art

river and canal, most of which apparently have sprung into existence since the opening of the latter, we were skimming along, about ten o'clock forenoon, towards the beautiful and picturesque scenery around Little Falls. . . .

There are a number of beautiful and fanciful buildings and dwellings in the village, which have a sure and solid foundation, being planted on the various shelves and elevations of the rock to the north of the stream; altogether, the village and scenery around is one of the most romantic and lovely of all the ten thousand glens, hamlets, and waterfalls which we visited during our sojourn in the west. It seemed, in the passing sunny glimpse which we got of it, the perfect Eden of a poet's heaven. We were luckily afforded a good opportunity of enjoying this feast of fancy, for the packet having to ascend six different locks in the canal, we had leisure to wander for miles through the most imposing scenery in all the wild

and luxurious garb of unshorn Nature. Every striking feature of the landscape was brought in a few seconds within the range of the eye, from the
brawling water roaring over the rocky depths of the dark ravine below, to
the sun-bright foliage which crowns the mountains above. It is impossible
that any one could long remain insensible to the charm, which seems to
pervade this masterpiece of Nature's unstudied composition. . . .

Soon after passing Little Falls, we fell into a state of moving mediocrity. We were drawn slowly along, while the view was completely
bounded on each side by the forest, and nothing behind or before but the
lazy length of the watery highway, which, from the long perspective, ter-
minated in a mere point at each end. Above our heads we had a similar
view of the blue sky, which, in its turn, was reflected below our feet, giving us at times an idea, as we gazed down, that we were gliding along a
diametrical division of the globe; for the heavens below appeared as fair
and bright as the zenith from which they were reflected.

After passing several places with high-sounding names, we arrived
at the city of Utica; and although it is well enough as an American city of
third, or perhaps fourth-rate importance, on visiting places with such
names, we seldom failed to entertain an idea that we had before us a quiz-
zical representation of the classical, historical, and important cities of the
Old World; for, alas! in nine out of ten instances, they were but sorry sub-
stitutes for the venerable originals. As an instance of the mistakes which
are made by travellers drawing their impressions of the character of
places from the names they have received: — I parted with one of my travelling friends at Schenactady, he to follow in another boat. I agreed to
wait for him at [New] *London,*[2] unconsciously deeming that such a town
would be a pretty prominent landmark, on the banks of a canal at least;
but I found, on enquiry, that were I resolved to step on shore at this
doughty nameson of our British metropolis, it was more than likely I
would not get a bed! I therefore resolved to pass on, and enjoy the hospi-
talities of the more commodious city of Utica.

I took up my quarters for the night in the coffee-house, the door of
which, luckily for the transportation of my luggage, was within a few
steps of the canal. Here I would observe, for the edification of all worthy
sons of restlessness, that it is a sore and crying evil passing over the surface of the earth in the company of ponderous trunks and stuffed carpet

2. Gordon's *Gazetteer of the State of New York* (1836) describes New London as
having "2 taverns, 4 stores, and about 40 dwellings." Disturnell's *Gazetteer* (1843) says "it
contains about 200 inhabitants, 25 dwelling houses, 2 taverns, 6 stores and groceries, and an
extensive boat yard for building and repairing canal boats."

bags; I conceived, at times, that even the burden of a *better half* would have appeared, in comparison, but a light affliction, had I been able to make the exchange!

After securing a bed, I set out on a voyage of discovery through the city. The business parts seemed humming with life and activity; and there are several private streets, possessing small plots in front, decked with various shrubs and flowers, growing luxuriantly. There are nine churches, and only 10,000 inhabitants; so there appears to be no want of the means of grace, however they may be made use of. But perhaps the less we say about this matter the better.

While walking along one of the finest streets of the city, I met rather an unusual character taking the air on the pavement—a majestic elephant, which the keeper was leading along, while a young cub was playfully trotting at its side, like an early lamb, following its mother; with the slight difference, that in this case the pet happened to be about the size of a couple of well-fed oxen.

On returning to the coffee-house, we found an explanation of the appearance of the ponderous strangers, on perusing the contents of a huge bill in the bar-room, which being too long to stretch its length between the ceiling and the floor, had been separated in the middle, and the pieces placed side by side. It embodied an excellent specimen of Yankee puffing. Portraits of every ill-shaped brute which the caravan contained were displayed, with descriptions below each of the most wonder-working sort. There were to be seen lions that had swallowed whole bullocks, and monkeys twice as big as the human form divine; royal Bengal tigers, and pelicans of the wilderness, that were represented feeding their young with their own heart's blood. In the eyes of many a juvenile observer, the very bill, which hung in all its palpable length before them, afforded good proof of the truth of what was stated, for it was impossible, they thought, that there were not such animals to be seen, when their very portraits were grinning in fearful liveliness from the paper before them; and even seemed to be bellowing forth a confirmation of what was written below. No nation in the world understands the science of puffing more profoundly than the American, or practises it to more advantage or perfection.

UTICA IN 1840

In 1820 John Howison had thought Utica "a very extensive and flourishing village" of about 5,000 inhabitants. Two decades later Utica was a small city. The population had almost trebled, commercial life was lively, and Utica's attractions lured many British tourists into breaking their journeys for a few days. One of those many tourists was Archibald Montgomery Maxwell.

Maxwell, a British Army regular, was posted to New Brunswick as lieutenant-colonel to the 36th Regiment during the Anglo-American tensions of the Maine border dispute. He spent his leave in the autumn of 1840 dashing around the eastern United States and seeing the sights. His condescendingly good-humored account of America proves his description of himself as "a walking alchymist," finding pleasure of one sort or another in everything he saw or did.

An experienced traveler, Maxwell focused a good deal of attention on the military preparedness of the United States—indeed, his comments on Utica open with the annual muster of the local militia. But this professional interest forms only one element of his recollections. As a British officer at the time, he was cultivated by American Whigs, conservatives, and the whole spectrum of Van Buren's opponents. These local political concerns drew Maxwell into the spa society of Lebanon Springs and Saratoga, which he enjoyed immensely. In Utica, the city museum, fairly typical of museums of the time, diverted him, and he followed in the footsteps of dozens of his compatriots in paying homage to the delights of the scenery around Trenton Falls.

We walked through Utica, a city which has sprung up within a few years. Its situation is beautiful, being surrounded by an amphitheatre of undulating and fruitful hills. The streets are broad and regular; and the Mohawk River and Erie Canal pass through the town. In our stroll we saw hundreds of canal-boats, part laden with the produce of the interior, ready to start eastward; whilst others, full of foreign merchandise, were bound towards the west. The population is about 14,000: there are four academies, and numberless schools and churches.

In Chancellor Square, a very fine one, we saw more military manœuvrings; and certainly more awkward gentry I never beheld; but what can you expect, when only three days in each year are set apart for instruction? The chaps, notwithstanding the blustering of their military Mentor, were all whiffing cigars and amusing themselves. I admit that

From Archibald Montgomery Maxwell, *A Run through the United States, During the Autumn of 1840,* 2 vols. (London: Henry Colburn, 1841), 1: 209–213, 228–29.

Utica, 1838. By William Henry Bartlett, from N. P. Willis, *American Scenery* (London, 1837–40). Collection of McKinney Library, Albany Institute of History and Art

some of the uniform companies are in a much better state of discipline. Their dragoons reminded me of the times of Oliver Cromwell; for these cavaliers have red jackets, or jerkins, cut in the oldest fashion, with yellow doublets, and yellow breeches, and immensely long red feathers, stuck on most uncooth-looking caps.[1] We had "Patrick's Day" and "Yankee-Doodle" from every band we fell in with; and where there was no band, an outrageous thumping of drums supplied the deficiency.

We visited the Museum, to look at two white negroes born of jet black parents. They certainly had the woolly hair and flat noses common

1. Another professional soldier, Richard Levinge, was equally unimpressed by the uniforms of the Utica dragoons in the early forties. "They wore a sort of contrivance on their heads like a watering-pot, from which sprang a cloud of ostrich feathers of diverse colours" (*Echoes from the Backwoods,* 2: 75).

to the African race, yet still were perfectly white; but I was more taken
with the long-boat of the celebrated Bill Johnston, who was so troublesome a customer among the hundred islands in the years 1837 and 1838.[2]
It is a splendid ten-oared gig, — for so it might be called from its length
and narrowness. The collection of the birds, shot in the immediate neighbourhood, is very interesting, and from their plumage they would all appear to belong to the species met with in tropical climates.

I was surprised at finding in this republican museum a representation of the "Martyrdom of Louis XVI." I thought it in bad taste; for surely
the most zealous republican must regret that his favourite form of government should have been preluded by so revolting a tragedy. My humble
opinion is, that the day is not distant when the monarchial principle will
be re-established and triumphant through this great continent. Every
thing, as it appears to me, tends to this, as well as to the termination of the
federal government.

Our landlord having procured us a carriage, we left our luggage with
him and drove across the Delafield Hills by the road that leads to
Sackett's Harbour on Lake Ontario. Turning off from this, we passed
through the village of Trenton, and were put down at the Rural Retreat at
Trenton Falls, the thunder of which I could hear distinctly as I smoked a
cigar and sucked a mint julep to refresh myself; whilst my more sober
friends regaled themselves with tea.

Never in my life did I quit any place with more regret than Trenton
Falls this morning. It is one of those spots which a man falls in love with,
and fancies he would be delighted to pass all the remainder of his days
there. The situation of the hotel is singularly beautiful: it has a dense
wood in its rear, which comes up close to it, and which no sun can penetrate; you have the noise of the rushing waters in the distance to soothe
you; the gardens and shrubberies are delightful; and the tree-covered hills
which surround you are now beginning to put on their autumn tints;

---

2. Bill Johnston achieved some notoriety as a pirate in the late thirties. He was based
in the Thousand Islands during the undeclared war waged by American sympathizers along
the St. Lawrence River at the time of the Canadian rebellion. "Bill was originally a Canadian farmer at Bath; but a considerable amount of his property having been confiscated, as
he says, improperly, for alleged smuggling, he left Canada, went to the States, and vowed
revenge against the British. . . . Bill, in 1843, was about sixty years of age, but was hale,
and straight, and ruddy; his nose was sharp, as were his features generally, and his eyes were
keen and piercing; his lips compressed and receding; his height about five feet ten inches; he
wore a broad-brimmed black hat, black stock and vest, frock and trowsers of dark duffle"
(Alexander, *L'Acadie,* 1: 309, 311).

whilst the variegated contour of the more distant mountains completes the grandeur and beauty of the scene.

Before breakfast I walked to the mill-dam and the pretty little fall formed by it, and watched for some time a sad bungler in the sublime art of Izaak Walton. I regretted at the moment that I had not brought my rod and tackle, that I might have given him a lesson; but one can't do everything; neither did I intend my tour to be a sporting one: had such been my intention, I might have been present yesterday at the Delafield races, which took place about five miles from Trenton; but the mountain-road to it was execrable, and we all agreed that the wild woods and sequestered dells of Trenton were worth a hundred race-courses.

A JOURNEY WEST OF UTICA IN THE MID-1830s

British forces in North America spent a good deal of the eighteenth century killing Indians or paying them to kill one another. In the early nineteenth century, after the military threat posed by the tribes and nations of the eastern seaboard had been broken, British travelers became sympathetic toward the plight of the aboriginal remnant. They were the topic of much fantastic speculation on both sides of the Atlantic: the idea that Indians descended from the lost tribes of the Jewish diaspora was especially popular among clergymen, for example, while George Catlin convinced himself that the Mandan Sioux resulted from a lost medieval Welsh expedition to North America. The fewer Indians, the more was written about them, and the greater the sympathy they evoked.

The Iroquois nations of New York had been confined by treaty to a few areas of reserved land by 1800. Most popular among tourists was the Tonawanda Seneca reservation, near Buffalo, but the great rush of westbound travelers saw, and commented copiously on, other Indian lands in central New York. The Oneida nation held land west of Utica, and Henry Caswall, going to study theology at Kenyon College, left this fairly typical description in his America, and the American Churches. *"These poor people had recently embraced Christianity, and their condition was said to be much improved. I noticed their dwellings, which were ingeniously covered with the bark of trees. I saw their council grove, which consists of twenty or thirty trees of the walnut species. In the distance their church was visible, and its spire rising above the trees gave interest to the scene, and suggested pleasing emotions" (p. 16). But, he records, the American government was about to move the Oneida to the unsettled Midwest, where he feared they would lose their newly adopted religion (which he terms "civilisation").*

In the mid-thirties, Richard Weston, by now roundly hating all things American, took a brief western jaunt before returning to his beloved Scotland. He stayed overnight with a "Nadir" (probably Oneida, though the mistake is telling) band west of Utica, and treated them in his recollections with a simple tact notable by its absence from his accounts of the doings of the "pale faces."

I went on to Utica, which the Americans call the imperial city of the west. It is a busy place; the stores are well filled; but the people have a pale, sallow, and ague-like appearance. The water is brackish, soil sandy, undulating. The Erie or Western Canal, which runs through it, is not above four feet deep, the boats being long, narrow, and flat-bottomed. The town is built mostly of wood, though there are many brick houses, and a few of stone. If you examine even their outward appearance, you will easily conceive they have not the comfort within that ours have. Some of the windows have shutters on the outside even of the upper stories; some have blinds not unlike our venetian ones; and others have paper hanging inside of the glass, to darken the room in order to keep away the flies which are partial to light. The people use fly-traps here to thin them; but notwithstanding the numbers killed in this way, they are not perceptibly decreased. I took up my lodging in a bar-room, a place which is only suited for a talker and a drinker; but I had no choice; and I always like to have an opportunity of studying the American character. I got the usual stare from a number of loungers; and observing a newspaper, took it up, seating myself on a form in the recess of the window. I always preferred being nearest the light, as I had little faith in the Americans. One is quite surprised at the catalogue of crimes, of every enormity, recorded in the American newspapers. Our crimes are no doubt manifold, yet I think they are far greater here; and owing to the thinness of the population, how many must be perpetrated that never come to light! But we need not wonder at all this, when we consider the character of the population; for there is no place where the maxim of doing unto others as we would they

From Richard Weston, *A Visit to the United States and Canada in 1833 with the View of Settling in America. . .* (Edinburgh: Richard Weston and Sons, 1836), pp. 245–46, 251–55.

should do to us, is less attended to than in the wide and extensive land of liberty. . . .

I left Utica in one of the line-boats on the Western Canal, from which I used occasionally to step out and view any of the public works that were going on. I found that the labour performed was chiefly done by Irishmen, the Americans in general appearing to be unfit for hard work; indeed, were it not for the emigrants, they would have fewer canals and rail-roads. Observed some men scooping up the sand from the bottom of the canal; a great deal of business is carried on through this waterway.

I went and visited the salt-works at Onondago. The lake of that name is upwards of four hundred miles from the sea; yet, notwithstanding, if you put a pump into it twenty feet below the surface, you will bring up strong salt water. There are wooden tanks built on the ground to contain it, previous to filling the cisterns, which latter are composed of lines of troughs, having lids to cover them during rain or at night. Evaporation goes on by the influence of the sun, for, as the wood is now getting scarce, government has interdicted boiling. The troughs, which are also made of wood, are raised a little from the ground. Officers appointed by government are in attendance to see that the salt is well made; it is of weaker quality than what is manufactured in Europe; and the Americans have to import the article, though the duty is very high, to cure their butter.

The Cayuga Flats here, as well as many others, remind me of the fens in England, and are as unhealthy. The soil is alluvial generally, and produces good crops, the salt acting as a manure. The water is brackish, and the insects numerous and troublesome. I spoke to a farmer, who was sinking a well at fifteen feet and came on a spring of salt water, remarking that I wondered how he could live there with such bad water. He answered that he did not care a cent for water if he had good crops; and that he had a ready demand for all kinds of farm produce by the canal. . . .

I went along a wooden bridge here nearly a mile long, over a swamp, the surface in many places being covered with a green mantle. Malaria was thinning the population at a great rate; farms were deserted, and houses shut up, owing to the pestilence, yet new adventurers were pouring in.

Clyde, a low-lying sickly town, on the line of the canal. In coming to this place I had to pass over a large marsh, wood in some places being laid across the road to make it firm, the water on each side covered with a green scum, from which proceeded, by the action of the sun, a close fog that produced a choking kind of effect on my breathing. Two persons had died that day in the house next to the bar where I took up my lodgings for the night; they were put into a box, and buried within four hours after their decease. In another house a few doors from it, a father and mother, along with two children, also died shortly after I arrived, and were likewise put into boxes, and buried in pairs. The deaths, I was informed, averaged fifty per day. It was like the city of the plague — no ceremony there at burial.

A number of Indian children would occasionally accompany our boat along the banks of the canal, running so as to keep up with it; the passengers now and then throwing out a cent on the bank to induce them to come farther. Most of them had the usual accompaniment, the blanket, over their shoulders. Having been told that they belonged to the Nadir [Oneida?] tribe, a thought struck me that I would visit their settlement, and remain with them all night if I could procure lodging; after which I could join the line-boat next day. I accordingly got hold of one of the boys, giving him a cent, and went in his company to their village.

As we approached the place, I remarked that the trees in the orchard are not planted in rows like those of the pale faces, but irregularly; and the same with the Indian corn. In the latter I thought the Indians have the advantage over the pale faces, as by this means they effectually puzzle the crows, which will begin sometimes at the end of a row in the straight planted fields, and with mathematical exactness step from place to place, and dig up and eat the seeds as they go along, to the dismay of the farmer.

The Indians are not so fond of dollar-making as are the pale faces, seldom planting more than they need for their own consumption. They are simple in their dress, and have not the suspicious and inquisitive American stare. I observed an infant lying on a board, to which it was tied by the shoulders with a strap, another being fastened across the lower part of the body, the arms and legs being free. There was a blanket covering the child, and a woman beside it. I thought at first it was dead; but afterwards learnt that the young children are always strapped to a board of this kind till they are able to walk.

The adults have a hobbling gait in walking, appearing to lean more on the heel than the toe; they stand erect, their shoulders squared — whether the lacing be the cause of this I do not know. Their spine does not appear to have the same curve as ours; their hands, in place of hanging in a line with the thighs, rather fall behind them. In a word, you would think it very easy to drive them over. I have noticed a few men in Edinburgh walk very like them.

I saw their chief, a female, who was dressed something like the rest; her hut had no distinguishing feature about it that I could observe. She was treated by her vassals with great respect, although not an Indian herself. This tribe had captured her father and mother when she was quite a child, and having taken them to their territory, put the father to death, but not in the presence of herself or her mother; she still, however, remembers having heard his screams. Her mother was murdered sometime after, having always expected it since her husband's death; the daughter heard them debating her death, though she did not witness it, and even her own, which was only prevented by the chief's squaw, who afterwards adopted her. The old chief having died, his eldest son married her, after consulting the tribe and obtaining the consent of his mother. He was shot soon after by his brother, who wished to obtain her hand; and the heads of the tribe, having met, decided that he should be put to death for the crime. The old squaw was then made chief, and her daughter-in-law divided the honours with her, presiding over and settling the differences of the tribe; and she was made sole chief on the death of the former. Many offers had been made to induce her to enter into wedlock again, but she declined them all. The state also have offered her a pension to leave them, but she declines it; she says that though they murdered her parents, she is aware it was during a time of war; that they have been kind to her, and that she is fond of them, and will not leave them.

I observed one of the men at the door of his hut making snow shoes. They are formed thus: A strong twig is bent into a kind of oval narrower at the toe than heel; the hoop is covered across with skin. It is six times or more the size of the foot, in order to cover a quantity of snow, that it may not sink readily; and the foot is laced in with straps something like our skates. The Indian hut, though meaner than the log-house, is superior to the shanty.

ONTARIO'S WEATHER SHORE

Before the Erie Canal, Utica had marked the western boundary of intensive settlement. Frances Wright, traveling the Genesee Road in 1818, noted in her Views of Society and Manners in America *how the landscape itself suddenly changed. "Leaving Utica, the country begins to assume a rough appearance; stumps and girdled trees encumbering the inclosures; log-houses scattered here and there; the cultivation rarely extending more than half a mile, nor usually so much, on either hand. . ." (p. 179). Despite the "roughness," however, she was to be as charmed by Canan-*

*daigua and Geneva as her many successors would be, and more sanguine
in her predictions of wealth for the fertile country than many.*

*In comparison, the growth of the communities on the weather shore
of Lake Ontario was largely ignored. The main roads, the canal, and the
railroads all carried passengers coming west from Utica south of Oneida
Lake and through the Onondaga valley. Nevertheless a few accounts of
the area were published. British Army officers, usually in a futile pursuit
of deserters from the forces stationed in eastern Ontario and Quebec,
provide a few scant accounts of Watertown and the mouth of the Black
River. Sackets Harbor received attention from naval officers immediately
after 1814, but thereafter was generally ignored. Oswego expanded with
the huge carrying trade from central New York coming up the canal spur
from Syracuse, but tourists were almost always more interested in the
steamer service across Lake Ontario than in Oswego itself.*

*Little traveled, the area offered nothing to the amateur of land-
scape, for whom the falls at Trenton and Rochester whetted the appetite
for the feast at Niagara. Little known, its fertile farms attracted surprisingly few writers for emigrants — though a rare letter from a poor immigrant to Oswego County did see print, it was for reasons that had to do
with English public policy, not to recommend the intrinsic merits of the
area in which he had settled.*

*The feeder canals to the north opened for business too late to affect
to any significant extent the typical journey of the British tourist of the
first half-century. The three extracts that appear here can only be described
as exotics in the vast and increasingly homogeneous literature of British
travel in New York state.*

JEFFERSON COUNTY IN 1843

*The late 1830s brought political uproar and sporadic armed rebellion to
British North America. The Canadian rebels received great popular support in the northern and western counties of New York State. The "Patri-
ots War" culminated in an attempted invasion of Prescott in November
1838; relations would continue to be strained through much of the following decade. One of the major points of controversy would be the status of
deserters from the British forces in Canada. Article Ten of the Treaty of
Washington, 1842, attempted to regularize the extradition of military deserters along the frontier, but, as James Edward Alexander (1803–1885)*

discovered, public opinion in Jefferson County was still strong enough in the mid-forties to thwart the treaty's provisions.

Alexander, a Scot, was among the most widely traveled of nineteenth-century British Army officers. By 1840 he had already seen active service in India, Burma, Persia, Turkey, Portugal, and southern Africa; and he had traveled privately in South and North America. He would later see service in the Crimean War and in New Zealand. In 1841 he was posted to Canada with the 14th Foot and was stationed in Kingston, Ontario.

Desertion from the harsh conditions in the military was not an unusual occurrence in the nineteenth century. French Creek, in Jefferson County, was only twenty-four miles from Kingston, and the high wages of the United States attracted many disaffected soldiers. A corporal and private having stolen a skiff, a gun, and a watch, Alexander decided to test the effectiveness of the extradition treaty. He pursued the deserters to French Creek, where they escaped from American custody, then followed them to Watertown, where they were again arrested; but an anti-British jury acquitted them of the charges against them. In this account of Alexander's futile mission I have omitted most of the legal detail.

The journey to Watertown in a two-horse waggon was an excessively tedious one; the country was white with snow, among which appeared at intervals the log and frame houses of the farmers, portions of the ancient forest and snake fences everywhere. The road was so cut up that all that could be mustered generally in the way of speed was three or four miles an hour, and the snow fell nearly the whole time. In talking about deserters never enjoying happiness, even if they made good their escape, and acquire property, the driver turned round, and pithily remarked, "Because they aint to hum;" that is, they have separated themselves for ever from home and friends.

At Depeauville and Brownville, through which the party passed, there were long and earnest arguments among the people assembled at the bar, as to the comparative merits of some new candidates for the offices of Senator, Sheriff, &c., and dollar bills were freely betted. One man, in the heat of argument, most irreverently said, "We'll carry our election in spite of God Almighty."

From James Edward Alexander, *L'Acadie; or, Seven Years' Explorations in British America,* 2 vols. (London: Henry Colburn, 1849), 1: 305–307, 319–21, 323–24, 331, 333–34, 341–42.

Brownville, Jefferson County: cotton mills on the Black River, c. 1820. From Jacques Milbert, *Itinéraire pittoresque* (Paris, 1828–29). New York State Museum, Albany

Watertown, containing many handsome buildings, and also cloth and cotton factories, tanneries, leather factories, &c. &c., and then inhabited by twelve thousand inhabitants, is situated on the banks of a stream with a swift and full current and excellent "water privileges," called the Black River, from its rocky bed and banks and dark-coloured water. It rushes impetuously towards Sackett's Harbour, distant twelve miles. The factories attract many deserters, who there find employment. They do not get much money wages, but are found and get an order for necessaries on particular stores, also they get nightly an allowance of whisky, and some we saw there were miserably drunk every night. There were about fifty deserters in and about Watertown; some of these men had, doubtless, been tempted to desert, and were furnished with clothes to do so, in order that their labour might be available in a country where manual labour is so dear and so difficult to be procured. But deserters soon find to

their cost that their labour is little esteemed, many respectable people refuse to employ them on any terms, and those who do, treat them with deserved scorn and contempt. . . .

Among others of the public buildings which I took the opportunity
of visiting during my detention at Watertown, was an excellent establishment called the Black River Institution,[1] where persons of both sexes receive a liberal education on easy terms. They are generally young persons,
though all ages may be found receiving instruction, from seven to forty
years of age, and once a father and son were being taught at the same
time! The former after failure as a merchant, having a wish to read for the
church. The Rector was very civil, and showed me the halls of study; the
apparatus for expounding the science of natural philosophy, the collection of minerals, the young ladies under instruction in reading and
history, and who were attending to music, drawing, algebra, &c. In one
room I remarked that the two sexes were receiving lessons together on
light, refraction and reflection, by a Scotch Professor, Mr. Ramsay; and
the Rector said to me, "You are probably surprised to see young men and
young women, some of them sixteen years of age, receiving instruction
together, as you know we are very particular about these matters in the
States. There was a great prejudice against it at first, here also, but it is
now found to be attended with no bad results; on the contrary, the presence of the young ladies has a humanizing effect on the young men. You
observe they enter by different doors, and sit apart, and their eyes *ought*
to be directed to the black board only, and not to one another."

I complimented the worthy Rector on the general excellence of the
system pursued at the Black River Institution, at the same time I was constrained to point out that the health of the pupils did not seem to be sufficiently attended to, particularly in the matter of ventilation. The advantage of pure cool and moist air was altogether overlooked; every hall of
study was heated with that "hellish" invention, a close stove, and without
a tin of water on it for evaporation. There was no ventilation, and the
lungs inhaled for hours (as is usual in the Northern States in winter) a
burnt air, which, and not the peculiarity of the climate, I am convinced,
lays the foundation of most of the cases of consumption in the States.

After the Institution, several of the factories were visited; the cloth
factory, where strong and good broad-cloth was being fabricated with ex-

1. The Black River Religious and Literary Institute was incorporated in 1836 and occupied a building on the corner of State and Mechanic streets in Watertown. It was renamed
the Jefferson County in 1846. Its founding principal was the Rev. James R. Boyd, who
served until 1848, when he returned to the ministry.

cellent machinery. The leather factory and tannery, where raw hides were in steep below, and harness-making going on above; an iron foundry, where stoves were extensively made, also every sort of machinery, a pump factory, &c., &c., all dependant on the full and rapid current of the Black River, falling in a great sheet at one place over a high dam; at another, rushing and boiling over an inclined plane of shelving limestone rocks. . . .

It is now time to proceed to the justice's room, to attend the examination of the prisoners charged with felony. The apartment is a small one, a large and hot stove is in the midst; three benches are on one side, on which sit many of the old deserters, (now working in the various factories), and other sympathizers of the prisoners — all bearing a villanous look of scorn and hatred of the prosecutor, and taunts and threats were muttered, as thus, "We don't care a b____y curse for any officer out of Canada, and if these men are surrendered, we won't let them go without bloodshed." But my cause being a good one, it behoved me unflinchingly to do my duty.

The prisoners are introduced in charge of two rough-looking constables, and are seated to confront the prosecutor, the chief constable and the sergeant (the latter the principal witness against them). No less than three counsel have been provided for the prisoners by their sympathizing friends; and there being a notion that this would be the case, the prosecutor had been advised to provide himself with a counsel also, which I did in the person of a very intelligent lawyer, Mr. Moore, jun. The justice now turned round from writing at his table, and calling the court to order, he commenced proceedings. . . .

I think I was a good deal indebted to masonry for my safety at Watertown, where I was in the midst of many miscreants. One day a tall and stout master boot-maker, an Irishman, came to me, and finding that I was a mason, he said, "There is a party here which intends to thrash you and your Sergeant, but as you are a mason never fear. I have got a party as strong as the other, and we won't see you come to any harm." Of course I was very much obliged to him for his kind intentions . . .

While I tarried at the American hotel,[2] a wedding took place in the house. A respectable farmer came in from some distance and married the cook. The bridegroom was about fifty, and the bride was thirty years of age. The landlord and many of his boarders assisted at the ceremony, which was performed in the evening, and those of the boarders who had not been present, were invited in afterwards by the bridegroom to partake

2. The American Hotel was built in 1827 and burned down in 1849.

of wine and cake. After all were charged he gave this sentiment, "Friendship to all, love to a few, and hatred to none." So systematically were matters managed, that next morning the bridegroom was sitting at the stove in the bar at seven o'clock, and at half-past seven breakfasted as usual at the public table, at which, of course, his wife, the cook, did not appear, and in the afternoon the happy pair left for their home. The farmer took the numerous jokes which were bandied about on the occasion, very good humouredly, and when I asked the landlord what the wife was like, he answered, "she is as pretty as a picture, and straight as a candle."

Two brother farmers, and of a respectable exterior, were pointed out to me one day in a waggon, as possessing one wife between them, after the manner of the nairs of India.[3] But generally speaking, the decencies of society are well preserved in and about Watertown, and one owner of an extensive factory, said, that among all the women employed by him during thirty years,[4] there had been only one instance occurred of an illegitimate child.

[The prisoners were discharged by the Watertown jury, and Alexander prepares to return to Canada.]

Before I left Watertown, after breakfast, I had an opportunity of seeing the manner of voting by ballot in the States. It was the election for senator, sheriff, &c., altogether quite a field day. The evening before I had attended a meeting of the Whigs — synonymous with Conservatives — in the States, to arrange their proceedings for the morrow, and there were some amusing speeches delivered, in which the "loco-focos," or Radicals, were sharply handled.

In one of the lower rooms of the American hotel, a table was placed opposite a door-way, the door itself was taken off its hinges, across the door-way was nailed a board, the voters came along the passage, "brought up" at the board, handed over it their folded ticket (containing the name of the candidate they voted for) to a man who stood up beside the door inside, he slipped the ticket through a slit in a box, like a large tea-caddy, with a handle at top, and which stood on the table.

At the table sat two clerks who registered in books, the names of those who came forward to vote, whilst a fourth functionary sat at the table, with a 'tooth-picking air' and apparently observing all those who

3. The Nairs were a military and noble caste of Malabar, on the southwest coast of India.

4. The earliest large textile concern in the area, the Black River Cotton and Woolen Manufacturing Company, started spinning in November 1814, some thirty years before Alexander's visit to Watertown.

came forward to vote, and was ready to detect and check any irregularity. There was no noise or altercation while the business of balloting was going on, well dressed and indifferently attired voters came forward, all conducted themselves with decorum. Many of the tickets were printed on coloured paper, and stamped with the eagle or other devices outside, so as to show openly which side in politics the voters took, thereby rendering the ballot a mockery. After all had voted the scrutineers opened the box and examined and counted the tickets and declared the result.

OSWEGO IN THE EARLY 1840s

While the omission of Watertown, situated off the main tourist route, from British accounts of New York is understandable, that of Oswego appears to be less explicable. Oswego, like Schenectady, is seldom described: both cities were only interesting as transportation centers. Schenectady was the eastern passenger terminus for the Erie Canal; Oswego, the steamer depot for voyages across the lake into Canadian ports. Indeed, the author's missing his ship is the only reason that the extract appearing here was written.

David Wilkie's Sketches of a Summer Trip *suggests that Oswego had no intrinsic merits or novelty to set it aside from the other cities and villages of New York and gives it but brief notice. "We arrived at the village of Oswego, beautifully situated at the mouth of the river of the same name. Like all the infant cities of America, the houses are as gew-gaw and gingerbread-looking as one could desire, stuck together like so many rows of bright-coloured pasteboard boxes in a toy shop, calculated to trick little masters and misses out of their spare pence" (p. 236).*

The anonymous "Wanderer," son of an Edinburgh merchant, published his journals after retiring to the city of his birth. Most of the book is taken up by his account of a residence of several years in India during the 1820s. His notes on a six-week trip through the United States are desultory and mainly occupied with retelling tall stories of dubious provenance. The book as a whole has several eccentric inconsistencies. The Wanderer does not identify himself by name, for example, but his anonymity must have been severely compromised by the portrait that appears opposite the title page. Nor is the year of his trip to America given, though the days and months are carefully transcribed from his journal's pages. He seems to have made his visit some time in the early 1840s.

I passed several log-houses, where I saw the settlers with their patches of cleared land, the stumps standing, and a few sheep and pigs feeding hard by. The fences are of wood, placed in a zig-zag direction. When I arrived within about twenty miles of Oswego, I found the land along the road side was well cleared; but the stumps of the trees were in many places still standing. It takes seven years before the roots become rotten, and the stumps in a fit state to be removed from the soil. It was nine P.M. before I reached Oswego, thus taking seventeen hours to travel seventy-five miles. The steam-boat for Toronto had sailed half an hour before my arrival; and the Oswego steamer, which ought to have sailed next day, was so damaged, in consequence of having been driven on shore in a gale, that she was under repair, so the earliest conveyance I could have to Toronto was the steam-boat, on Friday evening, for which I resolved to wait. I took up my lodgings at the Welland House, or hotel, kept by Mr Spencer. It is situated on the banks of the Oswego river, which runs through the town, and is near the wharf, from which the steam-boats sail, and, on that account, well adapted for travellers.

29th May. I rose at ten A.M. and took a saunter through the town; in passing through one of the streets, I saw on a sign, "ready-made coffin warehouse." I stood looking at this strange, and to me, unusual announcement, for about a minute, when the store-keeper, no doubt thinking me a likely customer, stepped briskly forward and handed me his shop-bill, wherein he requests the public to call and examine the article for themselves; at the same time alleging that he is ready to preserve his customers, when dead, from all smell and putrefaction, in the warmest weather, for any reasonable time, say from one to ten days: N.B. "a respectable person will always be ready to lay out the dead."

Oswego is a small town, containing about 5000 inhabitants. The river of the same name, which here falls into Lake Ontario, runs through it. The river is about 150 yards wide, and is crossed by a bridge, which is supported by seven wooden arches. A charge is made of one cent. (½ d sterling) for each foot passenger who passes along it. The Welland House is an excellent house. I have a single-bedded room, which is a luxury I have not enjoyed since I left home; my shoes are cleaned by a man of colour; the board is excellent, and includes brandy, beer, and cyder; the charge by the day is a dollar; no extra charge for servants; and the master of the house waits upon us during dinner, along with the waiters. When I left the house, he sent my luggage on board the steamer with his own cart,

From Anonymous, *Journal of a Wanderer; Being a Residence in India, and Six Weeks in North America* (London: Simpkin, Marshall, 1844), pp. 154–56.

Oswego: south view of Oswego, c. 1840. From John W. Barber and Henry Howe, *Historical Collections of the State of New York* (New York, 1841). Courtesy of the DeWitt Historical Society of Tompkins County, Ithaca

and drove me down himself in his own carriage to the boat free of expense. The steam-boat, expected on Friday evening, did not arrive, which detained me at Oswego till nine P.M. on Saturday evening, when I set sail on board the St George steamer for Toronto.

AN IMMIGRANT COUPLE IN OSWEGO COUNTY, 1828

Published accounts of the lives of the mass of immigrants are extremely rare. The poor were unlikely to know Edinburgh and London publishers socially, and even if they did, the potential audience for their descriptions of America was too poor to buy them, and, anyway, semiliterate. That the following letter was published in England, in 1829, had to do not with its intrinsic interest but with the political aims of Benjamin Smith, the editor of the volume in which it appeared.

In the late twenties unemployment exacted, through the Poor Law Rates, a large and growing toll on the incomes of the English middle classes. The whole Poor Law structure was under intense scrutiny, the

royal Commissioners appointed to examine it were preparing their monu-
mental report, and the Poor Law Reform Act would pass the parliament
in 1832. A Malthusian calculation demonstrated that to ship off what was
euphemistically termed the "surplus population" of a district to the colo-
nies and the United States was cheaper than to support them for one year
at home and in the workhouse. An East Sussex gentleman, Benjamin
Smith, joined the Poor Law debate on behalf of this subsidized emigra-
tion by publishing twenty-four unanimously enthusiastic letters from
Sussex residents who had been helped to emigrate to America. He sent
two men out to find such letters, claims to have published the first twenty-
four that came to light without regard to their contents (which we may
reasonably doubt), and altered only the worst of the spelling.

Most of Smith's letter-writers had settled in New York, following in
the footsteps and benefitting from the experience of neighbors and rela-
tives who had previously chosen New York as their home. Among them
were a middle-aged couple, Thomas and Hannah Boots, who settled in
Oswego County on the northern shore of Oneida Lake. Their letter to
their children in England, recommending they also emigrate, was the last
that Smith collected for publication, and was written only months before
his book appeared.

Constantia,
December 2nd, 1828

Dear Children,

I now write for the third time since I left old England. I wrote a letter, dated October 8th, and finding that it would have 4 weeks to lay, I was
afraid you would not have it: and as I told you I would write the truth, if I
was forced to beg my bread from door to door, so I now proceed. Dear
children, I write to let you know that we are all in good health, excepting
your mother; and she is now just put to bed of another son, and she is as
well as can be expected. And now as it respects what I have got in America: I have got 12-1/2 acres of land, about half improved,[1] and the rest in
the state of nature, and 2 cows of my own; but if I had not got a good
friend in England, I could not have bought it. We can buy good land for

From Benjamin Smith, ed., *Twenty-four Letters from Labourers in America to Their
Friends in England* (1829; San Francisco: California State Library for the W.P.A., 1939),
pp. 44–46.
1. Another immigrant, Stephen Watson, writing from Albany on October 5, 1823,
specifies what "half-improved" meant: "When they clear land, as they call it, they chop the

18s. per acre: but buying of land is not one quarter part, for the land is as full of trees as your woods are of stubs; and they are from 4 to 10 rods long, and from 1 to 5 feet through them. You may buy land here from 18s. to 9 pounds in English money; and it will bring from 20 to 40 bushels of wheat per acre, and corn from 20 to 50 bushels per acre, and rye from 20 to 40 ditto. You may buy beef for 1-3/4d. per pound; and mutton the same; Irish butter 7d. per pound; cheese 3d.; tea 4s. 6d.; sugar 7d. per pound; candles 7d.; soap 7d.; and wheat 4s. 6d. per bushel; corn and rye 2s. per bushel. And I get 2s. 4d. a day and my board; and have as much meat to eat, 3 times a day, as I like to eat. But clothing is dear: shoes 8s.; half boots 16s.; calico from 8d. to 1s. 4d.; stockings 2s. 9d. to 3s. 6d.; flannel 4s. per yard; superfine cloth from, 4s. 6d. to 1 pound; now all this is counted in English money. We get 4s. per day in summer, and our board; and if you count the difference of the money, you will soon find it out. 8s. in our money is 4s. 6d. in your money. And among the good things of America, we have good laws, as good as they are in England, and much better attended to. For if a man comes to America with a family, and falls sick or lame within 6 months, the county must take care of them; if they have been here 6 months, then the town, which you call a parish, must keep them. So people need not fear of suffering; and people are a great deal more friendly here than they are, or can be, in England: because they have it not in their power as they have here; for we are all as one, and much more friendly. I have found plenty of good friends here, such as I never found in England, — only one. As it respects this world's goods, and in the regard to Christian privileges, I enjoy myself much more than I did in England. For we have preaching twice on the Sabbathday, and prayer-meeting in the week; and all within but a mile of my house. I forgot to tell you that I had built a framed house upon the land which I had bought. Now, I think if you can or do credit what I write, as it is truth, that it will suffice you. But among the conveniences of America, there is some ill-conveniences: first we have 2 or 3 miles to carry our grist to the mill; and 4 miles to go up to the store, which you call a shop; and when we get there, perhaps cannot get all we want; for where I live is a new country, and being so far from the sea, where the goods come on shore, they are very often out of goods. Another thing is, we have no brewhouse near; so we cannot get any yeast to bake with; so we are obliged to make risings; and if we do not use them just at the right time,

---

wood off about 2 feet from the ground, and then plough a row between the stubs . . ." (p. 15).

we sometimes make heavy bread. And the roads are very bad but with all the ill-conveniences, I bless God for sending me to America. Josia has had the fever-ague for 8 or 9 weeks; but we hope he has got rid of it. But them that I thought to find my best friends is not so. And all that wish to know the truth of America, let them help pay for the letters, because they cost a great deal: but let old Joker see them. Henry and his wife and 2 children are all well; he has just lost a little boy; he is gone into eternity about 7 months old. He gives his kind love to you all. Remember us to all our brothers and sisters; and let them know how we all are, and how we are getting on: and as soon as you get this letter, write to let us know whether you will come to America or not; as I shall leave it to your own judgment about it. And if you judge right, I think you will come if you can; and if you come, you will do well to go to Benjamin Smith, Esq., and get him to intercede for you, as he was my best friend. And you will want 1 pound 10s. to get up where I am, both young and old. And if you come, be sure to get the gentlemen to let you lay in your own provision; and not let that rogue C____ get it for you. And plenty of flour; plenty of hams of bacon: sugar, cheese, butter, plums; and the first of bread. Plenty of all this, and tea plenty; and bake a part of flour into hard bread as your mother did. And when you get to the Quarantine ground, have a letter wrote to send by the first steam-packet you see; to let me know when you shall be at Seracuse. The best way for you to come, is to come up to Albany in a tow-boat: when you get to Seracuse, call for entertainment at the sign of the Farmers' Accomodation; and if we get your letter will meet you there; and if not, come on to the town of Hastings, in the county of Oswego, and there you will find us out. And direct your letters, Thomas Boots, Hastings, County of Oswego, States of New York, North America. So no more at present from your

Ever tender and loving parents,
THOMAS BOOTS. HANNAH BOOTS.

Be sure if you come, come away in March if you can; for the sooner you come in the spring, the better.[2]

Mr. John Boots, Jun., Robertsbridge,
Sussex, Old England.

---

2. This was common advice. As Smith notes in his introduction to the volume, the annual average passage from Liverpool to New York was forty days; but the average was thirty-seven days in March, and only thirty in April.

THE LAKE VILLAGES

*West of Utica lay the new lands of the country's post-independent growth.
These areas gave British tourists the novelty of traveling where a long past
did not reverberate, in a land where living generations were responsible for
everything the visitor saw. And one of the surprises for British travelers
was that there was much to see — a line of charming villages, close to elegance, that marked the northern edge of the Finger Lakes, the state's world-
famous penal experiment at Auburn, the extraordinary salt industry in the
Onondaga Valley, and, through the center of all this, the great canal that
focused and stimulated the agricultural and commercial life of the area.*

*In short span journeys through central New York display the
changes in British travelers and what they looked for during the first half
of the nineteenth century. The earnest social investigator visiting the penitentiary and the political economist marveling at the salt industry become
increasingly identifiable as specialists by the 1830s, where previously such
interests had been common to all visitors. As British travelers become a
more homogeneous group with narrower and more predictably bourgeois
interests (or with less time to indulge their interests — which comes to
much the same thing), so, increasingly, they elevate the group of Finger
Lake villages that stretches from Skaneateles to Canandaigua, and pre-
eminently Canandaigua itself, as a vision made flesh; and it is a potent
English vision, the suburban and bourgeois romance of country life.
Against so powerful a fancy native to British writers the later-developing
city of Syracuse and the area's industries struggled in vain for attention.*

*Indeed, the only detailed description of Syracuse, which appears
here, comes from the late thirties in an account by a man with so little
imagination that he seems incapable of choosing amongst details — and so
he recorded everything he saw. James Silk Buckingham's earnest catalog
of Syracuse is followed by Edward Strutt Abdy's approbatory view of the
Auburn penitentiary and George Combe's notes on the village of Auburn.
On Canandaigua there is Frances Anne Kemble, and Alexander Mackay's
later trip eastward to Auburn encapsulates the area's attractions.*

SYRACUSE IN 1838

We left Auburn on the morning of Monday the 10th of September, at
seven o'clock, and travelled by the rail-cars on a wooden rail-road, drawn

Syracuse: the Erie Canal in central Syracuse, c. 1840. From John W. Barber and Henry Howe, *Historical Collections of the State of New York* (New York, 1841). Courtesy of the DeWitt Historical Society of Tompkins County, Ithaca

by two horses, to Syracuse, the distance being twenty-five miles, and the time occupied about three hours. We found comfortable accommodations at the Syracuse House Hotel, and remained there for two days.[1]

The town of Syracuse is one of the most recently settled of all the larger places along this route, it being not more than twelve years since the first house in it was built; yet it already possesses about 800 dwellings, many large warehouses and stores, an excellent hotel, with many smaller but still comfortable public inns, a bank, a court-house, seven churches, including Episcopalian, Presbyterian, Methodist, Baptist, Universalist, and Unitarian, and a population of nearly 7,000 persons. It is pleasantly situated, having the Onondaga lake, about a mile from its north-western edge, and fine undulating hills, with the elevated village of Onandaga, formerly the county-town, on its southern border; while gentler eleva-

From James Silk Buckingham, *America, Historical, Statistic, and Descriptive,* 3 vols. (London: Fisher, Son, and Co., 1841), 3: 149–54, 164–66.

1. The Syracuse Hotel, a simple brick structure, was built 1820–1822; much enlarged and rebuilt, it reopened as the Syracuse House in 1827.

tions, east and west, connect it with the level land that extends along the line of the great Erie canal, in these directions. Syracuse, indeed, like many other places along this tract, owes its first existence and its present prosperity to this canal, which has caused many villages and towns to spring up and flourish along its whole extent, that, without its agency, would not, for many years at least, have been erected.

At this moment Syracuse enjoys the benefit of lying both in the stage route, and in the line of canal conveyance from the Hudson to lake Erie; so that more than 1000 persons, by all the different conveyances, pass through it, on the average, in each day. A rail-road is in progress from hence to Utica, which cannot fail to increase this number greatly; and the elements of prosperity in and around the town itself are so abundant, as to make it certain that in a very few years its size and population will be doubled.

The streets are regular, and of great breadth, from 80 to 100 feet; the houses and stores are, many of them, of stone and brick; and few, except the original buildings, continue to be of wood. The court-house is a large and substantial edifice, though it lies beyond the verge of the town on the north, instead of being, as is usual in similar cases, in the centre. The cause of this inappropriate situation is said to have been a contest between the neighbouring villages of Salina and Syracuse, as to which should have the court-house, and thus bring to it the transaction of the county business; when the relative strength of the rival parties was found to be so nearly balanced that a compromise was recommended, which was agreed upon, and, like most compromises, satisfied neither party; for the Court-house now stands nearly midway between the two villages, and in a position equally inconvenient to both.

A fine academy for the education of male youths stands on the eastern verge of the town. It is a substantial brick structure, and cost 20,000 dollars in the erection. It has at present 60 pupils, and is increasing in reputation. It was founded at first by individual subscription in shares; but now receives, like other public institutions of this nature, an annual grant in aid from the legislature of the State, in proportion to the number of pupils engaged in studying the higher branches of education. A female seminary has also been just established at Syracuse, in which a classical and mathematical, as well as an ornamental education, will be given to young ladies on nearly the same plan, and at the same expense, as at the Ontario Female Seminary at Canandaigua; so rapidly are the means of education multiplying all around, to keep pace with the increasing population.

In the immediate vicinity of Syracuse are some remarkable Salt

Springs, which are producing great gain to their proprietors, affording extensive occupation to labourers, yielding a considerable revenue to the State, and attracting population every day to this quarter. There are four special localities in which these springs are at present worked; and around each, a village of some size has gathered. There is one at Salina, one at Liverpool, and one at Geddes, three villages surrounding the borders of the Onondaga Lake, (which is 6 miles long and 2 miles broad) distant from each other only two or three miles, and one at Syracuse, an equal distance from them all.

We visited Salina, the oldest and largest of these Springs, in company with the superintendent, Mr. Wright, to whom we had been introduced by Mr. Marsh of the Syracuse bank,[2] who accompanied us also in our excursion, and from both of whom we received every information and attention we could desire. It appears that the Salt Spring here was well known to the Onondaga Indians inhabiting the borders of this Lake, long before any white settlers had come among them; and they had discovered it in the usual way of tracking the wild deer to it, when they came at certain seasons, to lick the salt from off the surface of the earth; the spot being hence called, in the language of the country, "a deer-lick." Since the settlement of the whites, however, the value of this spring has became well known, and accordingly extensive works for the manufacture of salt have gradually sprung up all around; so that what the grain and flour trade is doing for Rochester, the salt-trade appears to be accomplishing for Syracuse.

The four Salt Springs, already named, are found at the depths of from 50 to 100 feet beneath the surface. From thence the water is pumped up by a water-power taken from the surplus or waste waters of the Oswego canal. It comes out of the earth in the purest and most transparent state of clearness, at the rate of about 300 gallons per minute; and here, at Salina, it is forced up to a height of nearly 200 feet above the level of the soil, to admit of its being supplied, from a general reservoir, to the salt-works of Salina and Syracuse, the latter a distance of a mile and half; as the Syracuse spring is not sufficiently abundant as to supply the works of the town, and the villages of Geddes and Liverpool use their own springs for their manufacture.

The mode of producing the salt is partly by solar evaporation of the water from shallow vats, partly by boiling the water in large cauldrons or kettles, imbedded over an extensive furnace, and partly by passing hot air in metallic tubes through the water in vats, instead of exposing it to solar

2. Moses S. Marsh ran the Onondaga County Bank, incorporated on April 15, 1830.

or furnace heat. The saltness of the water furnished by these springs may be judged of by the fact, that 40 gallons of it will produce a bushel of salt, by either of the processes named, whereas it takes 360 gallons of the sea-water of the ocean to produce the same result: the amount of actual salt in the spring water is just 60 per cent; the taste being that of pure salt, without any foreign admixture.

At Salina, the quantity of salt made, varies from 12,000 to 16,000 bushels per day; but from all the four springs, at least 25,000 bushels per day are produced. The quantity of wood consumed as fuel in the furnaces — though the greater portion of the salt is made by solar evaporation — is at least 600 cords per day, or not less, at the least, than 200,000 cords per annum, each cord weighing on the average about two tons. Already, indeed, the apprehension begins to be entertained that wood-fuel will be scarce, though the forests have been but a few years under the axe; and measures are even now in contemplation for bringing up supplies of coals, by the Ohio and Lake Erie, from the western parts of Pennsylvania. As the springs have never yet failed, or even sensibly diminished, and have never been known to freeze, the manufacture goes on throughout the entire year, where the furnace and the heated tubes are used; and those works depending on solar evaporation are only interrupted during the short period of extreme severity in the winter.

In the afternoon of our last day at Syracuse, we went to see the Museum, at which two fine large serpents, of the Anaconda tribe, were to be seen, just fresh from South America, imported in a ship to New York. This, like most of the museums we had yet seen in the country towns, was very poor in objects of natural history, or even in curiosities of any interest. They are not, as in England, attached to some literary institution, with a scientific man as a director, but they are the property of very unlearned persons, who use them as a sort of provincial theatre, for which they are in many instances a substitute. In the day-time a flag is hoisted on the building, or sometimes hung out of the window. A small band of three or four instruments is then employed to play at a balcony or other place in front; the band here consisted of a wretched violin, a hurdy-gurdy, and a long drum; but this seemed to attract passengers, who entered from the street, paid their shilling admission, gazed around their half hour, looked at the serpents, the stuffed beasts, and the wax-work figures, which attracted the largest share of attention, and then departed.

These wax-work figures, I observed, formed a prominent part of every provincial museum that I had yet seen. They represented, generally, prominent characters of the American revolution, and sometimes popular officers of the United States navy and army; but the resemblances were so imperfect, and the dress and accompaniments so awkward and ill-fitted, that the most intimate acquaintances would have found it difficult to recognize their friends, but for the inscription of their names over the figures themselves. There was one group here, however, which was even more attractive to the visitors than the figures of Washington, Franklin, and General Jackson; this was the Scriptural personages of King Saul, the Ghost of the prophet Samuel, and the Witch of Endor. The former was arrayed in all his royal robes, with his diadem on his head, though the Scriptural account of the interview represents Saul as disguising himself, by putting on other garments: the ghost of Samuel was dressed in a white calico sheet, thrown around his head and body, leaving only the face and beard visible: and the Witch of Endor was dressed in an old-fashioned English gown of black bombazeen, with a long waist and stays, her head covered with a pointed hat like the witches in Macbeth, and over her shoulders was a printed cotton handkerchief of Glasgow or Manchester manufacture! Yet this was thought an admirable group, and was evidently the most attractive of all the objects contained in the Museum. At night, a cheap theatre for farces, songs, dances, and similar entertainments, is opened; and this being frequented by labourers and children, forms the chief source of their revenue.

During our stay at the Museum, there were many Indians present, especially women and children, many of them very gaily dressed, with scarlet blankets, feathers, beads, and trinkets, and all appearing to enjoy the music very much, as well as to be greatly amused with the effect of a very poor electrical machine on those who held its chain. I ascertained, on inquiry, that these Indians belonged to the tribe of the Onondagas, who have a small settlement near Syracuse, and that free admission is given to them whenever they come to town; as the sight of them in the windows and about the buildings, draws strangers to enter, for the sake of seeing them more at leisure than they could do in passing the streets. The females were more than usually gay and attractive in their apparel, and appeared, from their smiling countenances and flaunting manner, to have learnt the art of coquetry from the whites, in which their visit to the Museum for the purpose of attracting others, gave them abundant opportunities of practice, without much improvement to their morals.

AUBURN PENITENTIARY IN AUGUST 1833

The state penitentiary at Auburn was begun in 1816 and departed sharply from English prisons in the treatment of prisoners. Beaufoy's reaction, though eccentrically sanguine about conditions in England, is fairly typical of early travelers. "For my part, I think the Americans show great good sense in making their prisons places of deprivation, hard work, and punishment; instead of following our plan in England of rendering them most comfortable and eligible houses of entertainment during the winter season" (Tour through Parts of the United States, *p. 66). Those in custody at Auburn were required to demonstrate their penitence through work, which coincidentally defrayed most of the costs of the establishment. Silence was enforced; immediate obedience to orders was demanded; and at night the prisoners were confined to solitary cells. While there is no evidence that this harsh regime brought anyone to sincere repentance, it did attract the attention of many Europeans.*

In 1833 the British government sent an official deputation to examine American prison discipline. They were accompanied by a Fellow of Jesus College, Cambridge, Edward Strutt Abdy (1791–1846). Abdy stayed in the United States for some eighteen months visiting many public institutions and published an account after his return to England.

Abdy reports on the penitentiary system in a rather neutral tone, though he found it progressive and relatively cheap. His interest, however, was concentrated on organization; Harriet Martineau, who looked at the people rather than the theory, saw a radically different place. The convicts were "without exception, pale and haggard," and she thought that allowing tourists to observe the incarcerated stripped away the prisoners' last vestiges of self-respect — leaving them either hardened or miserably wretched.

Charles Murray also thought the prisoners "miserable, jaded, desponding," but his was more the tourist's eye; he provides one of a very few descriptions of the outside of the building. "The mass of building is solid and imposing, and altogether well suited to the gloomy character of the place; but its effect is totally destroyed by an absurd nondescript set of pinnacles on the top of the building, in the midst of which is a representation of a sentinel with a musket. Whether he is meant as a scare-crow to the prisoners or not, I cannot tell; but I am sure that he and the litter of pinnacles around him are a grievous annoyance to the eye" (Travels in North America, *1: 63).*

Abdy had neither his humane impulses nor his aesthetic prejudices offended by Auburn penitentiary. Having already examined Sing Sing and Weathersfield, Massachusetts, he toured the central New York institution in August 1833, and his account lies at the crossroads between early enthusiasm for the American experiment and later distaste.

The next morning I visited the prison; the external appearance of which bears a much stronger resemblance to places of the same kind in Europe than any I had before seen in America. It was here, I believe, that the Penitentiary system was first tried. As the agent was out, the chaplain took me round the different parts of the establishment. There are altogether 770 cells; 220 of which are in a building lately erected on a better plan of construction than the old one; though, in both, the means of properly ventilating the cells are defective; as there is no aperture in any of them, like those at Singsing, for keeping up a current of air by an open communication from the back part of the room with the air at the roof. The space, however, between the dormitories and the wall, which forms the opposite side of the passage, is much larger than that in the old portion of the building.

There is a difference in the manner of securing the convicts in their cells between this prison and that at Singsing; each lock being separate, and the door too far withdrawn from the range in which the rooms are placed, to admit of any communication between them. The dinner, too, which at the latter is taken separately and in the cells, is here eaten in common, at tables provided for the purpose. One advantage, said to arise from this arrangement, is the facility with which the quantity of food can be regulated according to the exigencies of the prisoners; among whom the hard-workers require more than those whose employment is less laborious. This accommodation, however, might be obtained, if required, by a liberal apportionment of diet, as easily as in the other system, by sending the keepers with a supply along the line, and requiring the convicts to make the same signs through the bars of the cells, when they want more meat, that are here made at the public table with the same object. At Singsing the convicts have the same rations; but that is not a necessary consequence of eating separately.

There is a greater variety of manufactures carried on at this prison than at Singsing or Weathersfield; and the avenues, or covered ways, through which the keepers, by means of small slits in the wood-work, are enabled to see the men at work, are more complete; as, in most cases, they are carried all round the workshops. These contrivances not only afford the best security for the due observance of silence, and of obedience to other regulations, by impressing on the minds of all at work, that they are

From Edward Strutt Abdy, *Journal of a Residence and Tour in the United States of North America, from April, 1833, to October, 1834,* 3 vols. (London: John Murray, 1835), 1: 267–71.

under the immediate eye of vigilance and authority, — but enable visitors to see all that is going on, without occasioning any trouble or interruption to the business of the place. Out of 696 that were under confinement at the time of my visit, there were but eight in the infirmary — a greater number than the average. Here, as in other establishments of a similar kind, it is found that the sudden transition from immoderate indulgence to total abstinence, in the case of habitual drunkards, has a good effect upon the general state of health; shewing that reform, to be salutary, need not always be gradual; and that a remedy may be radical with the physician, and yet conservative to the patient.

The system pursued here is milder than that at the penitentiary on the North river. From the latter there have been transferred to the Auburn prison, at two successive periods, 120 convicts; and all of them have expressed a decided preference to the treatment that has followed the change. This testimony may be thought to favor the system it is employed to discredit; and, if capital punishments were the best, because a man would rather be flogged than hanged, severity of discipline would find its best advocate in the terror it excites. Other feelings, however, are to be enlisted in aid of reformation; and preventive checks to crime are not to be estimated by the tortures applied to the body or mind of the criminal. Any one can perceive in the countenances of the convicts at Auburn, much less of that ferocious and resentful feeling, which the "cat" at the Singsing penitentiary has left impressed on the features of its inmates.

A violent and ignorant outcry, which has forced its way from the workshops of the mechanics to the doors of the legislature, has been raised, particularly in the State of New York, against convict labor, from its supposed tendency to ruin trade by lowering its prices.[1] A slight consideration, however, will shew that no such injury can possibly arise from an open contract; the nature of which is to keep down the profits of the new competitor to the level of the general market. I was assured by a very well informed man, whom I met at a time when public attention had been directed to these disputes, that he could purchase shoes at Albany, of a commissioner at Lynn, — a town in Massachusetts, famous for its "cordwainers," — fifteen per cent. below what they would cost at Singsing, to which place he had gone under an impression that he could get them cheaper there. He added, that it was not an uncommon thing at Auburn, to procure household furniture from New York, rather than from the

---

1. The Auburn authorities sought outside contracts to provide labor for the penitentiary's inmates. Several proto-trade unions were formed to complain about the competition, which, it was feared, would drive down wages and result in unemployment.

prison in the neighborhood. Such are the fallacies and falsehoods relative to the work done in the penitentiaries; the inmates of which are accused of inflicting a fatal blow to the interests of honest industry. That this opinion is very general, is evident from the high prices at these places, occasioned by the influx of those who, while they entertain it, afford the best refutation of an error that will cure itself.

THE PENITENTIARY IN 1839

How could Edward Strutt Abdy and Harriet Martineau, whose visits were separated by a mere three years, come to such different conclusions about the Auburn penitentiary? George Combe's account of the place makes it clear that Abdy's focus on organization in the prison is far too partial — the personality of the prison's governor (the "penitentiary agent") largely dictated how the institution was run. Combe (1788–1858) visited Auburn one month after a particularly brutal agent, Captain Lynds, had been dismissed from his position for the second time, and witnessed the changes in the running of the prison that his more humane successor had introduced.

Combe's interest in Auburn was, in a sense, professional. An Edinburgh lawyer, he had been converted to the new science of phrenology after hearing its father, Spurzheim, lecture in 1815. Three years of intensive study followed, and in 1818 Combe began to involve himself in phrenology as a publicist, writing popular texts on the subject and participating in the controversies that it provoked. He retired from business in 1837 to devote his time to the cause and what he saw as its logical concomitant, a national, secular education system for Britain. He made a successful lecture tour of the United States between 1838 and 1840, and one of his interests at the Auburn penitentiary, which he visited in June 1839, was to examine the moral and intellectual organs of its inmates.

June 5. [1839] Ther. 54°. *Journey to Syracuse.* — A railroad is in the course of construction between Utica and Syracuse, but not yet serviceable. The road was described as very bad, and we were advised by our

From George Combe, *Notes on the United States of North America During a Phrenological Visit in 1838-9-40,* 2 vols. (Philadelphia: Carey and Hart, 1841), 2: 68-69, 71-75.

friends to travel by the boat on the Erie Canal. We started at eight o'clock in the morning, and proceeded at the rate of five miles an hour. The distance is fifty-three miles, and the canal runs for a part of the way through a low, marshy, unsettled, and uninteresting country. It rained the most of the day. After dinner, a brisk young man entered the boat, and in a loud voice asked if any lady or gentleman wanted to have "corns cured." He was asked his terms, and said they were half a dollar for one corn, and less for each additional. He offered to remove the corn by the root instantly, without pain, and engaged that it should never grow again. After a great deal of bargaining and bad wit, one passenger made an agreement with him to have one corn extirpated, for which he was to pay 25 cents (1s. sterling). The operator, who was dubbed by the passengers "the Doctor," pulled out a bottle, borrowed a pen-knife, applied some sulphuric acid to the corn, received his 25 cents, paid 18 cents for his fare, and left the boat. The lent knife was destroyed by the acid, but "the Doctor" was fairly beyond reach before its owner made this discovery. The best piece of wit elicited on the occasion was a remark that this was in every sense "a toe-boat." The master of the boat told me that "the Doctor" had done a small business to-day, but that yesterday he had cleared $9 in the boat going east. . . .

There is no lock on the canal from Utica till within one mile of Syracuse, where three descending locks occur. We arrived at Syracuse at half-past eight o'clock, and found very comfortable accommodation in the Syracuse Hotel, close beside the wharf.

Syracuse. — We were again greeted by several highly respectable citizens of Syracuse who have embraced phrenology, and have formed a phrenological society. One of them kindly drove us in an open carriage to Salina, a village in the neighbourhood, which has received its name from its salt springs. These have all been reserved by the state, and they yield a large revenue, applicable to the expenses of the Erie Canal. The spring was known to the Indians, and was discovered by the resort of the wild animals to drink the water. It lies near the Onondaga lake, which is fresh to the bottom. The well at Salina, which was opened twelve or thirteen years since, is seventy feet in depth, and from it brine is raised, by means of forcing pumps worked by a water-wheel, to a reservoir eighty-five feet above the Oswego Canal. It is distributed to a great number of salt-works. . . .

June 7. Ther. 58°. *Railroad from Syracuse to Auburn.* — This railroad was opened only on 5th June, and we travelled on it in the third morning of its operation. It was not inclosed, and the domestic animals along the line had not yet become accustomed to the locomotive engines and trains. It was a curious study to mark the effects of our train upon them, as it rushed past. The horses in the fields generally ran away, carrying their heads erect, and their ears bent downwards and backwards; and they turned their heads alternately to the one side and the other to catch a glimpse of the dreaded enemy behind. One horse, however, turned round to us, and presented a bold and inquiring front. He erected his ears and turned them towards us, stood firm on his legs, and looked as if he would "defy the devil." The sheep and lambs fled in terrible agitation and confusion. The swine early took alarm, and tried to run from before us. When we overtook them, they endeavored, in an ecstasy of fear, to push themselves through the fences, if there happened to be any, or into the banks. The cows fled, but were speedily breathless, and gave up in despair. A huge breeding hen rose suddenly from her brood, and put herself in an attitude of defence, without moving a step. Another hen, without a brood, flew straight up into the air, in a paroxysm of fright. Fortunately none of these animals ventured on the railroad, and we arrived at Auburn, distance 26 miles, in one hour and ten minutes, without accident or detention. In a separate car were two stout, rascally-looking convicts, chained together, under charge of an officer, going to Auburn state-prison. They were merry and reckless, and came out at the half-way station to have their last supply of tobacco and whisky, before entering on the life of temperance that awaited them in jail.

Auburn State-Prison. — We visited this prison, accompanied by his excellency Governor Seward (to whom we carried letters of introduction), and saw its whole economy.[1] It was commenced in 1816, and is built on the plan of a hollow square, inclosed by four walls each 500 feet long. The convicts labor during day in large workshops, under the close surveillance of the officers of the prison, to prevent them from conversing. After work hours, they are locked up in separate cells. They move to and from their cells, and to and from the hall in which they receive their meals, in the lock-step, and are never allowed to communicate with each other. The system of treatment is essentially the same as that pursued at Boston and Blackwell's Island. . . . Here, however, the sleeping cells are lower in the roof, and have no ventilating chimneys communicating with the open air. The convicts dined during our visit, and we saw 650 of them in a large apartment, seated at narrow tables arranged like the seats in a theatre, so that the convicts at one table looked on the backs of those at the table be-

---

1. William Henry Seward (1801–1872) had moved to Auburn as a lawyer in 1823. He was elected New York's first Whig governor in 1838 and retired to the practice of law in January 1843. He would later serve as Lincoln's secretary of state.

fore. The keepers were stationed in the open passages to watch them. Their heads presented the usual development of criminals, viz., deficiency of size in many, deficiency of the moral organs in the great majority, deficiency of intellect in many, with large organs of the propensities in nearly all. One exception struck me. A man apparently above sixty presented an ample coronal region, with a good intellectual development, such as one very rarely sees in confirmed criminals. I mentioned the fact to Governor Seward, and he very obligingly made inquiries into his history. He learned that the man had been a "root doctor;" but in consequence of the removal of the late agent of the prison, and the recent appointment of Dr. Palmer in his place, no information could be obtained concerning the offence for which he had been convicted.[2] Among the convicts was a man in respectable circumstances, who, under religious delusions, had chastised his son, a child, to such an extent that he died. He is sentenced to seven years' confinement. His intellectual organs appeared to be of average size; those of Combativeness and Destructiveness to be large; and the moral organs rather shallow and deficient. In the hospital we saw a convict who, six days before, had voluntarily chopped off his left hand. Governor Seward asked him why he had done so. "Because," said he, "it had offended against God and man, and it was borne in upon me, that if I cut if off, as commanded by the Scripture, God would forgive me, and man also." In the hospital we saw likewise an interesting man, Mr. Rathbun of Buffalo, acting in the capacity of steward. He had been engaged in gigantic building speculations in the town of Buffalo, and at Niagara Falls, and failing in resources, he was a participator in forgeries, to the extent, as we were told, of nearly a million of dollars. He was a man of great talent, and of highly popular manners, and so bold in his undertakings, that he was a general favorite with the people. It was with great difficulty that the jury could be induced to find him guilty, although the evidence was overwhelmingly clear, and the frauds enormous in their extent. At last, however, they returned a verdict against him, and he was sentenced to five years' imprisonment. He has been appointed steward of the hospital as an act of grace. He obeys the prison rules, does not presume on his former station, discharges his duties, but keeps himself quite aloof from his fellow convicts.[3]

2. A War of 1812 veteran, Captain Elam Lynds, had been penitentiary agent from 1821 to 1826, when he was dismissed after a prisoner, Rachel Welch, died from a whipping. He became agent once more in 1838 on the strength of his reputation as a disciplinarian. He reinstituted the system of feeding prisoners in their solitary cells but was forced to resign after two more prisoners died. Dr. Noyes Palmer took over the office of agent on May 9, 1839.

3. Benjamin Rathbun (c. 1789–1873) had come to Buffalo from Sandusky in 1821.

Captain Lynds, the late agent of the prison, is described as having been a brave officer of the army, and the father of this convict-system. He had also managed the prison at Sing-Sing. He entertained the opinion that convicts were sent to prison to be punished, and that discipline could be maintained only by the lash. He acted on these views, and his proceedings had been so much at variance with the spirit of the age, that there arose a great public excitement on the subject, in consequence of which he had retired. Dr. Palmer had succeeded him, and the social dinner, which we saw, has been instituted since his appointment. . . .

Auburn. — After dinner, we hired a carriage and drove along the shores of the Owasco Lake, two miles from the town, and, but for an execrable road, would have enjoyed the scenery highly. Although its banks are low, the landscape of the lake is exceedingly beautiful, and at this season in its prime. We visited Judge Conklin of the supreme court, who has a residence near the lake, and enjoyed much interesting conversation with him and his family.[4] The more I see of the American judges, the higher becomes my estimate of their powers, activity, and attainments. . . .

We returned to Auburn in the evening. It is one of the most pleasing little towns we have seen, even in this land of pretty villages, and shows evident marks of prosperity. It has numerous mills and manufactories, driven by the stream which issues from the Owasco Lake. Its population now amounts to 6000. There are seven churches, an academy, a presbyterian theological seminary, a museum, two banks, a court-house, and a jail.

I made inquiry into the system of repairing the roads here, and was told that they are maintained by so many days labor assessed on each proprietor. It is performed in this month. The ruts are filled up with mud, and this is all that is done till the subsequent year. We saw them using the plough to mend some of the bye-roads in this state. . . .

June 8. Therm. 65°. *Geneva.* — At Auburn we met a family from Boston travelling westward, and along with them hired an "exclusive extra," or stage coach seated for nine persons, and drawn by four horses. We started at half past nine A.M., and found the road, although the great

---

He ran the Eagle Tavern until about 1830, thereafter pursuing an extraordinary career as a speculator and builder until arrested August 3, 1836 for forging a credit note. He blamed his brother and financial agent, Lyman Rathbun, who escaped from jail and was believed to have fled to Texas. The forgeries ran to well over a million dollars, and Benjamin was sentenced in September 1838 to Auburn, where he served a five-year term. His account of his career, "The Case of Benj. Rathbun," written in prison between 1836 and 1838, was first published in *Buffalo Historical Society Publications* 17 (1913): 227–70.

4. Alfred Conkling (1789–1874) was appointed by President Adams as federal judge for the northern district of New York in 1825, and he served on the bench until 1852.

high-way turnpike to the west, horribly bad. Here I realised the fact of having the crown of my head rudely beaten against the top of the vehicle, so dreadful were the jolts. Seven miles west from Auburn, we crossed the Cayuga Lake on a wooden bridge, one mile and eight rods in length. This lake is thirty-eight miles long, and from one to two miles broad. It is shallow, but a steam-boat navigates it daily to Ithaca, a thriving village at its head, thirty-six miles distant from the village of Cayuga, where we crossed it. Fifteen miles farther west, we entered Geneva, a small town situated on the bank of the Seneca Lake, and distinguished for its picturesque beauty. We dined here; and started again for Canandaigua, where we arrived at eight P.M., the distance being sixteen miles. Since we left Auburn the country has presented a rich soil, well cultivated, with every external indication of great prosperity among the people. C[ecilia] was feverish when we arrived at Canandaigua, in consequence of the pain occasioned by the excessive jolting which she had sustained.[5]

Canandaigua. — This village is situated at the distance of half a mile from a beautiful lake bearing the same name, and is itself one of that class of towns which I have seen in no country except the United States. Fifty years ago, it was in the heart of the forest; now its principal street is two miles in length, with two broad side-walks, decorated with trees. The houses stand in enclosures at a little distance from the road, and are ornamented with trees, shrubs, and flowers. The street is a long succession of pretty villas, of pure white, gleaming through the richest verdure. The houses and offices are built chiefly of wood; but they have a handsome appearance. . . .

The peculiarity of American villages consists in the beauty of the dwellings and the superior manners and education of the inhabitants compared with European villages. There is, however, not much society among themselves, but to strangers they are very hospitable. A number of Scotsmen are settled here, some of them in affluent circumstances, and their condition is such that I could not bewail their change of country. Some of them complain of trouble with their "helps;" but I strongly suspect that the meagre wages allowed to domestic servants (less than the common remuneration for labor in other departments of industry,) has much to do with these annoyances. When ample remuneration is given, I am assured that the native Americans will engage in service, and prove faithful, useful, and obliging.

5. Combe had married Cecilia (b. 1794), a daughter of the actress Sarah Siddons, in 1833. She brought with her a large inheritance and a desirable cranial formation (which Combe checked carefully before marrying her).

VILLAGES OF THE NORTHERN FINGER LAKES

The line of villages at the northern shores of the Finger Lakes, from Skaneateles in the east to Canandaigua in the west, were for most British visitors both aesthetic and physical relief during their journeys through New York State. These settlements came close to elegance after the commercial bustle of Rochester or Utica, and the cramped antiquity of downtown Albany — their prosperous, tree-shaded avenues of spacious houses suggested that trade and its mundane demands had been relegated in the lives of the inhabitants to a position comporting more closely with the idea of propriety that these bourgeois travelers held. Here the frenetic pace of life in the youthful cities was lacking; and Englishness of taste could be found in a careful regard for appearance and the minor landscapes of private gardens; and here, particularly at Canandaigua, the hospitality of American friends and acquaintances revealed something of the sober attractions of American society.

For many visitors, Canandaigua epitomized this quiet promise of civilized life. As early as Frances Wright's journey in 1818 and 1819, it had seemed a lovely place transported by inexplicable circumstance to the wilderness. The wilderness rapidly ebbed as the area was settled more extensively, but Canandaigua's attractions were not lessened. Its serene delightfulness is evoked here in pages from the journal of the actress Fanny Kemble (1809–1893).

Frances Anne Kemble was born into one of England's chief theatrical families and, though she always disliked acting, made a successful London debut as Juliet in October 1829. A two-year tour of North America ended in June 1834, with her marriage to Pierce Butler, who soon afterward inherited a Georgia plantation. The marriage proved a disaster, and in 1846 she finally left her husband, provoking two years later a notorious divorce case in which he sued her for abandonment. The marriage was legally ended in 1849, and Fanny Kemble thereafter divided her time between England and America, compromising her distaste for dressing up by giving dramatic readings from the works of Shakespeare.

Her account of Canandaigua was written in happier times. On her successful tour of Ameria in 1833 and 1834 she was accompanied by several other actors, and in particular her father; and in the midsummer of 1833 the party reached Canandaigua on a tour that would take them to Niagara Falls.

[Sunday, July 14, 1833] As the evening began to come on, we reached Canandaigua Lake, a very beautiful sheet of water, of considerable extent; we coasted for some time close along its very margin. The opposite shore was high, clothed with wood, from amidst which here and there a white house looked peacefully down on the clear mirror below: the dead themselves can hardly inhabit regions more blessedly apart from the evil turmoil of the world, than the inhabitants of these beautiful solitudes. Leaving the water's edge, we proceed about a quarter of a mile, and found ourselves at the door of the inn at Canandaigua; the principal among some houses surrounding an open turfed space, like an English village green, across which ran the high road. My father,[1] Mr. _____, and I went up to a sort of observatory at the top of the house, from whence the view was perfectly enchanting. The green below, screened on three sides with remarkably fine poplar trees, and surrounded by neat white houses, reminded me of some retired spot in my own dear country. Opposite us, the land rose with a gentle wooded swell; and to the left, the lake spread itself to meet the horizon. A fresh breeze blew over the earth, most grateful after the intense heat of the morning, and the sky was all strewed with faint rosy clouds, melting away one by one into violet wreaths, among which the early evening star glittered cold and clear.

We came down to supper, which was served to us, as usual, in a large desolate-looking public room. After this, we came to the sitting-room they had provided for us, a small comfortable apartment, with a very finely-toned piano in it. To this I forthwith sat down, and played and sang for a length of time: late in the evening, I left the instrument, and my father, Mr. _____, and I took a delightful stroll under the colonnade, discussing Milton; many passages of which my father recited most beautifully, to my infinite delight and ecstasy. By and by they went in, and _____ came out to walk with me.

Certainly this climate is the most treacherous imaginable: the heat this morning had been intolerable, and to-night a piercing cold wind had arisen, that would have rendered winter clothing by no means superfluous. We walked rapidly up and down, till the bleak blast became so keen, that we were glad to take refuge in the house. Our unfortunate carpet bags and their contents are literally drenched: many of my goods and chattels will never recover from this ablution; among others, I am sorry to say, _____'s beautiful satchel.

From Frances Anne Kemble, *Journal* [of a Residence in America], 2 vols. (London: John Murray, 1835), 2: 268–73.

1. Her father was Charles Kemble (1775–1854), who had become manager of the Covent Garden Theatre in London in 1822. His Hamlet had been a great success in New York City.

Monday, 15th.

Our breakfast, which was extremely comfortable and clean, was served to us in our private room; a singular favour: one, I hope, which will become a custom as the country is travelled through by greater numbers. Before breakfast, D____ had been taking a walk about the pretty village, and trying to beg, borrow, or steal some flowers for me. The master of the inn, however, succeeded better than she did; for he presently made his appearance with a very beautiful and fragrant nosegay, which I found, to my utter dismay, had been levied from a gentleman's private garden in my name. My horror was excessive at this, and was scarcely diminished when I discovered, upon enquiry, that they had been gathered from Mr. _____'s garden; that gentleman having large property and a fine residence here. He was not in Canandaigua himself; but, as we drove past his house, I left cards for his lady, who must have thought my demand on her green-house one of the greatest impertinencies extant. It was nine o'clock when we left Canandaigua: we were all a little done up with our two previous days; and it was unanimously settled that we should proceed only to Rochester, a distance of between thirty and forty miles, which we accomplished by two o'clock.

If Canandaigua was most frequently favored, other towns had their champions. The beauties of Geneva, highly praised by Tyrone Power, caused Alexander Mackay to break his journey through New York for a full three days. Mackay's account, which dates from the late forties, codifies some thirty years of unstinted praise for a fertile, lovely area — praise that escapes the limits of specialist interest and political complexion, and eventually becomes one of the commonplaces of British description of the State.

Early next morning I took a stroll through the village. The small towns, which so profusely dot the surface of Western New York, are in every respect the most charming of their kind in the Union. The country, which is of an undulatory character, abounds with exquisite sites, particularly that portion of it which lies between the Genesee and the upper waters of the Mohawk. The scenery is beautifully diversified by a series of lakes of dif-

From Alexander Mackay, *The Western World; or, Travels in the United States in 1846-7. . . ,* 2d ed., 2 vols. (Philadelphia: Lea and Blanchard, 1849), 2: 196-99.

ferent sizes, from twelve to thirty and forty miles in length, which follow
each other in rapid succession. The land around them is generally well
cleared, and the little towns which garnish their banks bespeak a degree of
general comfort which is only to be met with in the New World. As you
tread their broad and breezy streets, and every now and then catch a
glimpse of the elegant white houses with which they are lined, through the
waving and rustling foliage in which they are enveloped, you are apt to
forget that such a thing as poverty exists, and to give way for the moment
to the pleasing allusion that competence is the lot of all. One of the most
pleasing features about these towns is their faultless cleanliness. In this respect the Americans are in advance of every other people with whom it
has ever been my lot to mingle. An American house, both outside and in,
is, generally speaking, a pattern of cleanliness. The American likes to
make a good external show, and bestows great care, when circumstances
will admit of it, upon the outside of his dwelling. The neat little garden
which fronts it is not, as with us, walled from the sight of the public. It is
generally bounded towards the street by a low wall, which is surmounted
by a light iron or wooden railing, so that the public enjoys the sight of
what is within as much as the owner himself. This is what renders not only
the rural towns of America, but also the suburbs of its larger cities, so elegant and attractive; each resident, in consulting his own taste in the deco-
ration of his dwelling, also promoting the enjoyment of the public. How
different is the case in our suburbs and country towns! An Englishman
likes to have his enjoyments exclusively to himself; and hence it is that the
grounds fronting your "Ivy Cottages," "Grove Villas," and "Chestnut
Lodges," are concealed from the passer-by, by lofty, cold, and repulsive
walls. There cannot, in this respect, be a greater contrast than that presented by the private streets of an American town, large or small, and
those of our own villages and the suburban districts which skirt our great
communities. Nor let it be supposed that to this external neatness, in the
enjoyment of which the public thus participates equally with the owner, is
sacrificed any of the care which should be bestowed upon the manage-
ment of the residence within. An American is almost as domestic in his
habits as the Englishman is. His house is, therefore, the private sanctuary
of himself and family, and as much attention is generally bestowed upon
it with a view to rendering it comfortable and attractive, as in decorating
it externally for the common enjoyment of himself and his fellow-
citizens. In point of domestic neatness and cleanliness, the Englishman
certainly comes after the American. Would that I could find a high
place in the classification for the lower orders of my Scottish fellow-
countrymen!

Canandaigua is, in itself, perhaps the most attractive of all the towns of Western New York. There are others with more beautiful sites, but none presenting so fine a succession of almost palatial residences. It is situated on the long gentle slope which descends to the northern extremity of Lake Canandaigua, the most westerly and one of the smallest of the lakes alluded to. The main road between Buffalo and Albany, which passes through it, constitutes its principal street, from every point of which the lake at the foot of it is visible. The street, which is about a mile long, is exceedingly wide, and shaded on either side by an unbroken succession of lofty and magnificent trees. The houses on both sides, which are almost all detached from each other, are some distance back from the street, having gardens in front occupied by grass and flower plots, with clumps of rich green foliage overhead. The finest mansion in the town is the property of a wealthy Scotchman, who has been settled in Canandaigua for upwards of forty years.[1] It is really a superb residence, more like a ducal palace than the dwelling of an humble citizen. The business portion of the town is that nearest the lake, being a continuation of the main and indeed almost the only street of which it boasts.

The country being beautiful and the roads good, I preferred taking the common highway to Auburn, forty miles distant, instead of the railway. I therefore hired a gig, and drove that day to Geneva, sixteen miles from Canandaigua. On leaving the latter, the road led me close to the northern end of the lake; when it suddenly turned to the east, leading over a succession of gentle undulations of the richest country. Before the Erie canal was constructed, and, of course, previous to the introduction of railways, this was the great line of road between the Hudson and Lake Erie. Along it the earliest settlements were consequently made, so that now the aspect which the country on either side presents is more like that of an English than an American landscape. The farm-houses and farming establishments along the road are large, comfortable, and commodious; the farmers here being of the wealthier class of practical agriculturalists. Some of the houses are built of brick, others of wood; but whether of brick or wood, they are all painted equally white, which, in summer time,

1. John Grieg, manager of John Hornby's two-twelfths interest in the Pulteney Estates for most of the first half of the nineteenth century, was famous for his hospitality and figures in dozens of travelers' accounts of western New York. His great house in Canandaigua expressed for many commentators what America might achieve in gentility. As Colonel Maxwell puts it, " – an excellent library, a choice collection of pictures, a cabinet of fossils, cameos, and coins, an excellent billiard-table, splendid apartments, and hot and cold marble baths. Is not this a pretty comfortable sample of savage life for you?" (*A Run through the United States,* 1: 252).

Geneva: view across the lake, 1840. Lithograph by Henry Walton. Geneva Historical Society

gives them a refreshing effect, in contrast with the clustering foliage which environs them. The afternoon was well advanced when I approached Geneva; and never shall I forget the beauty of the landscape which suddenly burst upon my view on gaining the top of the last hill on the road, about a mile back from the town. Below me lay Geneva, its white walls peering through the rich leafy screens which shaded them. Immediately beyond it was the placid volume of Lake Seneca, from the opposite shore of which the county of Seneca receded in a succession of lovely slopes and terraces. Large tracts of fertile and well cultivated land were also visible on either hand; and the whole, lit up as it was by a lustrous and mellow autumn sun, had a warmth and enchantment about it such as I had but seldom beheld in connexion with a landscape.

Geneva is a much larger town than Canandaigua, and I know no town in America, or elsewhere, with so charming a site. Lake Seneca, like all the other lakes in this portion of the State except Oneida, is long and narrow, and lies in a northerly and southerly direction. On its west bank, at its extreme northern end, stands Geneva. The business part of the town is almost on the level of the lake; the bank, which is clayey, high and abrupt, suddenly dropping at the point where it is built. It is on the high bank, before it thus drops, that the remainder of the town is built, most of the houses of which command a view of the lake. The most eligible residences are those which skirt the lake, with nothing but the width of the road between them and the margin of the bank. They have an eastern aspect, and nothing can exceed the beauty of the view commanded from their windows, as the morning sun rises over the landscape before them.

I was so delighted with Geneva that I prolonged my stay there for two days longer than I had at first intended. On the evening of my arrival I took a small boat and went out upon the lake. It is about forty miles long, but scarcely a mile wide opposite Geneva. The air was still, but the western sky looked ugly and lurid. As it gradually blackened, a fitful light every now and then faintly illuminated the dark bosoms of the massive clouds, which had now made themselves visible in that direction. As they stole higher and higher up the clear blue heavens, the illumination became more frequent and more brilliant, and nothing was now wanting but the muttering of the thunder to complete the usual indications of a coming storm. I was then some distance up the lake, and made as speedily for town as possible. When I reached it, innumerable lights were gleaming from its windows upon the yet placid lake, whose dark, still surface was occasionally lit up for miles by the lightning which now coruscated vividly above it. The first growl of the distant thunder broke upon my ear as I stepped ashore; and, pleased with my escape, I hurried, without loss of time, to the hotel. In a few minutes afterwards the progressing storm burst over the town, and the dusty streets soon ran with torrents of water. The effect upon the lake was magnificent. It was only visible when the lightning, which now fell fast on all sides, accompanied by awful crashes of thunder, gleamed upon its surface, and seemed to plunge, flash after flash, into its now agitated bosom. You could not only thus distinguish the dark leaden waters, with their foaming white crests, but the shore on the opposite side for a considerable distance inland, and on either hand. The whole would be brilliantly lighted up for a moment or two, after which it would relapse into darkness, to be rendered visible again by the next succession of flashes which fell from the black and overcharged heavens. In half an hour it was all over, when the scene displayed itself in a new aspect, veiled in the pale lustre of the moon.

THE GENESEE VALLEY

Once western New York had been secured by military action and made accessible by road and canal, it developed with a rapidity that astonished American and European alike. The frenzy of settlement provoked every visitor to comment, often extensively, and for British observers the development both of the city of Rochester and of the fertile flats of the Gene-

see valley summarized in a few miles' span America's national phrase—
"Go Ahead."

The rapid peopling of the western part of the state demanded attention, and forced even the dullest travelers into the realization that they
were seeing something extraordinary. *It provoked lively passages in
otherwise commonplace accounts; as one example, take these few sentences from William Newnham Blane's* Excursion through the United
States, *a book generally marked by his monotonous, impersonal medita-
tions on the American character and the place of religion in the society
of the United States. He traveled west from Rochester in the late spring of
1823. "As a great many settlers had lately fixed themselves in this part of
the State, Log-cabins were rising in all directions, and the work of clearing was going on rapidly. Each little open spot was covered with masses
of burning timber; and the large trees that had been girdled the year before, were in many places in flames even to the tops, producing at night a
very extraordinary and splendid effect" (pp. 393–94).*

The epitome of this huge invasion of settlers was the city of Rochester itself. In 1812 it consisted of two log huts. By the late 1820s, it was, as
Basil Hall reports, rapidly expanding, its prosperity based on the numerous mill seats at the falls of the Genesee, its hugely fertile agricultural
hinterland, and its location on the Erie Canal. Growing with its export
markets, it would in less than two decades have shed its temporary, ram-
shackle appearance, and William Brown describes a rich and still-growing
city.

Those who came early to farm lands purchased or leased from the
Holland Land Company, the Phelps and Gorham Patent, and the Pulteney Estate waxed rich with the area. Of the farming of one especially hospitable Genesee Valley family, the Wadsworths, there are numerous accounts, represented here in Patrick Shirreff's notes on Geneseo on his
journey west to Lockport. The passage typifies those of scores of Britons
with limited time making for Niagara Falls.

THE NOTORIOUS CAPTAIN HALL VISITS ROCHESTER IN 1827

*Certain critical accounts of the United States rapidly achieved notoriety,
and their authors, eminent among them Basil Hall, were roundly anathe-
matized. Hall's* Travels in North America *certainly exhibits his splenetic
temperament and his ignorance (he boasts of having read nothing of
America before traveling there); but it is difficult now to explain the ex-*

traordinary outcry the book provoked, and the wild claims made about it — that he was a mercenary of the British government, or that he and Mrs. Trollope were one and the same person, interested only in libeling American achievements. Published at the height of partisan debate about reforming Parliament, the Travels *became a favorite weapon in the conservative arsenal, and its praise in the pages of the* Quarterly Review *heated a controversy about its accuracy that raged across the Atlantic until eclipsed by Mrs. Trollope's* Domestic Manners.

Hall (1788-1844) had entered the Royal Navy in 1802 and traveled throughout the world during the Napoleonic campaigns. Retiring as a captain in 1823, already a Fellow of the Royal Society, he married Margaret Hunter in 1825 and spent the rest of his life in traveling, writing, and scientific experiments. He, his wife, and their young child spent 1827 and 1828 in the United States, whose inhabitants he praised for their hearty hospitality and whose institutions, on which he wrote extensively, he misrepresented. His more vehement critics probably took some satisfaction in his spending the last few years of his life in an insane asylum.

Hall and his family reached Rochester in June 1827, and he describes the village in uncharacteristically detailed prose (his wife, Margaret Hunter Hall, may have written some of the passage). But even though the description is not critical, it contrasts in an interesting way with Edward Allen Talbot's account, written four years earlier. Talbot gives the sense of a solid core; for Hall, all seems frenzied periphery. Here is Talbot's account: "The streets of Rochester are laid out at right angles with each other. The houses are built of brick, and neatly painted red and pointed out with white: This embellishment, with Venetian blinds, piazzas, verandas, balconies, &c. gives the village a very delightful aspect, and designates the inhabitants as tasteful, enterprising, industrious, and opulent; but, I believe, it is more owing to the other qualities than to their opulence" (Five Years' Residence in the Canadas, *2: 338). This solid comfort exploded with the huge wealth and commercial expansion attending the opening of the canal in 1825. A mere four years after Talbot's account, Hall is taken not with the suburban comfort but the frenetic activity of the place.*

On the 26th of June 1827, we strolled through the village of Rochester, under the guidance of a most obliging and intelligent friend, a native of this

From Basil Hall, *Travels in North America, in the Years 1827 and 1828*, 3d ed., 3 vols. (Edinburgh: Cadell and Co., 1829), 1: 160–66.

part of the country.[1] Every thing in this bustling place appeared to be in motion. The very streets seemed to be starting up of their own accord, ready-made, and looking as fresh and new, as if they had been turned out of the workmen's hands but an hour before—or that a great boxful of new houses had been sent by steam from New York, and tumbled out on the half-cleared land.[2] The canal banks were at some places still unturfed; the lime seemed hardly dry in the masonry of the acqueduct, in the bridges, and in the numberless great saw-mills and manufactories. In many of these buildings the people were at work below stairs, while at top the carpenters were busy nailing on the planks of the roof.

Some dwellings were half painted, while the foundations of others, within five yards' distance, were only beginning. I cannot say how many churches, court-houses, jails, and hotels I counted, all in motion, creeping upwards. Several streets were nearly finished, but had not as yet received their names; and many others were in the reverse predicament, being named, but not commenced, — their local habitation being merely signified by lines of stakes. Here and there we saw great warehouses, without window sashes, but half filled with goods, and furnished with hoisting cranes, ready to fish up the huge pyramids of flour barrels, bales, and boxes lying in the streets. In the centre of the town the spire of a Presbyterian church rose to a great height, and on each side of the supporting tower was to be seen the dial-plate of a clock, of which the machinery, in the hurry-skurry, had been left at New York. I need not say that these half-finished, whole-finished, and embryo streets were crowded with people, carts, stages, cattle, pigs, far beyond the reach of numbers; — and as all these were lifting up their voices together, in keeping with the clatter of hammers, the ringing of axes, and the creaking of machinery, there was a fine concert, I assure you!

But it struck us that the interest of the town, for it seems idle to call it a village, was subordinate to that of the suburbs. A few years ago the whole of that part of the country was covered with a dark silent forest, and even as it was, we could not proceed a mile in any direction except that of the high-road, without coming full-butt against the woods of time immemorial. When land is cleared for the purposes of cultivation, the stumps are left standing for many years, from its being easier, as well as more profitable in other respects, to plough round them, than to waste time and labour in rooting them out, or burning them, or blowing them up with gunpowder. But when a forest is levelled with a view to building a

1. Mr. Grainger of Canandaigua, according to Margaret Hunter Hall (*Aristocratic Journey,* p. 54).
2. This same image appears in Mrs. Hall's letter about Rochester.

Rochester: village of Rochester, 1827. From Basil Hall, *Forty Etchings from Sketches Made with the Camera Lucida* (Edinburgh, 1829). Cornell University Library, Ithaca

town in its place, a different system must of course be adopted. The trees must then be removed sooner or later, according to the means of the proprietor, or the necessities of the case. Thus one man possessed of capital will clear his lot of the wood, and erect houses, or even streets, across it; while on his neighbour's land the trees may be still growing. And it actually occurred to us, several times, within the immediate limits of the inhabited town itself, in streets, too, where shops were opened, and all sorts of business actually going on, that we had to drive first on one side, and then on the other, to avoid the stumps of an oak, or a hemlock, or a pine-tree, staring us full in the face. . . .

After we had gone about a mile from town the forest thickened, we lost sight of every trace of a human dwelling, or of human interference with nature in any shape. We stood considering what we should do next, when the loud crash of a falling tree met our ears. Our friendly guide was showing off the curiosities of the place, and was quite glad, he said, to have this opportunity of exhibiting the very first step in the process of town-making. After a zig-zag scramble amongst trees, which had been al-

lowed to grow up and decay century after century, we came to a spot
where three or four men were employed in clearing out a street, as they
declared, though any thing more unlike a street could not well be conceived. Nevertheless, the ground in question certainly formed part of the
plan of the town. It had been chalked out by the surveyors' stakes, and
some speculators having taken up the lots for immediate building, of
course found it necessary to open a street through the woods, to afford a
line of communication with the rest of the village. As fast as the trees were
cut down, they were stripped of their branches and drawn off by oxen,
sawed into planks, or otherwise fashioned to the purposes of building,
without one moment's delay. There was little or no exaggeration, therefore, in supposing with our friend, that the same fir which might be waving about in full life and vigour in the morning, should be cut down,
dragged into daylight, squared, framed, and before night, be hoisted up
to make a beam or rafter to some tavern, or factory, or store, at the corner of a street, which twenty-four hours before had existed only on paper,
and yet which might be completed, from end to end, within a week afterwards.

On our way back again to the carriage, which had been left standing
on the avenue, or nick cut for the road in the forest, we fell in with a gentleman on horseback, rifle in hand, and bearing, in testimony of his successful sport, a large bunch of wild pigeons and sleek-skinned black squirrels, tied to his saddle-bow. He had been gunning, he told us, for a couple
of hours; in the course of which time, he had first lost his horse, and in
looking for it, had missed his marks, and so of course lost himself. "And
now," continued the sportsman, "that I am fairly out of the thicket, I am
almost as much at a loss as I was before. For," continued he, jestingly to
our companion, "you have been getting up such a heap of new work here,
a man does not know the land from day to day. You have placed such a lot
of taverns and houses on the skirts of the forest; so many lime-kilns, gro-
cery stores, and what not, side by side, or jumbled altogether, amongst
the trees, that, for the life of me, I don't know scarcely where I have got
to, more than I did a while ago when straying amongst the trees after my
horse."

After our new acquaintance had rode on, I asked who he was. My
friend desired me to guess. I thought it might be the baker? the butcher?
the attorney? the bookseller? "No! no! none of these." The mason? said
I, or some such indispensable personage? "No — you are still wrong." Had
I guessed all night, I should never have thought of naming the dancing
master! but so it was. After laughing a little, I don't know well why, I ac-
knowledged myself well pleased to have witnessed so undeniable a symp-
tom of refinement peeping out amongst the rugged manners of the forest.

I spoke this not disrespectfully—quite the contrary. At first sight, certainly, it would seem, that where people are so intensely busy, their habits must almost necessarily, according to all analogy, partake in some degree of the unpolished nature of their occupations, and, consequently, they must be more or less insensible to the value of such refinements. I was therefore glad to see so good a proof, as far as it went, of my being in error.

ROCHESTER IN THE MID-1840s

Rochester's mushrooming growth is chronicled in dozens of British accounts, extracts from many of which appear in Myrtle Handy and Blake McKelvey's "British Travelers to the Genesee Country" (Rochester Historical Society Publications 18 [1940]: 1–73). Few observers, however, had the inclination or the time to examine the details of that growth. William Brown, brought up to the Yorkshire wool trade, visited Rochester in the mid-forties, and his grasp of the political economy of the settlement's expansion is rare in its exactitude.

Little is known of Brown apart from his book. He moved among the commercial middle classes, in contrast to the Marryats and Buckinghams of American travel, and spent four years in North America—two years in Cleveland, two in Toronto—making his living as a tavern keeper. That perhaps suggests an urban bias to his recollections; but he had a sharp eye for farming and its problems, and as a writer he is rare in appreciating the interconnectedness of town and country in the economic health of the areas he visited. His hard-headed, realistic account, America, was composed from notes and memories after his return to England and issued by a small Leeds publisher.

Brown traveled through western New York with his family one late August, on his way to Ohio; he does not specify the year, but the chronology of his American life strongly suggests 1843 or 1844.

Rochester is a city of the third magnitude, in America; it is situated upon the Erie Canal and the Genessee River, about two miles from its mouth upon Lake Ontario; and here steamers arrive continually from various

From William Brown, *America: A Four Years' Residence in the United States and Canada; Giving a Full and Fair Description of the Country, As It Really Is. . .* (Leeds: William Brown, 1849), pp. 9–12.

parts of the Lake, not only from the ports belonging to the Union, but also from Canada. The city contains about 28,000 souls. This city is famed for the falls of the waters of the whole river Genessee taking place here, of which the inhabitants are taking the utmost advantage, in turning the stream to manufacturing purposes. The flour mills are here on the most extensive scale of any in the Union, and the construction is superior to any in the world. I counted from twelve to fourteen mills, all in operation, some of which had a complement of ten runs of stones, and each pair capable of turning off from twelve to fourteen bushels of wheat per hour. Every operation in these mills is more like clock-work than anything else; very few hands are employed, everything is done by the water; the grain is hoisted up by power, carried to the smut mill, then to the hoppers, then to the stones, and from the stones to the cooling frames, and so on to the dressing or bolting mills, which latter are here preferred to the dressing mills of the old country; from the dressing mills it is shot into barrels, which when filled and weighed are immediately "ended up," branded, and ready for market. It is really pleasing to see such order and regularity in any manufactory; it is here done without bustle or hurry, and so clean and perfect, that the Rochester brand for flour stands pre-eminent in the markets of the whole world.

The river, coming down from the high lands towards the city, is channelled off in portions through the town, as well as a great part into the canal basin. These goits are carried direct to the mills, which are generally situated upon the banks of the river below the falls, and if you stand upon the bridge, you will see the water shooting out from scores of water-wheels in a sheet of white foam, making a clear jump of perhaps 200 feet perpendicular height into the channel below. Of course, this immense fall in the tail goit is at present lost, but in the course of a few years this spare force will be economised and brought into use, by mechanical contrivances, in which the Yankees are as much gifted as any nation in the world. There are also two or three woollen factories established here, which make cloth suitable for the wear of the farmers in the neighbourhood, as well as a large quantity sent to Canada and worn there. There are also card makers, machine makers on a large scale, as well as steam engine makers, steam boat builders, and locomotive engine manufacturers. Furniture, carriage, chair, and sash factories are in abundance; in fact, almost every craft which requires power is carried on here in very great perfection. The markets are well supplied with animal and vegetable provender in the greatest abundance, and the apples of Rochester are without exception the finest I had ever seen in my various travels through the kingdoms of Europe: — they are much superior to those brought to Liverpool from New York, and which are grown upon Long Island, and are called New Town Pippins, both in size and flavour, and are so cheap that you may buy a bushel for one English shilling. Rochester I consider the best city in the union for an Englishman desirous of settling in the States, as from its contiguity to the lake, and from its immense traffic by the canal and on the railway, it will always command a good trade, and a great portion of the English from Canada West pass through on their journeys to and from the Mother Country, almost every day.

In travelling by canal a stranger very naturally enquires of every one he sees, where the good land is, as what he sees from the banks is the most wretched specimen he ever saw. The answer invariably is "As you go west you will see good land," and west you may go till you come to the antipodes before you can see any considerable tract of land which an Englishman would consider GOOD LAND. I made enquiries respecting the produce per acre of wheat, and I found that around Rochester ten or twelve bushels per acre was about the average; but there is no other place upon this canal where the average will stand as high. In Indian corn thirty to forty bushels are produced, and oats and barley may be reckoned about half as much more as wheat. In fruit and garden stuff they reap abundant crops, especially fruit. The gardens, if cultivated as English gardens are, would be as prolific as any in the world; but there are no pains taken here in them; the plough is generally used instead of the spade, and every other operation is done in a very rude and primitive style. In many fields on the banks of the canal, the white Mexican bean is grown, but we were a day or two before we could find out what was growing, from the immense quantity of weeds, which you may safely average at a hundred stalks, as high again, to every plant of the beans. You had therefore to clear away the weeds to come at the crop; these weeds also infest the wheat and other grain crops, and were it not for the Yankee invention of the smut mill to clear the grain from weed seeds, the flour would not be useable for human food. This machine, however, does its work perfectly, and when the grain has undergone the operation and is ground into flour, it is equal if not superior to any produced in the world.

There are also large tracts employed in the cultivation of broom corn, the bushy straw of which is required in large quantities for brushes and brooms, and most beautiful articles are made from it for domestic purposes, and nothing can exceed their utility for either sweeping the floor or brushing the clothes. Most of the prisoners confined in the prisons, if not fit for any other occupations, are taught to make these articles, and by the produce not only earn their own living, but, having a strict account taken of their work, are enabled on leaving prison to draw a consid-

erable sum of money to start them off west, and set them up in some honest calling, which gives them an opportunity of redeeming their characters
and of becoming good citizens. Large quantities also of chicory are produced, which the land seems particularly well adapted for; as well as
beets, cucumbers, pumpkins, squashes, and melons in endless varieties.
Some of these latter plants attain an enormous size, especially the large
melon squash, the fruit of which I have measured and found to be from
six to seven feet in circumference, and to weigh from 150 to 170 lbs. A
smaller sort nearly resembles in colour and conformation oranges,
lemons, and other fruits. These look really beautiful climbing up the ve-
randah in front of a neat frame cottage; and though they are worthless as
human food, yet you cannot help being reminded by them of the enchanted gardens of the Hesperides.

A very great drawback upon most of the farms in the western part
of New York is the progress of the Canadian thistle. This is fearfully en-
croaching, and infests the land for hundreds of miles; it proceeds at the
rate of two or three miles a year, and when this blast comes upon a farm,
it is all over for growing wheat or almost any other crop; the land becomes almost worthless, and can only be beneficially employed in growing Timothy grass or in pasturage. The evil is of such a magnitude, that it
is impossible for the farmers to contend with it, and in consequence they
give up the struggle in despair, and by this means fearfully increase the
calamity. Although this weed is called the Canadian thistle, yet, during
my residence in Canada, I scarcely ever saw it in large quantities; but in
New York State it is rapidly extending itself, and it is to be feared that before long the whole of the Eastern States will be desolated by it, and there
is as yet no remedy found against its ravages.

The city of Rochester contains many well built streets, generally of
brick, elegant shops, and churches; the aqueduct of the Erie canal is a
splendid and magnificent structure, the engineering works of which are
equal to anything I ever saw. Indeed, according to my opinion, this city is
the best specimen of the go-a-head principle that can be found upon the
face of the earth.

THROUGH THE GENESEE COUNTRY IN 1833

*British farmer-writers quite frequently traveled in America on behalf of
relatives and friends; one of them, Patrick Shirreff, of Mungoswells, East*

Lothian, was unusually qualified to write an overview of agricultural prospects in the New World. Using James Stuart's Three Years *as a guidebook and with his younger brother's interests at heart, he saw much of America in a rather brief tour and measured his observations against long experience of agricultural improvement. An intelligent writer with a discriminating eye for telling detail, he was related to the Scottish agricultural surveyor and writer John Shirreff (1759–1818), and his understanding of practical problems is exemplified in the latter half of his* Tour, *which is full of sensible advice for emigrants. In this passage he speeds across New York from Geneva to Lewiston, providing on the way an assessment of the Wadsworth farms.*

Canandaigua is situated near the outlet of the Lake of the same name, which is navigated by a steam-boat. The principal street extends back on rising ground nearly two miles, and consists of separate villas, as white and clean as paint can make them, with green Venetian blinds, situated at some distance from the street, and surrounded with umbrageous vegetation, which at this warm season imparted an appearance of coolness and luxury. Besides a garden in front, crowded with rose bushes bearing a profusion of flowers, many villas have a considerable extent of ground behind, capable of maintaining animals, and affording every family convenience. The buildings and beauty of Canandaigua surpass any place I have seen out of New England; and the wealth and comfort of its inhabitants may be owing to its early erection and situation in the Genesee country, the most celebrated wheat district in America.

The Genesee country was sold by the State of Massachusetts to Messrs Gorham and Phelps, who obtained 6,000,000 acres, at about eightpence sterling per acre; but finding difficulty in fulfilling their bargain, the land passed into other hands, and part of the country now belongs to the Pulteney family of England.[1]

We left Canandaigua by a stage-coach at three o'clock in the morning, and suffered considerably from cold. When day dawned, a little after

From Patrick Shirreff, *A Tour through North America; Together with a Comprehensive View of the Canadas and United States. As Adapted for Agricultural Emigration* (Edinburgh: Oliver and Boyd, 1835), pp. 81–87.

1. Phelps and Gorham sold one million acres to Robert Morris in 1790, from whom the Pulteney group bought about one-half million acres the following year. For a brief history of the western lands, see David M. Ellis et al., *A History of New York State*, rev. ed. (Ithaca: Cornell University Press in Cooperation with N.Y.S.H.A., 1967), pp. 150–56.

four o'clock, my thermometer, exposed on the outside of the stage, indicated 43°, and at Allanshill, on the outside of the hotel window, 45°. On different occasions I experienced inconvenience from variations of temperature in America, which are greater and as frequent as those of Britain. We reached the village of Genesee early in the forenoon, and from the courts being then sitting, could not be received where the stages stopped. The landlord and driver were not accommodating, but we soon found a very attentive hotel-keeper in a different part of the village.

The surface of the country, from Canandaigua to Genesee, is undulating and picturesque, but ill cultivated. The wheat crops generally good, and a considerable extent of ground preparing for fallow, by breaking up grass land which had been depastured. In some cases, four oxen and a horse were dragging a plough, a boy riding the horse in front, and a driver to the oxen. In every case, a driver was employed with oxen, and horses generally ridden by boys when in the plough, which, I supposed, was owing to their being little accustomed to this kind of labour.

I had observed the wheat crops of America abounding with a species of grass passing by the name of chess, which I imagine to be the *Bromus secalinus* of botanists, and which I have seen in the wheat crops of Surrey, England, and south of Ireland. A passenger between Canandaigua and Geneva, stated, that chess was reverted wheat, and originated from an inclement season, or bad seed, an opinion which I found pretty general in the States and Canada. This doctrine was made known to me by letters in the Genesee Farmers' newspaper,[2] published at Rochester, numbers of which I received in Scotland, but it is so different to my observation and reflection, that I told the passenger, I would as soon expect a horse to become a pig, as wheat chess. From extensive observation in remote parts of America, I have not a doubt of chess being indigenous to the soil, and hence its growth amongst wheat crops, where the farmer did not sow its seeds. . . .

Having heard much of the Genesee flats, I proceeded to call on their owner, on arriving at Genesee. Mr Wadesworth had gone to a distant part of the country, one of his sons being the only member of the family at home, and who had rode out after breakfast. On calling a second time, the young gentleman pointed out the way to the flats, where he said he would join us in an hour afterwards.[3]

2. The *Genesee Farmer,* published and edited in Rochester by Luther Tucker, started on January 1, 1831.

3. James Wadsworth (1768-1844) and his family are portrayed in Alden Hatch's *The Wadsworths of the Genesee* (New York: Coward-McCann, 1959).

The Genesee flats belonging to Mr Wadesworth, are rich alluvial soil, ornamented with aged trees, deposited in groups and at intervals; and perhaps no gentleman's park in Britain equals them in fertility and beauty. They differ from the rest of the surface in this part of the country, by having been cleared by nature, and are chiefly in grass, affording the richest pasturage I ever saw, with exception of some fields in the neighbourhood of Boston, Lincolnshire, England. On examining some parts which had never been subjected to the plough, red and white clovers were particularly abundant, also timothy grass (*Phleum pratense*), and several kinds of poea. Cocksfoot was less common, and a few spikes of tall oat-like grass (*Holcus avenaceus*). Rye-grass or yellow-flowering clovers were not visible. A field was pointed out which had been mown for hay thirty-five successive years, without top-dressing, and the grasses were still in vigour of growth, interspersed with red clover nearly thirty inches high.

The young gentleman joined us on the flats, and pointed out every thing deserving of notice. The sheep were a mixture of Merino and Saxon breeds, and not fat looking. There was a fine shorthorn bull, intended to improve the dairy stock, which I did not see. This contemplated improvement originated from perusing the writings of the Rev. Henry Berry of England;[4] and I took the liberty of advising the cross to be tried on a small scale, believing the shorthorns the worst milking breed in Britain. This opinion was new to the gentleman, who said he would keep it in view, and proceed cautiously in intermixing the breeds. The grazing cattle were extremely numerous — four-year-olds, which had been bought in spring, and kept on hay till the arrival of grass, on which they are to be fatted. Mr Wadesworth intends to cultivate wheat extensively; and one enclosure, as a beginning, was bearing an indifferent crop. I have often observed wheat not succeed well on very rich ground, and that, in Britain, the United States, and Canada, soils which have been long under cultivation, yield the best crops of this grain when properly managed. There was a variety of implements which brought to recollection those at Holkham, Norfolk, England. Amongst others, a mowing machine was exhibited and descanted on. We were shown a fine oak-tree growing on the banks of the river, and said to be twenty-four feet in circumference.

We passed the evening at the house of Mr Wadesworth, in agreeable and instructive conversation with the young gentleman, whose acquirements and intelligence were of a superior description. He expressed regret at the necessity of leaving home next day, but offered to place at my

4. A writer on stock improvement now known only for his book *Improved Short-Horns, and Their Pretensions Stated* . . . (London, 1830).

disposal his father's carriage, horses, and driver, with introductory letters
to his friends in the neighbourhood, and said he himself would show us
the country on the day following. Time would not admit of embracing the
kind offer, and I notice this attention as creditable to a person of the
highest influence and station, on whose good offices I had no claim. It
has been my fortúne to experience attention from eminent agriculturalists
in all ranks of life in Britain, and while the heart must be held as the seat
of kindness, I can bear testimony to having found true agricultural
knowledge, distinguished from what is empirical, connected with expansion of mind and liberality of sentiment.[5]

Next morning we left Genesee and passed through Avon, frequented for its mineral springs, and beauty of situation. While the horses
were changing, we found many people indulging in copious draughts of
water, which I prevailed on my friend D____ to taste, when he amused the
bystanders by making a wry face, and exclaiming in a serious tone of
voice, "Do people really drink that for health?" We dined at a stage
house, and were much annoyed by a tipsy person whose impertinence
called for an exercise of patience. He was descended of Irish parents, said
to possess property, and seemingly an excellent customer to the bar-room.
On reaching Rochester, I remarked to the driver, that he seemed to be traversing the same street twice in setting down passengers, and learned that
he was afraid to cross a certain bridge, through which one of his horses
fell a few days before and broke a leg. Few things in America appear more
striking to a Briton than the wretched state of the wooden bridges, a material which he does not associate with strength or durability. We took up
our quarters at the Eagle tavern, the landlord of which was attentive and
accommodating. . . .

We lost no time in viewing the sights of Rochester, the chief of which
is the fall of the Genesee river, ninety-seven feet in height, and celebrated
by the ill-fated leap of Sam Patch in 1829.[6] We enjoyed a walk down the
banks of the stream on a lovely evening, but the scenery in the neighbourhood of the fall has been injured by the erection of machinery propelled
by the water. The flour mills are numerous, and on the most extensive
scale, said to be capable of manufacturing 12,000 bushels of wheat in
twenty-four hours. There is an arcade, extolled by the inhabitants, but
possessing no attractions to individuals who have seen those of other

5. Shirreff had already been hospitably received by two of New York's agricultural
luminaries, Dr. Hosack of Hyde Park, and Jesse Buel of Albany.

6. Sam Patch (c. 1807–1829), born in Rhode Island, was a New Jersey cotton-spinner
famous for jumping from great heights. He died at the Genesee Falls on November 13, 1829.

Rochester: Genesse [sic] Falls, Rochester, 1838. By William Henry Bartlett, from
N. P. Willis, *American Scenery* (London, 1837–40). Collection of McKinney
Library, Albany Institute of History and Art

countries. Rochester is one of the many places illustrative of the growing
wealth and population of the United States, and which some English travellers ridicule for want of antiquity, on the principle a withered old beau
affects to despise the freshness and elasticity of youth. The first settlement took place in 1812, and the population is now estimated at about
14,000. The situation of the town, communicating with Lake Erie, and
the extensive waters to the west, by means of the Erie canal, which is carried over the river in the middle of the town by an aqueduct of free stone,
800 feet long — with Lake Ontario by a railroad — with Montreal by the St
Lawrence, and with New York by the Hudson, together with its splendid
water power, renders its increase of wealth and population almost without limits.

Next morning we set out for Lewistown by way of Lockport, travelling on what is termed the ridge-road, a natural formation extending round the south end of Lake Ontario, at a distance of eight or ten miles from the present waters, and nearly a hundred feet higher. It is from twenty-five to fifty feet wide, fifteen to twenty feet above the surrounding country, and composed of sand and gravel. The road is supposed to have formed the margin of the lake at some remote period of the world, but I had not sufficient opportunity to form an opinion on this point.

The country through which we travelled, after leaving Rochester, is more recently settled than any yet seen, the fields being thickly covered with black stumps overtopping the wheat crops; and the felling and burning of trees was going on in all directions. The houses were mere log-huts, and wanting in external comforts. The warm state of the weather induced the inhabitants to throw open the doors and windows, affording an opportunity of seeing the internal arrangements, and I can testify to their well-stored tables and general neatness. The crops were bad, and much of the soil so inferior as not likely to repay those engaged in clearing it of timber.

After a fatiguing ride, we reached Lewistown, a thriving village, at midnight, and found the bar-keeper and porter of the hotel intoxicated, which was the only instance of the kind I met during my transatlantic tour. By this time we had learned to take things as we found them, and in a few minutes our baggage and selves were in bedrooms without assistance.

The Niagara Frontier

O H MY GOD! how I was stunned and unable to comprehend the vastness of the scene!" wrote George Moore on seeing Niagara Falls in 1843. His is an extreme reaction, but one which, in some degree, morose conservatives shared with liberal reformers and literal-minded scientists with bubble-headed socialites. Niagara's was an appeal beyond dispute.

Yet the falls were in a strange sense familiar. As early as 1791 Patrick Campbell decided not to describe them in detail because so many visitors had tried before him and failed to capture the wonders of the place in words. Travelers trekked there from all over North America, and even the persistent minority disappointed with the falls bear, in their very disappointment, testimony that Niagara Falls was more than merely a local sight. To visit the falls, then, was not to discover the unknown but to confirm what one already knew — and in this sense British reactions to Niagara Falls epitomize much of British travel in the United States.

Physically the falls became rapidly accessible in the early nineteenth century. Hotels, guides, and souvenir shops began to encrust the banks of the Niagara, though fullscale development at the falls themselves came surprisingly late. On the American side manufacturing concentrated up river in the mills at Whitehaven, on Grand Island, and the busy industries of Manchester; in Ontario there was little more than a small aggregation of hotels and occasional houses until the "City of the Falls," a paper project even in the late thirties when Buckingham visited.

More generally the Niagara Frontier developed later than most of New York State; later, indeed, than parts of Ohio and Michigan. Delayed first by hostile Indians, then the proximity of British forces during the revolutionary war, later the confusion over land titles and unextinguished

Indian claims in the 1780s and 1790s, and finally the destruction of the
War of 1812, the growth of the Niagara Frontier waited on political security and the opening of the canal. But when it finally came the growth of
the area was, especially in the case of Buffalo, spectacular. British travelers were acutely aware of the relative backwardness of British Upper Canada, just across the Niagara River, and the Niagara Frontier provoked
reams of policy suggestions, especially about providing government assistance to populate Canada with would-be emigrants from Britain.

The swarming energy of Americans was the plainer for being recent
and the great locks of the canal at Lockport exemplified the young
nation's achievements for travelers such as Henry Tudor. For the falls
themselves there is no better collection of British accounts than Charles
Mason Dow's *Anthology and Bibliography of Niagara Falls,* published
by the State of New York in 1911. Here a brief memoir of tourist exertions
by the anonymous "Wanderer" stands for the hundreds quoted in Dow's
compilation. James Silk Buckingham visited Buffalo from the north, and
John Fowler came in from the east; their accounts of the city are supplemented by James Edward Alexander's military tour of an area that had
seen several threats of war with Britain after 1812 and would see more.
This was Alexander's second visit to the area: a dozen years earlier he had
traveled from the Ohio border up through Fredonia, observing the vast
tides of immigrants that was funneled westward through the great port
city of Buffalo.

LOCKPORT IN 1831

*The five pairs of locks that carried the Erie Canal over the ridge at Lock-
port were an engineering marvel, but they received little attention in most
travelers' accounts because of their proximity to the greater, natural mira-
cle of Niagara Falls. Liberal writers, however, briefly adopted them in the
late twenties as a symbol of democratic achievement. William Lyon Mackenzie, soon to become infamous as a leader in the Canadian rebellions,
lays out this interpretation clearly in* Sketches of Canada.

I seated myself on a large grey stone, on the high ground
above the canal basin, on the morning of the 1st of December
[1825], and surveyed the scene around me—the canal—the
locks—stone and frame houses—log-buildings—handsome

farms — warehouses — grist-mills — waterfalls — barbers' shops — bustle and activity — waggons, with ox-teams and horse-teams — hotels — thousands of tree stumps, and people burning and destroying them — carding machines — tanneries — cloth works — tinplate factories — taverns — churches. What a change in four short years from a state of wilderness! Kings build pyramids; but it was reserved for a popular government to produce a scene like this. (pp. 144–45)

More commonly, the locks were seen as evidence of human, rather than specifically democratic, skill and determination. So argued Henry Tudor, a barrister who had gone to America to restore his broken health. Having largely enjoyed his visit, he published his letters after his return to Europe in order to do some justice to a nation he felt was being unjustly slandered by unsympathetic travelers such as Basil Hall. This extract comes from a letter dated July 25, 1831, written at Lockport.

I left Rochester, in the company of the interesting family whom I have introduced to you,[1] for Lockport, distant sixty-five miles; and was delighted, on leaving the town, to enter on what is called the "Ridge Road," which, for its extent of nearly eighty miles to Lewiston, is, beyond all comparison, the finest road in the country. Without intending to cast a gibe or jeer in the faces of my American friends, I must say, that the road is thus excellent because *nature* has made it and not *man*.

As this inartificial turnpike is evidently of natural formation, and runs parallel with Lake Ontario, at an average distance of, perhaps, seven miles, towards which the slope of the ridge constantly inclines, it is regarded by geologists as the ancient shores of the lake. It is slightly elevated above the surrounding country, which presents a level surface nearly the whole way, and is skirted by the boundless forest on each side, whence an undulating tract of land has been won, extending from a quarter to three-quarters of a mile in breadth, and in length through the whole line of our route. These patches of newly cultivated ground are formed into

From Henry Tudor, *Narrative of a Tour in North America. . . . In a Series of Letters, Written in the Years 1831-2,* 2 vols. (London: James and Duncan, 1834), 1: 230–34.

　　1. Tudor had attended a temperance meeting in Rochester with the head of this Albany family. "The party consisted of a highly respectable and talented barrister of that city, his wife, equally amiable as himself, his little daughter, and also his brother and his lady, two agreeable persons resident at Geneva" (1: 223). They are not named.

all the imaginable varieties of curves, squares, semicircles, and other shapes that the fancy of the new settler had suggested. The scene was highly interesting. Nature here offered to the imagination what might easily be conceived to be a picture of man, just emerging from a state of savage life into the arts of civilisation. All was wildness, rudeness, and disorder: rough outlines of plans, half begun and none finished, and the effect increased by myriads of burnt, chopped, and girdled trees, similar to what I have before mentioned. Here and there, the half-formed enclosure was surrounded by a zig-zag, or, as it is called, a snake fence, constructed of split trees, and exhibiting a singular appearance. This is seen in all parts of the States; being the universal boundary of property in all their sections. I need scarcely observe, that the beautiful, verdant, and ever diversified ornament of hedges, so refreshing an object to the eye in English landscape, was not to be found here; since, in the most cultivated district of the Union, they are never to be seen; a deficiency in picturesque effect that is greatly felt by the English traveller. Perhaps a greater libel than any that has been attributed, by the Americans, to Captain Basil Hall, I heard pronounced by an American gentleman himself, when alluding to this great *desideratum* in American scenery, and seeming as if he wished to apologise for their absence—namely, that the soil of his country would *not produce them!*

Of Lockport, a tolerably correct idea may be formed, by considering it the counterpart of the country through which I have just been leading you. Indeed, its foundations are but just laid; and it looks, at present, like the element of order struggling with, and rising out of, chaos. Its history is concise enough. Five years ago, or thereabouts, it existed not; a wide waste of wilderness occupying its site—and now there are between 300 and 400 houses, of which it owes, entirely, the existence to the presence of the Erie Canal that runs through it. One thing, however, may be safely predicted, that in ten or twenty years from this time it will have become a handsome, wealthy, and important town. Though in its infancy, it possesses, notwithstanding, the finest work on the whole line of the Erie canal, in the splendid locks whence it derives its designation. This gigantic work consists of ten locks, of fine hewn stone, formed in a double range of five in each, placed in juxtaposition, and which have been constructed for the purpose of surmounting the rocky ridge dividing the two levels on each side of it.

These locks, formed of the very best workmanship, graduate a fall of about sixty-five feet, and are built in two tiers, in order to prevent the serious delay that would ensue, in consequence of the immense traffic on the canal, if the ascending or descending boats—whichever it might be—

Lockport: Lockport, Erie Canal, 1838. By William Henry Bartlett, from N. P. Willis, *American Scenery* (London, 1837–40). Collection of McKinney Library, Albany Institute of History and Art

had to wait the passing of those coming in the opposite direction before they could proceed. It is an interesting sight to behold one boat gradually rising to an elevation of sixty-five feet, while another is seen, at the same moment, sinking to an equal depth towards the spacious basin below.

In continuation of this stupendous work, and running immediately from it, is the grand excavation that has been cut through the mountain ridge to an extent of three miles, and of which the labour of hewing a passage through a solid rock of twenty feet in thickness, and for so great a distance, was, as you may suppose, enormous. It was here that the greatest obstacles of the whole 363 miles had to be encountered; and it certainly strikes the beholder with astonishment, to perceive what vast difficulties can be overcome by the pigmy arms of little mortal man, aided by science and directed by superior skill. In many places, the explosive power of gunpowder alone could have torn asunder the massive and deeprooted rocks, which seemed to defy the power of all except the great Being who created them.

A NIAGARA FALLS TOURIST IN THE EARLY 1840s

Niagara Falls became increasingly accessible to tourists in the early nineteenth century. Slowly improving roads and the opening of the Erie Canal, followed a little later by railroad service, brought thousands of tourists where dozens had previously traveled. By the 1840s, steamship service across the Atlantic had vastly increased British visitation, for Niagara Falls, unlike much of New York, did not lose its preeminent position as a place that demanded to be seen.

As more people arrived, so the immediate area was shaped to accommodate their viewing of the falls. Inconvenient trees were felled; bridges were constructed to allow observation from Goat Island; stairways permitted views from the base of the falls and the first Maid of the Mist *brought boatloads of passengers to a close appreciation of the falls' grandeur and power; and hotels multiplied on either bank. Niagara Falls was made a safer and more convenient "sight" as visiting it became more ordered, more routine, and less strenuous.*

Yet this tidy, "convenient" setting for the falls' splendor did not please everyone. British tourist accounts provide a varied inventory of emotional highlights (and occasional disappointments) and, as the decades passed and the area became more civilized, increasing numbers embraced the opportunity to grapple with the falls. Going behind the main chute was the usual form that this more muscular tourism took; and, in this extract, which stands for hundreds, the anonymous "Wanderer" of the early 1840s momentarily captures an earlier sense of the area, when aesthetic satisfaction resulted not from a tamed and uninterrupted view of the falls, but from the tourist's hard work in overcoming inconvenience and hardship.

9th June. During my stay here I paid morning and evening visits to the Falls to contemplate the sublime cataract; and every day I felt more and

From Anonymous, *Journal of a Wanderer; Being a Residence in India, and Six Weeks in North America* (London: Simpkin, Marshall, 1844), pp. 175-79.

more reluctance to leave. This morning I visited them for the last time; and on that occasion I summoned up resolution to venture behind the great sheet of water. Before descending the spiral stair which leads to the waters below the Falls, I was shewn into a room to undress, and I was supplied with a complete suit from the keeper's wardrobe, which I put on; and then the guide conducted me to the bottom of the stair by a rough path which winds along the bottom of the precipice, and leads under the excavated bank which overhangs about thirty or forty feet. The path was very slippery from the wet, and just as I passed the entrance into the cavern I stumbled and nearly fell. Before I had gone three yards more, I was completely drenched with the spray, and I felt a sensation of dread caused by a strong current of wind tossing me from side to side, and the gloom and thick mist which enveloped me. I felt as if I was in a shower bath. I saw several snakes crawling among the crumbling rocks of the cavern, unmoved amid the fearful convulsions of nature. The shock from the falling spray took away my breath for a few minutes, and to avoid falling, I leaned against a rock. My guide not thinking otherwise than that I followed close at his heels, went forward, and left me standing alone. He soon returned to me, and I saw his lips moving, but if the tongues of a thousand archangels had been given to him, the mighty roaring of the falling waters would have silenced them all. However I "guessed" he was urging me forward, and I followed him close up till I reached as far as I could go. This point is called Termination Rock, and is 153 feet from the commencement of the volume of water at Table Rock. After standing about two minutes, I found my situation so disagreeable that I retraced my steps as fast as possible, and came out as completely drenched as if I had been immersed in the foaming cauldron at my feet.

A cloud-like smoke overhangs the Falls, and gives to the white foam below the appearance of an immense boiling cauldron, and when the sun shines on the falling spray the ever-changing prismatic colours, so well described by the Poet, may be observed: —

> "An Iris sits amidst the infernal surge,
> Like hope upon a death-bed, and unworn
> Its steady dyes while all around is torn
> By the distracted waters, bears serene
> Its brilliant hues, with all its beams unshorn,
> Resembling, 'mid the torture of the scene,
> Love-watching madness, with unalterable mien."[1]

1. The lines are Byron's, from *Childe Harold's Pilgrimage* canto 4, stanza 72. They refer to the falls of the Terni, in central Italy. By coincidence, Iris Island was the name proposed by Augustus Porter after the War of 1812 for what is still known as Goat Island.

Niagara Falls: bridge across the Rapids, 1827. From Basil Hall, *Forty Etchings from Sketches Made with the Camera Lucida* (Edinburgh, 1829). Cornell University Library, Ithaca

The amount of water which passes over the Falls is estimated at 100 million of tons in an hour. The depth of water at the principal Fall cannot be ascertained; it is supposed by some to be 600 feet. It is said that when a boat approaches within a certain distance of the Falls it is difficult to arrest it, by reason of a magnetic attraction towards the precipice. Hence the tradition of the Indian, who finding his canoe within the influence of this attraction gave up all hope, laid down his paddle, swallowed the last drop in his flask, shrouded himself in his blanket and was precipitated over the Fall.

A few years ago an old vessel was purchased by the Hotel-keepers at Niagara for the purpose of being precipitated over the Falls. The circumstance was widely advertised, and a great assemblage was gathered together to witness the novel spectacle. The vessel was filled with animals consisting of bears, wolves, dogs, cats, geese, ducks, &c. The vessel struck on the rapids above the Falls, when the bear got overboard and swam to the shore; shortly afterward the masts fell overboard, and she filled with water; the poor animals were dreadfully frightened, they gathered together on that part of the deck which was the highest out of the water, but in a few seconds the vessel and all on board were hurled over the falls, and of all the crew and passengers aboard, a solitary cat and a lame goose were alone picked up alive. The vessel was shattered into a thousand fragments.[2]

2. The derelict sailing vessel *Michigan* was filled with animals and sent over the Horseshoe Falls on September 8, 1827. The event was watched by a huge crowd, variously estimated between fifteen and thirty thousand people.

I was charged for the use of the suit of clothes and the guide, half a dollar. My name was inserted in the book for registering the names of those who have passed behind the Falls, and I received the following certificate: — "This may certify that J____ R____ has passed behind the great falling sheet of water to Termination Rock. Given under my hand at the office of the general register of the names of visitors at the Table Rock, this 9th day of June 18 —

(Signed) Jea. Graskey.

IMMIGRANTS ON THE SHORES OF LAKE ERIE, 1831

It is seldom that British travelers describe the hordes of European immigrants who flooded into New York, and through New York State to the western territories, in the first half of the nineteenth century. The society of the United States tended for literate visitors to be white, English-speaking, and protestant, and exceptions to this general rule — Irish gardeners, German farmers, French storekeepers — usually appear in travel books as peripheral individuals, a touch of color rather than evidence of some wider, non-Yankee community. (Blacks, of course, elicit far more interest, especially among the abolitionist writers, but seldom in descriptions of New York State.) This impression of a homogeneous society is sharply contradicted, however, by the few writers who describe what must have been a common-enough sight: family and even village groups moving overland to their new home in America.

The James Edward Alexander who chased deserters in Watertown in the 1840s was then on his second visit to the United States. His first had been over a decade earlier. In 1831 he was unattached to a regiment and already the published author of a couple of travel books, on Persia and India. He took an extended leave to travel in South and North America, partly from curiosity, partly to pass the time before taking up a new command as a captain in the 42nd Royal Highlanders. Having spent some months in South America, he made for New Orleans from Cuba and traveled up the Mississippi and into Ohio.

In his overland trip around the south shore of Lake Erie, he came across frequent evidence of Europe's year of disorder and social convulsion, 1830. Although the parties of immigrants he witnessed from Belgium, Ireland, and Switzerland were only one small fraction of 1831's harvest, his notes are quite unusual — they did not congregate at Saratoga, after all, nor could they afford the best hotels and an extra exclusive. Not till the great famine and subsequent mass migrations from Ireland in the forties would immigrants provoke general interest among more genteel British visitors.

We arrived at the town of Erie, and found in the principal hotel (the Mansion House) a party of thirty-five Belgians, men, women, and children, at the head of whom was a Count Leo. They intended to purchase a tract on the Ohio. These foreigners excited a good deal of interest among my companions, who crowded in to see them eat, as if they had been *ferae naturae.*

The next stage was Fredonia, where I halted. The others went on. Fredonia is lighted with natural gas; a river runs by it; and if a light is passed over the surface of the water in particular spots, flames rise like those from the waves of Infernal Phlegethon.[1] In a small house on the banks of the stream is the gasometer; a square reservoir for water has been dug under cover of a roof; in this floats a large wooden box without a bottom; the gas rises in this, and the weight of the box forces the gas into tubes, which distribute it over the village.

Two neat churches stood side by side in Fredonia, a Presbyterian and a Baptist. I attended the former, and heard a tall young preacher deliver an excellent discourse. He censured those hearers who are more ready to criticise the orator than attend to the truths which he delivers: — "'He is not a smart man,' say some of a particular preacher, and neglect altogether the doctrines he endeavours to inculcate. How absurd it is," said the Minister, "for those who are starving to refuse food because it is offered to them in vessels whose form they do not like; equally foolish is it in those who reject the word altogether because the minister may not be personally approved of."

From Fredonia I went in a waggon to Dunkirk, on the shores of Erie, and found a house full of Irish emigrants, waiting an opportunity to proceed up the lake to Amherstburgh. I was delayed here nearly two days, and wandered about in the woods and along the beach, visited an American light-house, and spent a few pleasant hours with some lively and in-

From James Edward Alexander, *Transatlantic Sketches, Comprising Visits to the Most Interesting Scenes in North and South America, and the West Indies,* 2 vols. (London: Richard Bentley, 1833), 2: 138–41.

  1. Phlegethon is the principal river of Hades and runs with fire rather than water.

telligent ladies I accidentally met, and shall never see again "on this side of time."

> "The star which shines so fair at e'en,
>   Lives but the hours of night;
> It glows on many a fairy scene,
>   But fades at morning light.
> 'Tis like the joys which mortals taste,
>   They're but in slumber given;
> And when we wake, in life's dull waste,
>   The golden spell is riven."

At last I got an opportunity to sail down the lake to Buffaloe, and on the voyage thither, observed the rocky south shore of Erie, fringed with dark pines and a few scattered log-houses among them. Erie is two hundred and seventy miles long, twenty-five broad, and two hundred feet deep: it sometimes freezes in winter.

Arrived at Buffaloe, I found myself in a comfortable hotel, the Buffaloe House. I walked about the town, and saw that, phoenixlike, it had risen from its ashes, and exhibited no traces of the fire which had consumed it in the last American war. The commencement of the great Erie canal, connecting the Hudson with the Canadian lakes, is at Buffaloe. . . .

When embarking at Buffaloe to sail down the Niagara river to Chippaway, I saw several families of Swiss peasants who had just arrived from New York. The men wore blue smocks and forage caps with large peaks, and the women had the usual full petticoats, in shortness rivalling the kilts of our red-shanks.[2] The weather was very cold, yet these mountaineers looked cheerful and happy. In sailing out of the harbour, we passed a handsome pier, formed by filling coffers of wood with stone, and then building on them.

THREE VIEWS OF BUFFALO

Joseph Ellicott, the Holland Land Company's surveyor and agent, had laid out the plans of the village of Buffalo in the first years of the nine-

2. Scottish highlanders.

teenth century, but its development would prove more spasmodic and un-predictable than that of virtually any other New York settlement. Initially strong, profiting from rapidly increasing commerce on the western Great Lakes, it was razed by British forces in December 1813. Its rebuilding was rapid, stimulated greatly by the construction and opening of the Erie Canal. The canal provided regular, cheap transportation for goods mov-ing east to the Atlantic seaboard markets and for people moving west in massive numbers to settle the western states. Buffalo prospered as the great entrepôt for the trade of the middle lakes, gaining a preeminence that even the Welland Canal could not challenge.

The effects of the financial panic of 1837 were compounded in west-ern New York by the bankruptcy and eventual imprisonment for fraud of Buffalo's main speculator and builder, Benjamin Rathbun. (George Combe, visiting the Auburn penitentiary, saw him there in 1839.) War fever reigned at the same time, indignation over the British burning of the American vessel Caroline *at Niagara Falls in December 1837 threatening briefly to boil over into active, sustained American involvement in Cana-da's rebellions.*

But so strong was Buffalo's economic position that it proved resil-ient even in the face of these several setbacks. James Silk Buckingham, visiting the city in 1838 after enjoying Niagara and Grand Island, reports no evidence of financial distress and indeed notes the "apparently pros-perous condition" of even the black inhabitants. John Fowler had visited from the east at the end of his fact-finding tour of the state in 1830, and the gap between the village he witnessed and the city of Buckingham's ac-count bears testimony to Buffalo's growth—and, incidentally, to Rath-bun's achievement. James Edward Alexander came across to visit his fellow-officers in the early 1840s from his station in Niagara Falls, On-tario. His description of American military preparedness underlines the still occasionally tense relations between the United States and the British in Canada.

GRAND ISLAND AND BUFFALO IN 1838

James Silk Buckingham, having taken in and wondered at Niagara Falls (and having written some rather undistinguished verse on the occasion), traveled south to Buffalo before heading by private carriage—an "extra exclusive"—for Rochester. Despite its recent financial adventures, Buf-

falo seemed to be thriving, and it was still an arena for wholesale specula-
tion. The Panic of 1837 had delayed one of the city's more grandiose proj-
ects, the University of Western New York, but, as Buckingham suggests, a
massive confidence abounded in the area and bankruptcies and financial
disorder seemed to the inhabitants temporary and insubstantial annoy-
ances, merely delaying the inevitable for a few months.

The village that has sprung up on the American side of Niagara, is called
Manchester, because it was hoped by its founders, that the great extent of
waterpower which could here be brought into operation for mills and
manufactories, would make it the Manchester of the West. This expecta-
tion has not yet been realized, however, nor does it appear probable that it
ever will. At present there is a large paper-mill on Goat Island, which
makes about 10,000 reams of paper annually; and there are some saw-
mills, flour-mills, and a hat manufactory on the bank; but the village is
very insignificant, and derives all its importance from the visitors to the
Falls.

On the Canada side, there is at present no town, though a place has
been mapped out on paper, in the American fashion, called "The City of
the Falls;" but not a single house of the projected city has yet been
erected. There are three hotels on this side, the Clifton, the Pavilion, and
the Ontario. The last is at present occupied as barracks or quarters for the
officers of the 43d regiment of the British, the troops being encamped on
the heights; and the second is occupied chiefly also by the officers for
their mess, so that the Clifton is the only one now much frequented by
visitors.

The hotels on both sides, like all those we had stopped at in our
journey across from Saratoga to Niagara, are all built on too large a scale
for comfort. There are spacious drawing-rooms, vast dining-rooms, ample piazzas, and large bar-rooms and halls; but the bed-rooms are all miserably small and ill-furnished; and the provender, though abundant
enough in quantity, is worse in quality, badly cooked, carelessly served
up, hacked and torn to pieces rather than carved, and handed about by
disgustingly dirty waiters. From the great length of the tables and the
number of dishes to set on, and from the absence of covers and warm
plates, the first dish is always cold before the last is brought on. . . .

From James Silk Buckingham, *America, Historical, Statistic, and Descriptive*, 3 vols. (London: Fisher, Son, and Co., 1841), 2: 512–13, 540–42; 3: 10–14.

[Grand Island] was originally purchased of the Indians who inhabited it, for a trifling sum; but it is now the property chiefly of a company
of wealthy men at Boston, who bought it for its timber; and some few individuals residing in Buffalo and elsewhere, have portions of it also. The
price asked for land upon it now is from 20 to 30 dollars per acre, though
no part of it, I believe, is yet cultivated. The finest trees growing upon it
are chiefly white oak, hickory, bass-wood, black walnut, white-wood,
ash, elm, sugar, maple, and beech.

The Boston company[1] have recently erected sawmills at a point on
the east side of the island, nearly opposite the Erie canal, which they have
called Whitehaven, and where we landed while the steamboat was taking
in wood for her fires. We saw several large oak-trees under the process of
being sawed into planks of from 2 to 5 inches in thickness. The machinery
was worked by steam, and one set of saws, all acting together so as to
divide the tree into as many planks as might be thought proper, would effect as much in the same space of time, as thirty men using saws in pairs.
Some of these trees were five feet in diameter; and instances had occurred
of some exceeding six feet, or eighteen feet in girth.

These are the trees of the primeval forest, where no wood has ever
been cut down before, and which trees are no doubt the growth of centuries. In the recesses of these thick forests are found, even now, deer in
abundance, as well as other game; and the larger birds, such as pheasants,
quails, partridges, and pigeons abound, as well as fish in great variety.
When the first growth wood is all cleared away, the island will, no doubt,
be cultivated; and it is more than probable that before the commencement
of the next century several large cities may occupy its banks, its position
being extremely favourable for that purpose, and its fertility sufficient to
sustain a large population.

From the Whitehaven timber-yard there have been already sent to
Boston, besides the oak plank going off almost every day, three complete
ships, which were cut out in frame here, including all the necessary tim-
bers and planking; and these being conveyed by the Erie canal to Albany,
thence to New York by the Hudson, and thence to Boston by sea, were put
together at the ship-yards of Boston in perfect vessels, one of which was
sent to South America, one to the Mediterranean, and one to India.

---

1. The East Boston Company bought sixteen thousand acres of Grand Island in
1833, mainly from supporters of Major Noah's Ararat scheme and including the substantial
holdings of Samuel Leggett. The company was only interested in the island's white oak
stands, which they felled to supply the shipyards of Boston. By 1850 the island had been
stripped, the sawmills dismantled; and the company moved on to other timberlands.

Buffalo: Buffalo harbor from the village, 1825. By George Catlin, from Cadwallader Colden, *Memoir of the New York Canals* (New York, 1825). Courtesy of History of Science Collections, Cornell University Libraries, Ithaca

It was on this island that Major Noah,[2] the present editor of the New York Evening Star, and author of a work endeavouring to establish the descent of the Indian race from the lost tribes of the house of Israel, proposed to build a city to be called "Ararat," for the purpose of collecting together all the Jews, now scattered over the world, into one spot, and fixing on this as their permanent home and abode till the coming of their expected Messiah. The plan, however, was not sufficiently popular among the Jews themselves to receive their approbation, and it accordingly fell to the ground; but the Major, himself a Jew, has thought the project of sufficient importance to deserve a permanent record, and accordingly, at this station of Whitehaven, where the city was intended to be built, a monument has been erected, with an inscription in Hebrew, for the information of all succeeding generations.

2. Mordecai Manuel Noah (1785–1851), a Philadelphia Jew, was U.S. consul in Tunis from 1813 to 1819, when he returned to America, dabbled in writing plays, and edited several of New York's major newspapers. He selected Grand Island in 1825 as the site for the New Jerusalem, a home for the Jews called Ararat. Despite large public displays in Buffalo and the carving of a commemorative monument in sandstone, the scheme was stillborn.

After completing our supply of wood, we passed beyond Grand Island, keeping close to the Canada shore, passing the small villages of
Waterloo and Fort Erie, with British sentinels at each, till coming opposite to the light-house of Buffalo harbour, we stood across for the American shore, and, arriving at the wharf about seven o'clock, having been
about five hours in performing 22 miles against a current running nearly 6
miles an hour, we went to our former quarters at the American Hotel, and
were delighted with the change, which its ample and wellfurnished apartments, good beds, and other agreeable auxiliaries, afforded us, in contrast to those with which we had so recently been familiar. . . .

The ground on which Buffalo stands, rises by a very gradual ascent
from the edge of the lake, up to a fine and extensive level; and while the
harbour, pier, wharfs, docks, canal, and warehouses, occupy the lower
part of the town, all the principal streets and public edifices occupy the
more elevated portion.

The city is well laid out, the streets being of ample length and
breadth, and arranged with great symmetry. Main Street, which exceeds
two miles in length, and is about 120 feet in breadth, is of finer proportions than the Broadway at New York, and has on each side of it massive
piles of buildings, in shops, stores, dwellings, and hotels, which may vie
with those of any other city in the Union, either for elegance of design,
solidity of construction, internal comfort, or external appearance. Several squares are agreeably interspersed in different quarters of the town,
enclosed by railings and planted with trees, on an area of beautiful lawn;
while the views of the expanded surface of the lake and the more restricted area of the strait, which are seen from almost every part of the
town, add great interest and beauty to the scene.

Of public buildings there are, the City Hall, a theatre, and 15
churches, of which the Presbyterian, the Baptist, the Episcopal, and the
Methodist, are the principal. These are all large and substantial structures; and, like all those I have yet seen in America, they are remarkable
for great neatness in their interior, and ample accommodation and comfort for their congregations, though of very irregular styles of architecture.

Of the hotels, the American is not only superior to all the others in
Buffalo, but better than any that we had yet been at since our landing in
America. In all its rooms, space, elegance, and comfort were united; the
drawing-rooms were furnished in the first style of a private dwelling, the
bed-rooms were lofty and airy, and the beds excellent. The table was
the best furnished and best attended of any at which we had yet sat,
though this was the feature in which it was least excellent; and all its subordinate appointments were well maintained. If good cooks could be

added, it might rank with any hotel in London, Liverpool, or Bath; but the Americans, as a nation, certainly do not appear to understand the difference between well-fed and tender, and ill-fed and tough provisions, whether in fish, poultry, or flesh-meats: and their modes of preparing and serving up that which they have, are so inferior to the processes used in England, that it will require many years to bring them to a standard of equality with us in this particular.

The population of Buffalo, now consisting of about 20,000 is almost wholly white. We did not remember to have seen 20 coloured people in the place, so thinly are they scattered; but these were well-dressed, and in an apparently prosperous condition. The bulk of the inhabitants are engaged in trade and commerce, though, of course, there are some few professional men, as physicians and lawyers, among them. Dutch and German emigrants abound, and Irish are not less numerous. It is from the former, that the domestic servants are chiefly taken, and the latter supply the daily labourers of the place. The general appearance of all classes indicates competency and comfort; but there is none of the style and fashion so apparent in the equipages and dresses of New York, Philadelphia, and Baltimore. The private parties of the more wealthy inhabitants exhibit, however, a happy union of ease and elegance, with more of social frankness, and less of pretension and etiquette, than those of the larger cities, and therefore, to us at least, they were far more agreeable.

Among the buildings projected here, but not yet completed, is a chartered University, to be called, "The University of Western New York," and an Exchange, of more colossal proportions than those of London, Paris, Lisbon, or Amsterdam. The elevation of this edifice, gives, among its dimensions, the following: Frontage 245 feet, depth 200 feet, diameter of the pillars of the portico, 10 feet 2 inches; height of the pillars and entablature, 86 feet; platform above the roof of the building for support of a dome 93 feet square, and 40 feet high. Circular section above the square, 60 feet diameter, and 58 feet high; surrounded by a colonnade of 16 pillars, 4 feet 2 in diameter, and 32 feet high; dome above this, 60 feet diameter, and 34 feet high; entire height, from the side pavement to the centre of the dome 222 feet. Those who are conversant with architectural measurements will at least admire the *scale* of this edifice as to size: it was estimated to cost 5,000,000 of dollars, or upwards of a million sterling; and but for the recent derangement of all monetary operations, the sum would have been raised, and the building erected before this time.

In the neighbourhood of Buffalo are some agreeable rides, and many pretty villas of the more wealthy citizens, some finished and occupied, and others in a state of progress. The presence of the lake not only furnishes pleasing views in all directions, but supplies a never-failing breeze from the waters, in the morning and in the evening, and makes the nights always cool; so that we suffered less inconvenience from the heat here, with the thermometer at 90° in the day, than we did at Philadelphia and Albany with the thermometer at 85°.

ENTERING BUFFALO IN AUGUST 1830

Journal of a Tour, *published in 1831, alone rescues a man named John Fowler from oblivion. Its pages reveal him to have been an experienced traveler in England and a sociable member of the mercantile middle class.*

It is only through good fortune that his impressions ever reached an English publisher. He sailed for Liverpool from New York City in October 1830, on board the Robert Fulton. *The Fulton was badly damaged in heavy seas while going to the aid of the barque* Standard *of Whitby, in mid-Atlantic, and only through a combination of good seamanship and favorable weather was she able to beach on the rocky island of Flores, in the Azores, after a tense week at sea. Fowler enjoyed the hospitality of the American consul on Fayal for ten days, found an orange-boat heading for Plymouth, reached Liverpool a few days before Christmas, and "was welcomed by many kind friends and acquaintances as one arisen from the dead." These same friends, he claims in the preface to the book, prevailed on him to publish his account of New York state and the wreck of the* Fulton.

A political liberal in his views, Fowler traveled across New York in the summer of 1830, reaching Buffalo in late August. The city had been almost completely destroyed during the War of 1812, but the tide of western emigration and the great commercial stimulus of the canal had combined to guarantee its rebirth and rapid expansion.

Before arriving at Buffalo, travelling became, indeed, no sinecure, it being our hard destiny to pass over what the Americans call a "*corduroy*

From John Fowler, *Journal of a Tour in the State of New York, in the Year 1830; with Remarks on Agriculture in Those Parts Most Eligible for Settlers.* . . (London: Whittacker, Treacher, and Arnot, 1831), pp. 117-20, 123-26, 130.

road," than which nothing can be conceived more direfully hostile to the comfort of either man or beast, or the safety of the vehicle. It is, in fact, a *road of logs,* of trees felled on the spot, and placed in contact with each other from side to side; the genuine corduroy rib, to be sure; coarse enough for horse jockey taste, however extravagant: but the thing mentioned, no farther delineation is needful — the cause is adequate to any thing, and the effect does no discredit to the cause. Poor Peter's pilgrims with their peas were well off, by comparison, even when the driver, in pure tenderness of heart towards us, condescended to limit his speed to two miles per hour; but when that speed was accelerated to five and six, why, then, good bye to description, and to *seats of honour,* and *all other seats;* 'twas rather too much for a joke: the reader's imagination, if tolerably fertile, will best help me out. Finally, however, we escaped without loss of life or limb, which is saying as much as will be received without suspicion, and I gladly wave the *traveller's license* of adding more; — would that I could even dismiss the recollection!

But after all, sad as the confession, if the road *is* to be passed, I know not how it could be otherwise accomplished. The soil of these woods has no consistency beyond that of decomposed, or half decomposed, vegetable matter, wholly inadequate to sustain the weight of carriages at any time, and, in the wet season, mere bog. Still you are strangely tempted to think, or, at least, to wish that these said logs had some earthly covering or other upon them; but then again, you are told of a newly settled country, and the value of labour; the latter, according to Dr. Smith,[1] a poser for every thing, so I may as well hold my tongue, and patiently "endure what can't be mended;" — be the name of *corduroy,* however, for ever infamous!

The day was fast wearing away when we entered the village of Buffalo. It had been remarkably fine, and the wind happening to meet, instead of to follow us, rendered agreeable what would, otherwise, have proved a choking affair indeed. Throughout nearly the whole of the way, the log road excepted, whenever we were in motion, there was nothing to be discerned in our rear but one dense cloud of dust; trees, houses, and even villages, as soon as we had passed them, were lost to our view, and woe betide those who chanced on this day to be shaping their course in an opposite direction: it would require very familiar acquaintance to pronounce upon their identity with any thing like certainty, when landed at their respective destinations.

1. That is, Adam Smith (1723-1790), the Scots economist from whose work stems the labor theory of value.

We were driven up to a splendid hotel at the south end of the village, called the *Buffalo House,* kept by *E. Powell, jun.:* it is less than a mile from the Lake, which in twenty minutes after my quitting the stage I had found my way into, and enjoyed the luxury of a moonlight dip in its refreshing waters. On returning to the inn I learnt that the last *general* meal of the day had been long ago despatched, and I had, therefore, *hard fate,* to put up with a quiet repast by myself. In the few instances of my *delinquency* in this way, I have thought my hosts, for the time being, would have been quite as well pleased had I omitted to give them so much additional trouble.

I amused myself for some time afterwards in a reading-room belonging to the establishment, and on retiring was shown into an apartment which for neatness, and even elegance, I have not seen surpassed on my route, only equalled at Auburn.

August 29th. — After such fair promise it is almost needless to say that I have arisen this morning free from a *vermin visitation,* or other nightly annoyance; and, as if by contrast to the *solitude* attendant upon my last evening's meal, have breakfasted with some thirty or forty sitting down to the table, and *mine host* and *hostess* presiding. . . .

But to speak of Buffalo, — upon my first view of which, after the route I had pursued to it, I was filled with admiration and astonishment; and could I for a moment have suffered myself to lose all recollection of the *canal,* and retain only the idea of its *land* approach, I should have been almost tempted to believe that such an appearance as it presents, at the termination of a forest, had been rather produced by magic or supernatural than by human means. In point of size it only yields to New York, Brooklyn, Albany, Utica, and Rochester, and how long any of these places, but the two first, may be able to boast even such superiority, is, in my opinion, a matter of great uncertainty. The situation of Buffalo, however considered, is commanding and important beyond most. Standing at the foot of Lake Erie — now connected with Lake Ontario by the *Welland Canal* — it has a direct communication with the Canadas; is open to the mighty lakes Huron, Michigan, and Superior, and an almost limitless extent of western continent; and, on the other hand, at the head of what is justly termed the *Grand Canal,* it is equally connected with the Hudson River, New York, as well as all intermediate places, the Eastern States, and, in fine, with the shores of the Atlantic. It is, as it were, the rallying point for the agricultural produce of the west, and the migratory population of the east, the connecting link of the varied interests of a great portion of this vast empire, and embracing within itself most of the advantages which, separately, may attach both to inland towns and seaports, but which are rarely united as in Buffalo. . . .

Buffalo: Buffalo on Lake Erie, 1827. From Basil Hall, *Forty Etchings from Sketches Made with the Camera Lucida* (Edinburgh, 1829). Cornell University Library, Ithaca

Leaving general for particular; — Buffalo stands on a fine plain at the mouth of the *Buffalo Creek,* an outlet of Lake Erie, and at the head of the Niagara river. The canal commences near this outlet, and from it lateral canals are cut in various directions, upon which numerous and extensive stores and warehouses are already erected, and many more in progress. Like Canandaigua, it consists principally of one fine broad street, called *Main-street,* having besides three public squares; and much that I have observed of the character and appearance of the buildings, public and private, there, and at Rochester, may apply to Buffalo. I think there are fewer erections of wood than at either of those places, whilst they are equally spacious and elegant. It has two handsome churches, and a court-house, built in very good style, an academy, of which report speaks highly, and where there are 100 students; with printing establishments, libraries, public baths, &c.; and in the bar of the inn I am at, and *at* that inn, I see the play of *"Is he Jealous?"*[2] advertised for performance to-morrow evening; — so soon the refinements, luxuries, and dissipations of life succeed to its comforts and conveniences. The present population

2. A one-act operetta by Samuel Beazly (1786–1851), first performed in London in 1816.

amounts to more than 6,000. — And this is *the* Buffalo which has arisen
from *that* Buffalo, the British with the horrid brand of war reduced to
ashes, *leaving but one house standing,* in 1814! — Never may that execrable, that self-inflicted scourge of the human race, with all its long train of
evils and calamities, revisit its borders more, but, with the blessings of
peace, and the industry and enterprise of her sons, may Buffalo become
all that they can desire, or I anticipate — a great and highly distinguished
commercial town, the honour and ornament of their august republic! . . .
    August 30th. —

"The morn is up again, the dewy morn,
With breath all incense, and with cheeks all bloom;
Laughing the clouds away with playful scorn,
And living as if earth contained no tombs."

Swimming in Lake Erie at five o'clock. —
    I was diverted in passing along *Main-street* at observing the extreme
singularity of the names over the shop doors, &c.; a circumstance, indeed, I have often noticed elsewhere; and, in additon, you will mostly see
portrayed upon a sign suspended over, or at the side of the door, some
touch of the profession practised within; for instance, at a *doctor's,* I saw
a *mortar and pestle;* at a *bookseller's,* two large *folio volumes;* at a *Miss
Jeremiah's,* a most exquisitely trimmed *bonnet;* and at a *fancy dyer's,* a
board, upon which was announced the character of their establishment,
had every letter painted with *different coloured* paint; — so much for
customs.

MILITARY BUFFALO IN THE EARLY 1840s

*James Alexander was stationed with his regiment in southern Ontario,
near Niagara Falls, in the early forties, and he took advantage of the opportunity offered by improving relations with the United States to travel
in the Niagara Frontier. In particular he was interested in meeting the
Americans that he might some day have to face in battle.*
    *British officers often had difficulty in concealing their amused con-
tempt at the annual musters of volunteer local militia companies; but
American regulars were a different matter. British military visitors to*

West Point, of whom there were many, were usually impressed by the curriculum and the quality of the cadets, and in their accounts they treat the officers of the regular army with the respect due to equals. With common professional interests and similar social backgrounds, American officers were congenial company. The relatively comfortable life shared by the officer class of both armies contrasted with conditions for other ranks. Their life was Hobbesian—nasty, brutish, and short. As a result the regular army in the United States was plagued with desertions, a problem that Alexander appreciated only too well from his own experience with the British army in Canada.

Alexander left Buffalo with a more exact notion of the qualities of his professional counterparts. His account was written up for publication from diaries and recollections in the late forties, after the Mexican war.

We crossed over into the States, and to the thriving and bustling Port of Buffalo, with its numerous signs, awnings over the side-walks, and empty boxes, which had contained goods, encumbering the same; traders are fond of this foolish display, which is attended, however, with the most serious inconvenience to pedestrians; but as it is "a land of liberty," the police, if any there are, do not seem inclined to interfere. At the American Hotel, we became acquainted with a pleasant and intelligent officer, Captain Williams, of the Topographical Engineers, since then, to our great regret, slain in Mexico.[1] He was in high health and spirits when we saw him, and having a considerable taste for painting, his room was decorated with some very creditable productions of his easel.

Captain Williams drove us in a carriage about the town, and showed us the substantial pier and breakwater in course of construction, and of which he had the superintendance. He also took us to the Barracks, where there was a large area enclosed. The 2nd Regiment occupied them, under the command of Colonel Riley,[2] who told me that he turned out every

From James Edward Alexander, *L'Acadie; or, Seven Years' Explorations in British America*, 2 vols. (London: Henry Colburn, 1849), 1: 288–91.

1. William G. Williams, a South Carolinian, entered the U.S. Army in 1824 and was promoted captain in the Topographical Engineers in July 1838. He was killed in action at the Battle of Monterey, Mexico, on September 21, 1846.

2. Bennett Riley (1787–1853) had entered the U.S. Army in January 1813 and fought with distinction in the War of 1812. He was promoted lieutenant-colonel of the 2nd Infantry Regiment in December 1839 and fought in the Seminole War of 1840. He would later be military governor of California before its statehood (1848–1850).

morning at *réveillé,* when he expected an officer "per company" to attend him in going his rounds.

In walking through the barrack-rooms, I remarked that the men were well provided with good breakfast and dinner crockery, that the messes were good, with plenty of vegetables; but that the sleeping arrangements were still on the old and bad plan — wooden bedsteads of two tiers, four men occupying these, two in one bed. The kits, or necessaries of the men, were so closely packed in their knapsacks, that they apparently required a paper-folder to accomplish it; a new and flat pouch held only twenty-six cartridges; the musket was the long and light French one. In the canteen there was no liquor sold; this is as it ought to be, but there was a regular store of goods and groceries; there were also gardens for the men. I saw many defaulters in a "dry-room," and as only a few picked men, as they are termed, are allowed to go out of barracks, from fear of desertion, I do not think the life of a soldier in the American regular army, composed as it is of a mixture of Irish, French, and Germans, British deserters, &c., is much to be envied. . . .

A friend going to Buffalo sometime after this, found that the officers had established a mess in the barracks; they dined in the middle of the day, and afterwards adjourning to a billard-room, a considerable noise and clatter was heard in the mess-room, and on looking in, my friend saw that the servants, including a black man, had attacked the remains of the dinner, as seemed to be their custom "of an afternoon," though this is rather different from our English notions of "carrying on the war."

There was another peculiarity at Buffalo, which struck an Englishman not used to American manners and customs as singular, in walking into the street from his hotel, he saw a pair of boots with legs in them hanging out of a window, and on the soles were the figures 73, the number of the room which the owner of the boots occupied.

We continued our journey down the Niagara River to Tonewanta, and in the forest I was courteously greeted by a deserter from my own regiment, Drummer Kelly, who had an amiable weakness for liquor, and who was constantly in trouble in consequence. He seemed very glad to see me, and I asked him to go back, "to turn over a new leaf," and that I would speak a word for him; but he declined my invitation, and said he did not think he could ever soldier again, and was now going to play the drum or bugle at a circus in Buffalo. I much fear "that he went to the bad" in double quick time, a circus not being a school of reform for bad habits.

The Southern Finger Lakes
and Southern Tier

THE SOUTHERN TIER and southern Finger Lakes region of west and central New York scarcely figures in the pages of British writers, for reasons that have to do with the dynamics of tourism. The area was settled later than the rest of the state, save the Adirondacks, but intrinsically it was little different from much of New York, and its settlers faced problems common to their predecessors elsewhere. Military action "solved" the problem of the indigenous people at the same time as it did for the Genesee Country to the north, during the revolutionary war. Bankruptcies among early development speculators were common, and squatters further complicated securing legal title to land throughout the west. Physically, the area's forests hindered farmers much as they did elsewhere. On the positive side, the major waterways offered a profusion of mill seats, the land was no less fertile than in many other, more rapidly settled parts of New York, and politically the boundaries with Pennsylvania were if anything more secure than those with Upper and Lower Canada.

But the region's slightly later development, a matter of only a few decades, made it attractive to visitors only after New York's heyday as the main area examined by foreigners curious about the growth of the United States. By the forties, New York's established sights, seen at railroad speed, left little time for original travel: the American West called ever more loudly to the foreign visitor. (The phrase "railroad speed," common in travel books, points to another problem. Bankruptcies plagued and considerably delayed the southern rail route from the Hudson to Lake Erie.) And there were other problems associated with later settlement. Charles Lyell, traveling in the early forties, was puzzled by the village of Corning, so recently founded that it did not appear on his map. For all but a handful of British visitors the region might just as well not have existed.

As far as British notice goes, the area's disadvantage—if indeed it was a disadvantage, for an absence of tourists meant an absence of foreign libel—consisted in this: it did not straddle the route to a famous sight. Visitors were generally prepared to suffer, if with much complaint, the horrors of early nineteenth-century travel for the spectacle of a Niagara Falls; but it took something of that order to attract them away from the established routes. Meanwhile, the scenery of the Alleghany and upper Genesee rivers was virtually unknown. Alexander Mackay visited the Portage Falls on the Genesee in the late forties, and his enthusiastic account of their "indescribable grandeur" in *The Western World* is as of a virgin land. "Scarcely one traveller out of a hundred who makes the tour of the Union either sees or hears of" them, he notes (2: 159), and that he can refer to "*the* tour" is one reason for their obscurity.

As the accounts by Emmanuel Howitt and Edward Thomas Coke graphically illustrate, the discomforts of traveling in a new region could be intense. The main transport routes in the Southern Tier funneled traffic north and south, and to go east and west, the usual direction for the visitor, was inevitably to travel through the backwoods. The route further northward, along the line of the Genesee road and the Erie Canal, was considerably easier and much quicker.

Accounts of New York helped define the tourist route through the state. Through their concentration on the sights of the northern route across the state, they passively accumulated the oblivion of the Southern Tier. The few hardy souls who did travel out of the ordinary way must have actively discouraged others from following in their footsteps (often literally, through a lack of regular coach services): their accounts can be read as cautionary tales, bolstering the impression that no spectacular beauty or sublime experience awaited them to justify the hardships of the journey. In the average British tourist's mental map of New York, to go south of the well-traveled route from Syracuse to Batavia was by the mid-1830s to venture into a dark, obscure, and uninviting land.

From this stems the curious observation that there are more early accounts of the Southern Tier, before the itinerary through New York became established and predictable, than there are late. Francis Hall, William Dalton, and Emmanuel Howitt all traveled before 1820. Two later tourists, James Stuart and Edward Thomas Coke, risked brief adventures down Cayuga Lake to Ithaca; but they soon scurried back to the regular timetables and more comfortable hotels that tourists pressed for time were coming to expect in their visits to the United States.

FRIENDS IN CATTARAUGUS COUNTY, 1819

Curiosity and theory surrounded the Indians of North America, and per-
haps the oddest theory of all was that they were children of the Diaspora,
descendants of the ten lost tribes of Israel. An adherent of this eccentric
belief was Emmanuel Howitt, a member of an old Nottingham Quaker
family, who traveled on some unspecified business in the United States
during 1819. He wrote to friends and acquaintances from all over the
northeast and published the letters after returning home. One long letter
is devoted to the Israelite thesis, which he ascribes to William Penn.

Members of the Seneca nation from the reservation near Buffalo
had toured England in 1818; Howitt not only returned that visit but made
the arduous journey south to the lands of Cornplanter and Pleasant Lake
(though he notes nothing of Indian religious revival) on the banks of the
Allegany River near the Pennsylvania border. There members of the Soci-
ety of Friends from Philadelphia had been working since 1798, and there
Howitt spent several days with his coreligionists and dozens of pages on
their pupils and neighbors.

[August 11, 1819] . . . I took the road towards Concord, on foot, but was
overtaken by a gentleman of that place, with whom I rode in his waggon
38 miles, passing through Hamburgh and Boston. In Boston township,
we saw an ancient breast-work fortification, not less in the internal diameter than 40 yards. Some pieces of iron have been found about it, and the
trees upon it are as large, and appear as old, as any to be found in the
woods: a decisive proof that this work must have been cast up at a very
distant period, and that by a race of people, perhaps, not of a more martial spirit than the present, but acquainted with more formidable modes
of warfare, — acquainted with iron, that reputed criterion of a great advance in civilization, and accustomed to the erection of works that bespeak habits of labourious activity, and an acquaintance with the mechanical powers. . . .

My journey, the next day, from Springville to the Cataragus land office, (18 miles,) was through an unbroken desert for 16 miles. It was the

From Emmanuel Howitt, *Selections from Letters Written During a Tour through the United*
States, in the Summer and Autumn of 1819. . . (Nottingham: J. Dunn, 1820), pp. 135–39,
141–43, 144–46.

most fatiguing journey I ever experienced, and one that I almost despaired
of ever accomplishing, — having no track, but marks on the trees. . . .

On the 13th, I reached a Squire Green's, on the Great Valley Creek,
ten miles from the Cattaraugus land office. The soil, along this valley, appears particularly rich, by the luxuriance of plants as well as of timber,
but as yet unsettled. Here I ordered a skiff, for which I waited till next day
at noon: it was a few boards nailed together, and a cover, raised to defend
me from the worst of the weather, for which I paid four dollars. With
this, I prepared to navigate the Great Valley Creek, and afterwards the Allegany river, being heartily tired of traversing this wilderness on foot.

At this place, provisions were excessively dear; wheat, 4 dollars per
bushel, — butter, 25 cents, — and every thing else in proportion; in provisions for my voyage, I paid accordingly; dried venison, 1s. 6d. per pound,
&c. Here are four saw-mills, which cut a vast quantity of boards for the
Pittsburg, Cincinatte, and New Orleans market, and are sent down the
Great Valley Creek to the Allegany, and thence down the Ohio. On this
route, I set out at noon; But the creek being very low, and filled with slabs
from the saw-mills, I was obliged to wade most of the way, and push my
skiff before me. It was four o'clock when I reached the river, which I
found extremely variable in depth and rapidity: in some places very deep
and still; in others shallow, narrow, and rushing over rocks and stones
with a strong current. Over these I was obliged to wade; and, by these
means, my progress was extremely slow. It was my intention to reach this
settlement [Tunesassah][1] that day, which is distant fifteen miles; but, owing to these impediments, (to having my skiff upset and filled with water,
which I was obliged to lade out with a pint tin, as I stood 2 hours up to the
middle in water,) I was compelled to seek the first lodgings I could find.

Pondering my solitary way, wet, and completely weary, as it grew
dark, I perceived a light, and, drawing up my boat, made towards it. I
found it an Indian village, and entered a wigwam, where several of them
were sitting. They took no notice of my entrance, but continued their
talk. I told them I was a benighted traveller, and must be indebted to their
hospitality for lodgings. They still continued their discourse, unmoved. I
then added, — I had travelled a long way, and was faint and in want of
some refreshment. They still continued their apathy and discourse. On
this, I repeated my request with some emphasis, to a young man near me.
He coldly asked me what I would have: I replied, some bread and milk.
He then rose and fetched me some of their bread, made of Indian corn,

1. The Quakers' first settlement was at Genesinguhta (Old Town) in spring 1798. In
1804 they purchased 700 acres 2 miles from Old Town on the Tunesassa Creek.

pounded in a mortar, and baked, husk and all, on the hearth, — and some thick butter-milk. I was really excessively hungry; but when I tasted of the bread, rough and husky, and thought of the nasty squaws by whom it was made, I could not eat: the butter-milk was still more intolerable, — and I dare say they thought my conduct as saucy as I thought their fare bad. . . .

I staid breakfast at an Indian's hut, where I boiled my kettle and frizzled my venison. Here I was informed, that "the friends lived only eight miles down the river". . . .

I reached this track just as friends were sitting down to meeting, and afterwards spent the day very agreeably with them. Jonathan Thomas had spent the greater part of the last 23 years in the work of civilization in this wilderness.[2] Joseph Elkinton,[3] the schoolmaster, informed me, — I am the only friend, except the Indian Committee and a particular friend of his, who have visited this secluded place during his residence. Our dinner was a perfect luxury: green Indian corn, potatoes, milk, bread and cheese, and blackberry pye. The afternoon past most agreeably, in listening to the account of improvements made by friends, among this part of the Senecas and Oneidas. On retiring, I could not help feeling most sensibly, the blessing of having had an education amongst friends, — and deep thankfulness for meeting with some of them in this vast wilderness, whose kindness to me, a perfect stranger, will ever be gratefully remembered.

The next morning, I walked with Jos. Elkinton to the Indian School and village, about three miles off. He has here a room built, which serves both for a school and house: for here he cooks his own meals and makes his own bed. A small birth is taken out of one corner where he sleeps, and above there is another small bed, for a benighted traveller, like myself, as sometimes happens. He had that day but six Indian scholars, who appeared to be making rapid progress in the English language, — writing, reading, and accounts. . . .

The young are accustomed to agriculture, the handicraft arts are introduced amongst them, the bow and arrow are laid aside, and it is highly gratifying to see the superior cleanliness, comfort and industry, in the habitations and manners, of those who have been educated by friends.

---

2. Jonathan Thomas worked in the Indian missions from 1796 to 1821. He had come to Tunesassa in 1809.

3. Elkinton, a Philadelphia Quaker, came to Tunesassa in summer 1816 at twenty-two years of age. He founded a school in his first year, which was briefly closed in the early twenties by an opposition to his teaching in English. He spent sixteen years in the colony, eventually to die in 1868 at the age of seventy-four. His grandson, Joseph Elkinton, recounted the early history of the mission in "The Quaker Mission among the Indians of New York State," *Buffalo Historical Society Publications* 18 (1914): 169–89.

The tract of land purchased by the Indian committee, has two good mill seats upon it. One saw, and one grist mill, are already erected and at work. The former cuts 4000 feet of pine timber in one day, which is here worth 5 dollars per thousand, and about 10 dollars in Cincinati. I. Thomas assures me that there is sufficient pine timber here, to serve 30 years, at that quantity per diem. The mountains covered with this pine appear but indifferent land, but the flats are excellent. After school was over, Joseph Elkinton introduced me to Tekianda, a chief, at his own house. He like the rest of his brethren, who spend their lives in these woods expressed his astonishment at the vast distance I had come, and during my stay repeatedly recurred to it. He furnished me with a few porcupine's quills, which they dye with brilliant colours of their own production, to ornament their mocasins. Some specimens of their paint, 2 of their ear-rings, and as a peculiar token of friendship, a tuft of feathers of the hen hawk, smeared with red earth, which he had worn all the last war; This chief is a great warrior. His presents I very willingly received, and was glad to replace by others; but when he offered me as a particular token of amity, his tomahawk to smoke out of, no considerations of offence to the old man, could subdue my horrid loathings, while my imagination figured to me the mangled brains of numbers, into which it had doubtless been dashed. A fine cucumber which he offered me, (though I did not want it,) was a far more acceptable present. His garden was in its first year, yet it is well stocked with all the varieties of cucumbers, melons, squashes, and other vegetables common to American gardens. Joseph Elkinton endeavours to excite a spirit of horticultural emulation amongst them, by using every exertion to excel them in the production of his garden. They look upon him as a most excellent "corn plant," and their attempts to equal him will not be without the best effects. The more I see of the effects produced by friends amongst these people, the more I am convinced of the unrivalled wisdom of their system.[4]

FROM BUFFALO TO ELMIRA IN 1816

The War of 1812 had disrupted life and destroyed several of western New York's small settlements, but the effect was merely temporary. Francis

4. Howitt here quotes an approbatory comment by Mrs. Grant of Laggan on the Quaker missions. "Of this humane community it is but just to say, that they were the only

Hall, one of the earliest Britons to venture a tour in the United States af-
ter the peace, found Buffalo bigger than ever and the focus of a thickly
settled area that was bustling with energy.

After leaving the phoenix Buffalo, he headed southeast from Avon
for Philadelphia. Before better roads and canals and railroads, the direct
route was for the single horseback rider usually the quickest. A decade la-
ter visitors going from Buffalo to Philadelphia would almost inevitably
travel via Albany and New York City, and save time, money, and physical
discomfort into the bargain.

Hall may have had some trepidations about his likely reception, es-
pecially given that he was an officer in the British Army, but the Ameri-
cans he met treated him with generous hospitality. His account, written as
a journal-cum-gazetteer on the spot, is rare in its frank admissions that
previous British visitors had not only made errors of fact and interpretation
—a common complaint, and occasionally given as the excuse for publish-
ing another book about America—but had unjustly vilified the American
character. There would not be too many such assessments during the next
few decades, which Allan Nevins terms with some justice the era of "Tory
condescension."

[October 19, 1816] Buffalo was among the frontier villages burnt during
the war; not a house was left standing. It is now not merely a flourishing
village, but a considerable town, with shops and hotels, which might any
where be called handsome, and in this part of the country, astonishing. Its
situation is highly advantageous, forming the extremity of the new line of
settled country already described, and communicating by the Lakes with
the Western States of the Union, and the two Canadas. The American side
of Lake Erie is also settling fast, and Erie is already a thriving town. The
celerity with which Buffalo has risen from its ashes, indicates the juvenile
spirit of life and increase, that so eminently distinguishes the American
population from the exhausted tribes of our hemisphere, which seem, in
many countries, scarcely to preserve vitality sufficient to bear up against
the evils of inequality, and bad government. "The hot breath of war" is

From Francis Hall, *Travels in Canada, and the United States, in 1816 and 1817* (London: Longman, Hurst, Rees, Orme, and Brown, 1818), pp. 242–56.

Europeans in the new world who always treated the Indians with probity like their own, and
with kindness calculated to do honor to the faith they professed" (Grant, *Memoirs of an
American Lady,* p. 363).

scarcely felt here, or, like their own forest conflagrations, is succeeded by a livelier verdure, and richer produce.

I found the country as I went on, thickly settled, but dull, and uniform in feature, being an entire flat. The autumn had been dry, and water was so scarce in many places, that my horse was sometimes very grudgingly served with what had been fetched several miles. This is an evil not uncommon in newly settled districts: draining follows clearing; the creeks, no longer fed by the swamps, disencumbered also of fallen trunks of trees, and other substances by which their waters were in a great degree stayed, easily run dry in summer, and soon fail altogether.

The principal inn at Batavia is large, and yet upon an economical principle, for one roof covers hotel, prison, court-house, and assembly room. I observed several prisoners at the bars of a lower room, and inquired of an old German about the house, what might generally be their offences. "They had been most of them speculating too much." It seemed hard thus to punish men for the ingenious use of their wits, so I begged a further explanation: they had been forging bank-notes. This delicate definition reminded me of a farmer at Watertown, with whom we fell upon the subject of English deserters. "We don't want them here," said he; "they are too familar by half." Now, though I could readily believe of these my countrymen, that bashfulness had no part in them, it seemed an odd ground of complaint for a Yankey; so I repeated something wonderingly, "too familar!" "Aye," rejoined he, "they steal every thing they can lay their hands upon." There is an Episcopal Church building here by subscription; the cost of which is to be 20,000 dollars. My host offered me a "Stirrup Cup," at parting, a civility not unusual in the untravelled parts, both of the States, and Canada.

Allan's Creek, betwixt Batavia and Caledonia, seems, from the banks still remaining, at some distance from its present channel, to have been once a considerable river, as was its neighbour, the stream of Caledonia, by the same token.

Caledonia is a small, but flourishing village, and has a handsome inn, with very comfortable accommodations: close to the road is a sheet of water, covering seven or eight acres, called the Great Spring, from which a clear and rapid stream descends, through a pleasing valley, into Allan's Creek, before the latter unites with the Genesee River. Its banks are adorned with natural groves and copses, in which I observed the candleberry myrtle in great abundance. . . . This district has been settled fifteen years; cleared land is worth 50 dollars. per acre; uncleared about 15 dollars. Farmers reckon upon a return in crops of about twenty-five for one.

I halted a day at Caledonia to rest my horse, and shoot partridges, and the next morning went on to Avon, on the right bank of the Genesee, to breakfast: here let me record the fame of the little red-bricked tavern, on the right hand side, near the entrance of the village (I forget the sign). In fifteen minutes after my arrival I sat down to a breakfast which a Parisian gourmand might have envied me. — By the bye, the Americans excel in breakfasts, though their dinners are naught. — At Avon I quitted the main road, and following the right bank of the Genesee, began, soon after crossing the stream of Lake Comesus, to fall in with the spurs of the Allegany Ridges. The scenery here improves, and the roads proportionably deteriorate: wild even to savageness, mountain heights branch thickly across the country, with no seeming order or direction, like so many gigantic mole-hills. The only level ground is the narrow alluvion of the streams, which the road is, as often as possible, taught to follow; when it cannot do so, it affords a very practical illustration of the ups and downs of life; yet is this travelling preferable, perhaps in both instances, to the uniformity which causes no fatigue, and excites no emotion. If the height be toilsome the prospect is pleasant of the deep glens, and shades beneath, and of the blue hills smiling in distant sunshine. The valley is often encumbered with rocks, and its road deep and plashy; but the white broken torrent rushes agreeably through it: its verdure is deep and various, or its cultivation cheerful. The Genesee River seems to bound the limestone region in this direction. The Allegany Ridges, less rugged and precipitous than granite mountains, are bolder and more irregular than the limestone heights, which have a nearer resemblance to long terraces of masonry. M. Volney[1] considers the Freestone Mountains, called the Katskill, which fall upon the Hudson below Albany, as bounding the granitic region towards the East, and constituting the basis of the whole mountain country from thence to the Apalachian Ridges, and Georgia, fixing the sources of the Susquehanna, and the Genesee Country as the points of contact betwixt it and the Limestone Country.

The woods round the Genesee abound in large black squirrels, some of which are as big as a small cat; they are destructive to grain, and are therefore keenly pursued by sportsmen, who frequently make parties, and celebrate the destruction of several thousands at one chase: their flesh is considered a delicacy: they migrate at different seasons, and have the credit of ingeniously ferrying themselves over rivers, by using a piece of

---

1. Constantin François Chasseboeuf, compte de Volney (1757–1820), traveled in the United States between 1795 and 1798 before being forced to leave, suspected as a spy. His *Tableau du climat et du sol des Etats-Unis* was published in 1803.

bark for a raft, and their tails for sails. Olaus Wormius[2] tells us the same story of the Norwegian squirrels, and Linnæus[3] authorizes the belief, so I suppose it to be an indigenous talent, though it would not cost much to a builder of hypotheses to infer from thence the derivation of American squirrels from an European stock.

The road from Danville crosses a creek, winds for three miles up a mountain steep, heavily timbered, and continues through swampy forests to Canisteo. Close to the little village of Arkport the Tyoga branch of the Susquehanna rises, in a meadow by the road side. Arkport is named from the low flat boats called arks, which are built there, and used on the Tyoga, and Susqehanna, whose head-waters have depth for no other craft, and for this, during the rainy season only. It may be supposed that so rugged a country is very thinly settled; villages are separated by a distance of fifteen or twenty miles, with few intermediate cottages. Betwixt Canisteo and Bath there are not more than a dozen, though improvements are going on. The principal settlements are to be found on the narrow alluvions of the creeks and rivers; but even there the soil is of an inferior quality. The roads are bad enough, but I was surprised to see them deep and miry, having experienced but one wet day during the autumn. I found, however, that this calculation would not apply to the mountains, or to the country east of them, where there had been heavy falls of rain: a circumstance easily accounted for by considering that the clouds which come impregnated with moisture from the Atlantic, are frequently arrested by the mountains, and disgorged, without crossing into the Western country.

Bath is built on the alluvion of the Conhocto Creek, and embosomed in wild mountains: the principal houses are placed round the three sides of a square, or green, and being most of them new, white, and tastefully finished, have a lively appearance, agreeably contrasted with the dark mountain scenery which opens on the fourth side. It was court day when I arrived, and as the court was held at the tavern to which I had been recommended, I found it in a bustle, but I was not the less comfortably accommodated in a well-furnished carpeted parlour, in which dinner was neatly and expeditiously served.

Among the persons at the court-meeting was the Militia General, M'Clewer, who brought on his countrymen the destruction of their frontier, by his wanton burning of Newark.[4] He keeps a store in Bath, and suc-

---

2. Ole Worm (1588–1654) wrote voluminously in Latin on Denmark and Danish history, medicine, antiquities, and the natural wonders of Scandinavia.

3. Carl von Linné (1707–1778), the Swedish botanist, is best known for the Linnaean system of classification of natural species.

4. George McClure (c. 1770–1851) commanded American forces on the Niagara

ceeded to the command which he disgraced, either by accident, or through the want of a fitter man. He had lately been cast in 1400 dollars damages at Canandaigua, in an action brought by an inhabitant of Newark, for the destruction of his property. It would be judging the Americans unfairly to suppose they had regarded his conduct with indifference: for some time after it, he scarcely dared to show himself in his own neighbourhood; and being on one occasion recognized at a public auction-mart in Philadelphia, he was hooted out of the room.

There is a road from Bath by the shores of the Crooked Lake to Jerusalem, the village of the Elect Lady, Jemima Wilkinson, and her sect of Friends. . . .

The road from Bath to Painted Post, follows the alluvion of the Conhocto branch of the Tyoga, and though stony is tolerably level; it crosses the Creek twice in the last six miles. The mountains have a slaty appearance, with horizontal strata. I was disappointed at Painted Post to find the post gone; broken down, or rotted, within these few years.[5] It was, as may be supposed, an Indian memorial, either of triumph, or death, or of both. A post is not much, but, in this instance it was a record of the past, a memorial of, (may I be pardoned the expression,) the heroic ages of America!

When I was at Ancaster [Ontario] I was shown the grave of an Indian, among the woods near the head of the stream: it was covered with boards, and a pole erected at each end, on which a kind of dance was rudely painted with vermillion. The relatives of the deceased brought of-

---

Frontier during the War of 1812. In December 1813, he retreated from Canadian soil after burning Newark, Ontario, on the night of December 10. British retaliation was massive: Lewiston, Black Rock, and Buffalo were razed the same month. The claim for his unpopularity among Americans is questionable: he was appointed sheriff of Steuben County in 1815, and was three times elected state representative. He moved to Illinois in 1834.

5. "The following account taken from the narrative of the captivity and sufferings of Gen. Freegift Patchin, who was taken prisoner by a party of Indians under Brant during the revolution, is probably correct. 'Near this, we found the famous PAINTED POST, which is now known over the whole continent, to those conversant with the early history of our country; the origin of which was as follows. . . . [an] Indian chief, on this spot, had been victorious in battle, killed and took prisoners to the number of about 60. This event he celebrated by causing a tree to be taken from the forest and hewed four square, painted red, and the number he killed, which was 28, represented across the post in black paint, without any heads, but those he took prisoners, which was 30, were represented with heads on in black paint, as the others. This post he erected, and thus handed down to posterity an account that here a battle was fought; but by whom, and who the sufferers were, is covered in darkness, except that it was between the whites and Indians" (John W. Barber and Henry Howe, *Historical Collections of the State of New York.* . . [New York: S. Tuttle for the authors, 1845], pp. 530–31).

ferings to it daily during their stay in the neighbourhood; a vitality of sorrow truly savage.

New Town, or Elmira, (I put down both the names, for I went six miles about, from not knowing it had the happiness to have two,) is pleasantly situated on the edge of the Tyoga: its appearance, however, is far from gay, for few of the houses are painted, and wooden buildings, without this precaution, soon acquire a dingy decayed appearance. But New Town has better claims than mere good looks, to my grateful remembrance. Owing to some accidental delays, in the course of my journey, I found by the time of my arrival here, that I had not cash sufficient to carry me to Philadelphia, nor even much farther than New Town: I had bills on Philadelphia, and applied to a respectable store-keeper, that is, tradesman, of the village, to cash me one; the amount, however, was beyond any remittance he had occasion to make, but he immediately offered me whatever sum I might require for my journey, with no better security than my word, for its repayment at Philadelphia; he even insisted on my taking more than I mentioned as sufficient. I do not believe this trait of liberality would surprise an American, for no one in the States, to whom I mentioned it, seemed to consider it as more than any stranger of respectable appearance, might have looked for, in similar circumstances; but it might well surprise an English traveller, who had been told, as I had, that the Americans never failed to cheat and insult every Englishman who travelled through their country, especially if they knew him to be an officer: this latter particular they never failed to inform themselves of, for they are by no means bashful in enquiries, but if the discovery operated in any way upon their behaviour, it was rather to my advantage; nor did I meet with a single instance of incivility betwixt Canada and Charleston, except at the Shenandoah Point, from a drunken English deserter. — My testimony, in this particular, will certainly not invalidate the complaints of many other travellers, who, I doubt not, have frequently encountered rude treatment, and quite as frequently deserved it; but it will at least prove the possibility of traversing the United States without insult or interruption, and even of being occasionally surprised by liberality and kindness.

ITHACA IN 1828

Although James Stuart spent more time than most in the United States, his account of New York is only unusual in the depth of his sympathy for

*American traditions and American aspirations. In this intellectual sense
he was something of an explorer; in practical terms his tour was conventional. On one occasion, however, he did diverge from the normal tourist
route.*

*In early September 1828, during a leisurely western progress to Buf-
falo and Niagara, he circled Cayuga Lake and spent a few days in Ithaca
before returning to the standard tourist itinerary at Geneva. In his* Three
Years *the village of Ithaca is isolated from the rest of the state only in the
minds of foreign travelers. The settlement is easy of access (Lieutenant
Coke, four years later, will sharply contradict that impression), it has the
same amenities as other, more familiar villages, and the scenery has its
own noteworthy attractions.*

We found the regular supper was finished before we reached Mr Jones's
hotel at Ithaca. The hotel seemed crowded with boarders and strangers;
but the landlord, without our applying for it, gave us separate accommodation, and continued it, unasked, while we remained. Mr Jones is a most
attentive landlord in all respects, — offered us his services on the day after
we arrived, and which, too, we spent at Ithaca, to show us the village, and
every thing in the neighbourhood which we had any curiosity to see.
Ithaca is a very flourishing village, the centre of several great roads, with
a population of between 3000 and 4000, and buildings in rapid progress.
It is surrounded on all sides, but that towards the lake, by hills 300 and
400 feet high. The soil of the low grounds rich. Public or tea-gardens are
common in the American towns. In one of the gardens here, kept by an
Irish gardener, formerly employed by the Archbishop of Canterbury in
the gardens at Lambeth, we saw some fine fruit, especially grapes, of
which he sent us a liberal present to the hotel.

The falls of Fall Creek, a river of considerable size, which discharges itself into the Cayuga Lake, within a very short distance from Ithaca, almost in the environs, are very remarkable, — the descent being
about 350 feet in the course of a mile and a-half, the last fall tumbling
from a height of ninety feet; the river banks rocky, wild, and romantic.

There was a great deal of keen discussion in the bar-room of this
hotel, on the subject of the approaching election of a President of the
United States. Upon one occasion it was carried so far, and apparently as

From James Stuart, *Three Years in North America,* 2 vols. (Edinburgh: Robert Cadell,
1833), 1: 116–19.

methodically, as if a regular meeting had been arranged to debate the merits of the two candidates. Rather too great warmth was displayed, but we afterwards found that one of the parties was a gentleman travelling through the State in order to learn the general sentiments as to one of the candidates, and that on this occasion he had accidentally got into collision with a gentleman similarly engaged on the other side. They addressed each other, the one as judge, probably a justice of peace, the other as colonel.[1] A good many people were present, but took hardly any share in the disputation.

During the night we were disturbed by a band of music, — clarionets, hautboys, and wind instruments, — close to the hotel for several hours. Scots airs were chiefly played. Auld Lang Syne, John Anderson my Joe, &c. It turned out that a marriage had taken place the day before, in a house a door or two from the hotel, and that the friends of the party had ordered a serenade for them. We had not previously observed any public musical performers, not even an organist on the street, at New York, or anywhere else.

At the Ithaca hotel, both brandy and white wine were set before us at dinner, and though we partook of the latter, no separate charge was made. The bill, instead of stating so much for board for a certain period, as is usual, was made out at so much for each meal, — breakfast at 1s. 6d.; dinner, 1s. 6d.; tea and supper, 1s. 3d., and lodging, 8d. per night for each; so that the whole charge for two nights' lodgings; supper on the evening of our arrival, and meals during the next day, — at all of which there was animal food and poultry in profusion, — amounted, for three persons, to 5 dollars, 13 cents, or L. 1, 6s. 9d. No waiter or boots to be paid, nor extra charge of any kind. In general in this part of the country, we are told, that the charge per day for persons travelling is a dollar, — probably not more than three dollars a week for resident regular boarders.

We pursued our journey on the 5th towards Geneva. Looking back from a height about two miles from Ithaca, and to the north-west of it, we were delighted with a view of the village, the falls, the hills covered with wood, and the lake. We breakfasted at a hotel by the roadside, kept by a person of the name of Pratt. The farm-labourers were seated at table with us, but the breakfast was good. We were hungry, and we solaced ourselves after breakfast with as many fine peaches in the orchard as we chose to

1. These early public opinion pollsters are not otherwise identified. The election of 1828 saw John Quincy Adams — elected by the House of Representatives in 1824 after a four-way split in the election had prevented any candidate receiving a majority, although Jackson received more of both the popular and the electoral votes than Adams — lose the presidency to Andrew Jackson.

devour. Some of our fellow-passengers were not well pleased that matters should have happened so on account of the strangers, and were anxious to explain, that it was only at such a place as this, off the great roads, that it could have occurred.

We had the widow of a farmer in the stage with us, now herself managing above 150 acres. She gave us minute details of her agricultural operations, — her butter-making, cheese-making, and cyder; as well as maple sugar-making; but although she was, as generally happens here, the proprietor of the land she farmed, and had only taxes of the most trifling amount to pay, it did not appear that the high price of labour allowed her to do much more, than comfortably to bring up a family of half a dozen children. The only village we passed on our way to Geneva was Ovid, with its handsomely situated church, and fine piece of green turf between the church and hotel. The American villages are generally announced to you by the spires of their churches peeping through the trees on your approach. No religious sect is more favoured than others. Every church, whether consisting of Baptists, Methodists, Presbyterians, or Unitarians, has its spire if the funds be sufficient, generally of wood, frequently with a glittering roof of tin, and of better architecture than the church itself.

A TOUR OF CAYUGA AND SENECA LAKES IN 1832

By the early thirties the village of Ithaca was thriving, its economic health secured by abundant waterpower and its geographical position astride several major north-south trading routes. As commerce encroached on its natural wonders, however, its very successes lessened its attractions for tourists: the waterfalls were tamed to power infant industries, as Lieutenant Coke confirms.

Edward Thomas Coke (1807–1888) was, in his twenty-sixth year, a lieutenant in the 45th Regiment. Being dissatisfied with recent accounts of America, he explains in the introduction to his only book, he took extended leave with a friend, a Mr. B., to examine the place for himself. They spent several months in 1832 touring the eastern United States and Canada and covered thousands of miles, but the twenty-one from Ithaca to Watkins Glen were more frustrating and difficult than most. Despite the inconveniences, however, their tour of the lakes did have its compensations (if not enough for Coke's book to cause a massive southern flow of tourists) — the lakes' scenery, memoirs of the Universal Friend, and the falls around Ithaca. Coke set out from the village of Cayuga on August 8, 1832.

Proceeding to the village of Cayuga, situated near the northern extremity of a lake of the same name, we embarked in a steamer which plies upon the lake, and crossed to the opposite side, touching for some more passengers at a village connected with Cayuga by a bridge exceeding a mile in length, over which the western road passes. The extreme length of the lake is 40 miles by two at its greatest breadth. The scenery is tame and uninteresting, until towards the southern end, when it assumes a more pleasing appearance, the banks becoming high and craggy in some places, and in others cultivated to the water's edge. But throughout there is an overpowering quantity of dense forest, with an intervening space of eight or ten miles between villages. For the last few miles, the face of the country presented a singular appearance, being broken every hundred yards, or thereabouts, with narrow and deep ravines, formed by the heavy rush of water from the hills in the spring of the year. In some, the rock was rugged and bare; in others the grass had sprung up again, or, where the ground more easily yielded to the force of the torrent, there were long and heavy undulations, like the swelling of the sea.

At the head of the lake, entering a coach again, after a drive of two miles across a plain which had once formed part of the lake, we arrived at the pretty town of Ithaca, containing 3300 inhabitants, surrounded on three sides by hills varying from 600 to 800 feet in height, with their slopes and summits partially cleared and cultivated. The plain between the town and the lake is so densely covered with forest that the water is not visible from the former; and in many places it is so boggy and unsound that no houses can be built upon it. Two adjoining squares in the town, encircled with a wooden railing and a grove of trees, are quite occupied by churches, there not being fewer than seven of them. The Clinton House, in the vicinity of those squares, at which we put up, is one of the handsomest buildings of the kind in the States, but its bar-room is one of the dirtiest.

There are many factories and mills in and about Ithaca, on the small streams which pour their waters into the lake. A rivulet within a mile of

From Edward Thomas Coke, *A Subaltern's Furlough: Descriptive of Scenes in Various Parts of the United States. . . During the Summer and Autumn of 1832,* 2 vols. (New York: J. and J. Harper, 1833), 2: 7–16.

Ithaca: Ithaca from West Hill, 1839. Detail. Lithograph by Henry Walton. Courtesy of the DeWitt Historical Society of Tompkins County, Ithaca

the town forms two of the prettiest Falls imaginable. The lower one, about 80 feet in height, falling over a series of small rocky ledges, appears like so many flakes of snow upon the dark masses of stone; and, where the sun strikes upon the foam, it glitters like the sparkling frost on a December's morn, after the preceding day's thaw. The other Fall, 200 yards higher up the hill, exhibits more water; but the fall is not quite so high, nearly one-third of the stream being diverted through a tunnel 90 yards long in the solid rock, above the lower Fall, for the purpose of turning several millwheels; and in course of time the latter cataract will be reduced to a few gallons per minute, like the Passaic at Patterson. . . .

Not wishing to return up Cayuga Lake, and in fact having made a point of never returning by the same road when it could be avoided, we hired a carriage with two excellent horses, and at a quarter to three in the

afternoon, on the 9th of August, departed from Ithaca, ascending a steep
and long hill for two or three miles. While enjoying a most extensive and
charming prospect from the summit, we encountered one of the heaviest
storms of wind and rain I ever experienced. After struggling against it for
a quarter of an hour, we succeeded in gaining an open shed by the road
side, already filled with half-drowned pedestrians and equestrians, who
were seeking shelter from the pitiless peltings of the storm. Such an arrival as ours, with a carriage loaded with heavy trunks, a pile of carpet
bags and hat-boxes, with umbrellas, water-proof cloaks, and great coats
innumerable, would have attracted the curiosity of less inquisitive people
than thorough-bred Yankees. Five or six inmates of the shed busied themselves with examining the ivory Chinese handle of Mr. B.'s umbrella; and
a person, whom they designated as "Doctor," dressed in a threadbare,
shabby-genteel, frock coat, of blue cloth, with a collar originally black
velvet, but which, by wear and tear of weather, had been transformed into
a nondescript colour, observed that "they carved cleverly in New York."
The patent leather hat-box soon fixed their attention, and, my answer not
satisfying them that it was not made of wood, they took it out of the carriage and minutely inspected it both within and without. . . .

We . . . once more pursued our route towards the setting sun, over
a road where there was no road, over bridges where it would be much
safer to ford the stream, and through a country rich only in stones and
stumps; where land would be no bargain at half a dollar per acre. Half an
hour before sunset, when we gained the summit of a long dreary hill, the
great orb of day burst through the clouds in all his setting glory, and the
thin vapours were seen rising from the woods and valleys beneath us, and
floating gradually away before the fast subsiding gale. The road, too, at
the same moment improved, running over a firm earthen track; the driver
cracked his whip, and, smiling, observed that "we should be in by half an
hour after sun-down yet." The horses trotted merrily along; we threw
aside our wet cloaks and coats; while every thing to us wore a different
appearance, and we now saw some beauty in the vast and empty forests
which encircled us on every side, save here and there a solitary patch of
cleared land, the effects of the industry of some hardy settler, who, one
would almost imagine, had quarrelled with the whole world by seeking so
secluded a spot; but we were now in a humour to be pleased with every
thing. . . .

We were doomed, however, to still further disappointments; nor was
it until an hour past midnight, after having trudged about eight miles on
foot through deep and muddy pools, that we reached a small inn, at the
head of the lake, wet, weary, famished, and consequently out of humour.

After much knocking at doors, and shaking of windows, we succeeded in rousing the landlord from his lair. In half an hour's time, he spread out before us a "rudes indigestaque moles" of apple-pye, new cheese, sour beer, heavy Indian bread, and port wine which savoured strongly of logwood and brandy; but our appetites had been well sharpened by our wanderings, and we were in no humour to find fault. Sitting by the cheerful wood fire, we already began to laugh at the misfortunes and slow progress of our journey, having been more than nine hours performing a distance of twenty-one miles. Excellent beds being provided, in a few minutes the troubles of the past, fears and anticipation alike of the future, were alike forgotten.

On the morning of the 10th of August, embarking on board a steamer, we left Watkins, Jeffersonville, Seneca Head, or Savoy, as we heard the small village, where we had passed part of the night, severally called. Though commanding a much finer situation than Ithaca in every respect, with a canal running past it which connects the water of lake Erie and Seneca with the Susquehannah River by the Chemung Canal, yet there are not above twenty frame-houses in the settlement, arising from the mistaken policy of the proprietor[1] of the land, who will scarcely sell a rood[2] under a New York price; whereas, if he gave away every other lot for building upon, the increased value of the remaining lots would make him more than an adequate return. The head of Seneca Lake, like that of Cayuga, is black marsh, overgrown with bull-rushes and reeds. Several large streams, with fine water-falls enter it a few miles from the village, of which the Hector, 150 feet in height, and those at the big stream Point 136, are the most worthy of observation.

We considered ourselves fortunate in meeting with a gentlemanly, well-informed person in Captain Rumney, an Englishman, the proprietor of the "Seneca Chief," the only steamer which plies upon the lake. . . . The profits arise principally from towing the Erie Canal boats to the different points in the lake, the traffic on which will be much increased by the Chemung and Crooked Lake Canals, now nearly completed. The charge for towing vessels from one to the other extreme of the lake, a distance of forty miles, is six dollars, and it is performed in a few hours.[3]

At Rapeley's Ferry, a few miles down the lake on the western bank,

1. Watkins was part of the 250,000-acre area known as the Watkins and Flint Purchase, after the heads of the syndicate that bought it, Royal Flint and Samuel Watkins.

2. A rod, a local English measure, is about five and one-half yards. A rod of land is a plot of 40 square rods.

3. The Seneca Lake Steamboat Co. was incorporated in 1825 with $20,000 of capital. The *Seneca Chief* (which had carried Governor DeWitt Clinton during the celebrations

are the remains of a pier from which the celebrated Jemima Wilkinson proved the faith of her followers. She had collected them for the purpose of seeing her walk across the lake, and addressing them, while one foot touched the water, enquired if they had faith in her, and believed she could reach the opposite shore in safety; for, if they had not faith, the attempt would be in vain. Upon receiving the most earnest assurances of their belief that she could pass over, she replied "that there was no occasion then to make a display of her power, as they believed in it;" and, turning round, re-entered her carriage, and drove off, to the chagrin of thousands of idle spectators, and to the astonishment of her numerous disciples.[4] Captain Rumney, who was acquainted with her during her lifetime, described her as a tall, stately, and handsome woman; but of rather a masculine appearance. In her costume she much resembled a clergyman, having her hair brushed back, wearing a surplice and bands, with a Quakers' hat. She was a native of Rhode Island. . . . She was well versed in the Scriptures, and possessed a remarkably retentive memory; but, in other respects, was an illiterate woman. The creed of her sect is the Metempsychosis;[5] but since her departure the number of believers has considerably diminished, the present head of the Society, Esther Plant, not having sufficient tact to keep them united. . . .[6]

All the points of land in the lake (save one, which has a singular bush formed by the hand of nature into the exact representation of an elephant) are occupied by small villages, which possess excellent harbours, during heavy gales up or down the lake, and have about 20 fathoms of water within 30 feet of the shore. This one exception is the property of Esther, who will not part with it on any terms. The entrance to the Crooked Lake Canal is at the village of Dresden, a German settlement, eight miles west of which is Jemima's house. On the opposite shore in Seneca County is Ovid, situated on a pretty eminence, overlooking the water; also Lodi, Brutus, and various other classically named places. . . . The soil is a strong loam, and well adapted for wheat. Seneca is, however, an Indian

---

at the opening of the Erie Canal) started service on the lake in 1828; a second steamer, the *Richard Stevens,* began service in 1835.

4. Jemima Wilkinson, the Universal Publick Friend (1752–1819), had gone with her followers to Jerusalem Township in 1790 to found what was then the largest settlement in western New York. The oft-repeated story of her promising to walk on the water, known only through hearsay and without eyewitness verification, is discussed in Herbert A. Wisbey, Jr., *Pioneer Prophetess: Jemima Wilkinson, the Publick Universal Friend* (Ithaca: Cornell University Press, 1964), pp. 174–76.

5. The transmigration of souls.

6. Wisbey does not mention an Esther Plant in his biography of the Friend. Her legal heirs were Rachel and Margaret Malin.

name, although it might naturally be supposed to have the same origin, in imitation of antiquity, as the neighbouring towns of Marathon, Pharsalia, Homer, Virgil, and Cassius. The scenery upon the lake closely resembles that of Cayuga, being unvaried and uninteresting; the water is, however, beautifully clear, the pebbly bottom being visible in a calm day at the depth of 30 feet. Being principally supplied by springs, the ice upon it never becomes so thick as to impede navigation; during the severe frost of 1831, a thin sheet formed on some parts, but was broken up by the first light breeze which ruffled the water.

SCIPIO TO BINGHAMTON IN 1819

The Cumberland farmer William Dalton's omniverous interests in land, crops, and the state of trade in New York drew him to examine areas otherwise ignored by British travelers. He spent much of July 1819 in Scipio township, Cayuga County, probably drawn there by the fact that a successful local farmer, John Kellet, had himself emigrated from Dalton's home area, England's Lake District, in the early years of the century. Dalton's notes on rural architecture, farms for sale, cash crops and the silkworm craze, pasture, rents, and agricultural work build a detailed picture of the rural economy, which he intersperses with his opinions of the writings of other travelers.

From Scipio he traveled down the eastern shore of Cayuga Lake to Ithaca, and made his way thence to Owego. Before entering Pennsylvania he provided a brief account of infant Binghamton, a last souvenir of a journey unmatched in nineteenth-century British accounts of early New York State.

It has, I believe, been already noticed, that there are a great number of farms in the market at present. They may be purchased of every dimension, from the garden lot, to 640 acres. Buildings, for the most part, are neat and good. This township being, comparatively speaking, an old settlement, log huts have given way to the more elegant branches of architecture.

From William Dalton, *Travels in the United States of America, and Parts of Upper Canada* (Applesby: William Dalton, 1821), pp. 113–19, 210–21.

A good framed dwelling-house, with stone cellars, may be raised for 500 dollars. This will be "very comfortable and convenient," and better calculated to resist the wintry blast, than may be imagined. The cellar is dug out, and built with stone, upon which, as a foundation, the frames are raised. These are cased over with boards on the outside, and laths and plaster on the inside. In some instances the outer coat is made double. These boards are about six inches broad, are made smooth, and, when fastened, are generally painted white or green, and will last a century. In laying these on, they begin at the bottom of the building, the edge of the next boards lays upon (not joints in with,) the lower, and so on. It will be seen from the price of the chief material, (wood,) that the labour is the principal cause of expence in the building. Glass sells here at 10*d.* sterling per foot.

A corn crib, with a barn of framed timber, and covered with rough sawn boards, containing an area of two hundred square yards, and finished with stabling, will cost about eighty guineas. A log cabin four or five.

The price of farms in Scipio, with proper out-buildings, varies from 20 to 25 and 30 dollars per acre, according to circumstances. Some very choice situations with extraordinary buildings, would, of course, command more. I have been surprized to find so many fine farms offered for sale. I see no appearances indicative of poverty, and yet almost every estate in this township might be purchased. Grain of all kinds seems to sell higher here than in most of the new countries. Land, I believe, may be bought here twenty per cent. lower than on the banks of the Ohio, while at the same time it is demonstrable that grain is worth commonly from thirty to a hundred per cent. more here, than in the above-mentioned district. I see no way of solving this difficulty but by admitting that the price of land is less dependant on the quality of the soil and the commercial advantages, than on the number of purchasers. The spirit of emigration seems nearly sufficient to counterbalance any effect which might be produced by the numerous sales in this county.

Great numbers of silk worms are raised and fed in this township. One gentleman of my acquaintance, who, till lately, kept a great number of these valuable reptiles, says that he could manufacture silk for nearly the same expence as tow cloth. How far this assertion may be correct, I cannot take upon me to say, but I am certain, from the great quantity of mulberry trees growing in the neighbourhood, they may be kept at a small expence. I saw several thousands of these industrious creatures in one room.

Some farmers are accustomed to have their shoes made in their own houses, by men who travel, as tailors do in the country parts of Old England. The rate of charge is from 2*s*. 3*d*. to 3*s*. 6*d*. (English) per pair, the employer finding leather and victuals. A pair of Suwarrow boots are made for 18*s*. and when bought ready made, will cost about a guinea and a half.

The estimated cost of clearing wood land, is the same wherever we have travelled — about 14 dollars per acre. How this is done it may not be amiss to explain. I have already noticed, that the stumps of trees are invariably (except in the roads) left standing. The upper part, when cut off, is immediately "chopped" into about twelve feet lengths. As many rails as may be wanted are then split off. One man can make 200 of these in a day. They are piled up to a considerable height, so as to form a good fence, but these have an awkward appearance. The remainder of the wood is rolled into heaps, and burnt to ashes, which are sometimes sold to the soap-maker. As soon as the trees are cut down, and the ground cleared from every thing but stumps, the surface, unless the season is far advanced, which is seldom the case while the "chopping" lasts, is soon covered with white clover, which springs up spontaneously in great abundance.

We assisted in turning out some stumps, which had stood about eight years. They were quite decayed. Until these are got out of the way, the plough is seldom seen amongst them. The harrow alone prepares the ground for a crop or two of Indian corn and wheat; the field is then probably laid down, or perhaps, more properly in many instances, *suffered to lay,* it not being absolutely necessary to sow it with grass seeds. We were shown some fields covered with heavy crops of grass and clover, which had sprung spontaneously, this being the first year after a crop of grain. In this state is a field belonging to Mr. Kellett's estate,[1] which, having produced ten fine crops of grain without the aid of manure, was suffered to rest. It now bears a crop of grass little inferior to what might have been expected had grass seeds been regularly sown.

The fertility of the soil almost exceeds belief. Mr. K's horse-pasture of five acres, in which he had grazed four as good horses as I have yet seen, all this season, and also some cows and working oxen occasionally, is nevertheless covered with such a superfluity of grass and clover, as to appear at a distance more like a meadow field than a horse-pasture. This is not an exaggerated statement. This last-mentioned, as well as several

---

1. John Kellet (1777–1858), born in Westmoreland, had emigrated to the United States in 1803 and bought a farm in Scipio in March 1806. He supplied provisions to the U.S. Army during the War of 1812, became rich, and was well known for his generosity and hospitality. A portrait and brief biographical sketch appear in Elliott G. Storke, *History of Cayuga County* (Syracuse: D. Mason, 1879), insert before p. 365.

others of this gentleman's fields, are freed from stumps. It does not require much logic to prove, that such land as this is worth £6 an acre, or £7 with buildings included.

Some orchards here are of a considerable size—from six to twelve acres. It is not unfrequent for farmers to have 300 bushels of apples in one season, from which great quantities of cyder are made. . . .

July 26.

We took our departure from this highly interesting place (Scipio)— our course south, towards Ithica, in the township of Ulysses, at the head of Lake Cayuga.

This tract is tolerably well settled, and (much of the timber being cleared away) is considered very healthy. The face of the country is extremely uneven;—so much so, as to render, in many places, the operations of the agriculturist extremely laborious. The soil in Genoa, Salmon creek, and Indian fields, is good and fertile. Towards Ludlow-ville the quality is not above mediocrity,—often dry, light and sandy.

LUDLOW-VILLE— stands in a low valley, down which the Salmon creek, a small but rapid stream, pursues its devious ways. The gloomy pine hills, rising to a great height on every side, and the falls of the creek at the entrance of the town, give it a romantic appearance. This being the depot of a well-settled country, there is an appearance of much trade.

Near this place we were shown a farm lately bought for five dollars per acre, which now bears upon it grain worth thirty dollars per acre.

A tremendous thunder storm commenced whilst we rested here, accompanied by a deluge of rain, which rendered the roads to Ithica rather unpleasant for travelling. The roads here are bad. The soil of Ithica is generally poor, and covered with shrubby oak and pine. Towards the head of the lake, the road passes close under a waterfall about sixty feet in height. This river has been diverted out of its course, and made to run down a steep gravelly hill, driving along by its rapidity great quantities of stones, which it has deposited in an otherwise impassable morass—thus making a good road.

ITHICA—is about eleven years old, and contains a beautiful academy, several elegant public buildings, with about 150 neat-looking houses, and about 1,000 inhabitants. The streets are well planned, but not being paved, and the situation being rather low, are extremely disagreeable in wet weather.

We observe few signs above the doors of taverns without the eagle. At this place we noticed upon one of these boards the representation of an eagle mounted upon the back of a lion, whose eyes it was employed in picking out. This observation, though trifling in itself, may serve to throw some little light upon the character of this people. Jealousy of Old England, is a prevailing feeling. When a war with her is expected, the breast of an American seems to glow with an ardent desire to meet so noble a foe. A war with Spain is confidently anticipated, but the name of a Spaniard only excites contempt.

It ought however to be remembered here, that the track of a traveller is but a line drawn through the country. The manners and customs, and to a certain degree the dispositions, of these enterprizing people, vary considerably.

The reports of travellers, in giving the character of a people, should be received with caution. Taverns are not always the best places for the acquisition of knowledge. The Americans revolt at the idea of those loungers which infest the taverns, in some particular districts of the country, being considered as representatives of the great mass of the people. In some of the principal inns, more particularly in young flourishing towns, the society to be met with is very valuable. It is the practice of lawyers, attornies, merchants, &c., to lodge at such places, which are generally the best built houses in the town. The ringing of a hand-bell is the signal that dinner, supper, &c. are ready. At no place which I have yet seen, is it usual to take more than three meals a day.

This place being advantageously situated at the head of the lake, which is bounded by a country remarkable for its fertility, seems destined to become a town of some importance.

July 27. — We left this flourishing place, and proceeded to take a survey of a farm of 200 acres in the vicinity. The situation was high and healthy — the soil *piny, i.e.* not deep nor strong. One hundred and thirty acres of this are nearly clear of stumps, and now bear good crops. There is a tolerably good dwelling-house, with two barns, orchards, &c., upon the premises. The price demanded was £711 sterling. The value of produce varies considerably, according to the seasons and the demand abroad. At present, wheat flour is worth about 2*s.* per stone. This being comparatively an old country, the price of labour is moderate; — about one-third higher than in the North of England.

OWEGA. — To this place we passed through a poor, hilly, piny, dry country; — uncleared, except in the vallies, the roads very bad, and the settlers few. Here we first enjoyed a sight of the rapid Susquehannah, which at this place is not more than 100 yards wide.

From Owega we shaped our course eastward, by the side of the river. The soil in this tract is not good, with the exception of some low

holme-lands near the river. An extensive mass of pine timber, rising in
gloomy grandeur to a prodigious height, seems to be the principal feature
in the face of the country towards the head waters of this river. This land,
when cleared, seems favourable for the culture of barley and oats, some
crops of which are ready for the sickle. The pine (fir) here grows from 100
to 150 feet in height, and will girt nearly as much as fifty feet from the
ground as at the bottom. Trees in general seem to preserve their thickness
to a surprizing height. This circumstance may be accounted for by the
peculiar fineness of the climate.

There are many *lumberers* in this wild part of the Union. As the
American interpretation of this word varies considerably from its common acceptation in England, it may be necessary to explain its meaning
here. Wood in its rough state, and more particularly fir, is called lumber.
As there is a good market for timber in the Chesapeake, but little or none
here, many people find employment in cutting down these trees, and lash-
ing them together in the form of large rafts. Being made in a situation
which is below high water-mark, as soon as the freshets (floods) commence they mount these rafts, and, being provided with great store of
provisions, &c. will thus float down the most rapid rivers several hundreds of miles. They return by land, and being, generally speaking, men
of loose habits, it often happens that the money which they receive for
their merchandise, only barely suffices to bring them home again. So easily do men reconcile themselves to such pursuits and such an extensive
field of action, that these men will converse with the greatest sang froid,
of a voyage made in the above manner, of fifteen hundred miles from
home. These lumberers are, generally speaking, the most ferocious part
of the population in America.

BINGHAMPTON—commonly known by the name of Chenango
Point, is situated at the junction of the rivers Chenango and Susquehannah. The former is crossed at the entrance into the town, by a bridge of
thirteen arches. The town is handsomely situated, regularly planned, and
well built; and seems destined to rise, though probably by slow degrees, to
be a place of considerable size and importance. It contains about fifty
houses, two churches, &c, &c. Flour *now* sells at twelve dollars per barrel,
or 3s. 10¼d. per stone.[2] Corn at one-eighth of the above price. Wheat
will be considerably lower after the new crop is taken off, but the average
through the year is about 6s. 9d. sterling per Winch. bushel.[3] Oats are
worth *now* from 27 to 29s. per quarter; in the fall 15 or 16. The peculiar

2. One stone is equivalent to fourteen pounds weight.
3. The standards for many English measures were deposited at Winchester.

Binghamton: street scene, 1810. Watercolor by George Park. Broome County Historical Society, Binghamton

situation of Binghampton, in the midst of a wild uncleared country, will account for the high price of these, as well as other articles of provision. The great variation of the prices in different seasons, argues a want of capital in the grower, notwithstanding the many privileges which he seems to enjoy. I could not hear of any British settlers in this part of the country, although, from the high price of provisions, and the comparative lowness of that of labour, there appears to be good grounds for saying, that an industrious farmer would run little risk in settling in this neighbourhood.

We spent a delightful day in rambling round the adjacent country. We had a farm of 216 acres, situated about one mile from Binghampton, offered to us for twenty-five dollars per acre. The State road runs through it; and the noble Susquehannah washes one of its sides. About one-half of this estate has been under cultivation a considerable length of time; — the other moity is covered with pines, which are valuable here. The soil of the former is very deep and fertile. In sinking a well near the dwelling-house, the soil (chiefly alluvial) was observed to be seven feet deep; the sub-soil the same depth of black sand; below this a spongy sandy gravel. There is also a brick-kiln upon the estate. In the freshets, the river frequently over-flows that part of the estate which is under cultivation, to the depth of a foot. But as these floods are regular and periodical, the farmer is always aware of their approach, and consequently (as they never come in the summer season) suffers no real damage. In general, these ebbings and flowings of the rivers, by leaving water to stagnate in marshy grounds, are productive of disease. I could not, however, learn that this was considered an unhealthy situation; and, upon the whole, should have little hesitation in giving a most decided preference to an estate of this description, which might probably have been purchased for £1,000, over one completely cov-ered with timber, without a house of any description, and without any so-ciety in the neighbourhood, at the rate of one dollar per acre.

Bibliography

BRITISH TRAVELERS IN NINETEENTH-CENTURY AMERICA

This list contains only those travelers mentioned in this volume and makes no pretense of being a complete bibliography of British accounts of the United States.

Abdy, Edward Strutt. *Journal of a Residence and Tour in the United States of North America, from April, 1833 to October, 1834.* 3 vols. London: John Murray, 1835.

Alexander, James Edward. *L'Acadie; or, Seven Years' Explorations in British America.* 2 vols. London: Henry Colburn, 1849.

_____. *Transatlantic Sketches, Comprising Visits to the Most Interesting Scenes in North and South America, and the West Indies.* 2 vols. London: Richard Bentley, 1833.

Anonymous. *Journal of a Wanderer; Being a Residence in India, and Six Weeks in North America.* London: Simpkin, Marshall, 1844.

Barclay (of Ury), Robert. *Agricultural Tour in the United States and Canada.* Edinburgh: William Blackwood, 1842.

[Beaufoy.] *Tour through Parts of the United States and Canada. By a British Subject.* London: Longman, Rees, Orme, Brown, and Green, 1828.

Bell, Andrew ("A. Thomasen"). *Men and Things in America; Being the Experience of a Year's Residence in the United States. . . .* London: W. Smith, 1838.

Birkbeck, Morris. *Letters from Illinois.* London: Taylor and Hessey, 1818.

_____. *Notes on a Journey in America from the Coast of Virginia to the Territory of Illinois.* London: Ridgeway and Sons, 1818.

259

Blane, William Newnham. *An Excursion through the United States and Canada During the Years 1822-23.* London: Baldwin, Cradock, and Joy, 1824.

Boardman, James. *America and the Americans, By a Citizen of the World.* London: Longman, Rees, Orme, Brown, Green, and Longman, 1833.

British Subject, A. See [Beaufoy].

Brown, William. *America: A Four Years' Residence in the United States and Canada; Giving a Full and Fair Description of the Country, As It Really Is.* . . . Leeds: William Brown, 1849.

Buckingham, James Silk. *America, Historical, Statistic, and Descriptive.* 3 vols. London: Fisher, Son, and Co., 1841.

Burns, Jabez. *Notes of a Tour in the United States and Canada in the Summer and Autumn of 1847.* London: Houlston and Stoneman, 1848.

Butler, Frances A. See Kemble, Francis A.

Campbell, Patrick. *Travels in North America in the Years 1791 and 1792.* Edinburgh: Patrick Campbell, 1793.

Caswall, Henry. *America, and the American Church.* London: J. G. and F. Rivington, 1839.

Chambers, William. *Things As They Are in America.* London: William and Robert Chambers, 1854.

Cobbett, William. *A Year's Residence, in the United States of America.* 3d ed. London: William Cobbett, 1828.

Coke, Edward Thomas. *A Subaltern's Furlough: Descriptive of Scenes in Various Parts of the United States. . . During the Summer and Autumn of 1832.* 2 vols. New York: J. and J. Harper, 1833.

Combe, George. *Notes on the United States of North America During a Phrenological Visit in 1838-9-40.* 2 vols. Philadelphia: Carey and Hart, 1841.

Dalton, William. *Travels in the United States of America, and Parts of Upper Canada.* Appleby: William Dalton, 1821.

D'Arusmont, Frances. See Wright, Frances.

Daubeny, Charles Giles Bridle. *Journal of a Tour through the United States, and in Canada, Made During the Years 1837-38.* Oxford: Charles Giles Bridle Daubeny, 1843.

Davis, Stephen. *Notes of a Tour in America, in 1832 and 1833.* Edinburgh: Waugh and Innes, 1833.

Dickens, Charles. *American Notes for General Circulation.* London: Chapman and Hall, 1842.

————. [Unpublished letters on American topics.] In John Forster, ed., *The Life of Charles Dickens.* Vol. 1: *1812-1842.* Boston: Estes and Lauriat [1872?].

Duncan, John M. *Travels through Part of the United States and Canada in 1818 and 1819.* 2 vols. Glasgow: Glasgow University Press, 1823.

Englishwoman, An. See Wright, Frances.

Fearon, Henry Bradshaw. *Sketches of America: A Narrative of a Journey of Five Thousand Miles through the Eastern and Western States of America. . . .* 3d ed. London: Longman, Hurst, Rees, Orme, and Brown, 1819.

Felton, Mrs. *American Life: A Narrative of Two Years' City and Country Residence in the United States.* London: Simpkin, Marshall, 1842.

Fergusson, Adam. *Practical Notes Made During a Tour in Canada, and a Portion of the United States, in 1831.* Edinburgh: William Blackwood, 1833.

Fidler, Isaac. *Observations on Professions, Literature, Manners, and Emigration, in the United States and Canada, Made During a Residence There in 1832.* New York: J. and J. Harper, 1833.

Finch, I. *Travels in the United States of America and Canada, Containing Some Account of Their Scientific Institutions. . . .* London: Longman, Rees, Orme, Brown, Green, and Longman, 1833.

Fowler, John. *Journal of a Tour in the State of New York, in the Year 1830; with Remarks on Agriculture in Those Parts Most Eligible for Settlers. . . .* London: Whittacker, Treacher, and Arnot, 1831.

Grant, Anne MacVicar. *Memoirs of an American Lady. . . .* (1808). Albany: Joel Munsell, 1876.

Gurney, Joseph John. *A Journey in North America, Described in Familiar Letters to Amelia Opie.* Norwich: John Joseph Gurney, 1841.

Hall, Basil. *Travels in North America, in the Years 1827 and 1828.* 3d ed. 3 vols. Edinburgh: Cadell and Co., 1829.

Hall, Francis. *Travels in Canada, and the United States, in 1816 and 1817.* London: Longman, Hurst, Rees, Orme, and Brown, 1818.

Hall, Margaret Hunter. *The Aristocratic Journey; Being the Outspoken Letters of Mrs. Basil Hall Written During a Fourteen Months' Sojourn in America, 1827–1828.* Ed. Una Pope-Hennessy. New York: G. P. Putnam's Sons, 1931.

Hamilton, Thomas. *Men and Manners in America.* 2 vols. Philadelphia: Carey, Lea and Blanchard, 1833.

Howison, John. *Sketches of Upper Canada, Domestic, Local, and Characteristic . . . and Some Recollections of the United States of America.* 2d ed. Edinburgh: Oliver and Boyd, 1822.

Howitt, Emmanuel. *Selections from Letters Written During a Tour through the United States, in the Summer and Autumn of 1819. . . .* Nottingham: J. Dunn, 1820.

Johnston, James Finlay Weir. *Notes on North America Agricultural, Economical, and Social.* 2 vols. Boston: Charles Little and James Brown, 1851.

Kemble, Frances Anne. *Journal* [of a Residence in America]. 2 vols. London: John Murray, 1835.

Lardner, Dionysius. *Railway Economy; a Treatise on the New Art of Transport.* . . . (1849?). New York: Harper and Brothers, 1855.

Latrobe, Charles Joseph. *The Rambler in North America: 1832-1833.* 2d ed. 2 vols. London: R. B. Seeley and W. Burnside, 1836.

Levinge, Richard George Augustus. *Echoes from the Backwoods; or, Scenes of Transatlantic Life.* 2 vols. London: J. and D. A. Darling, 1849.

Mackay, Alexander. *The Western World; or, Travels in the United States in 1846-7.* . . . 2d ed. 2 vols. Philadelphia: Lea and Blanchard, 1849.

Mackenzie, William Lyon. *Sketches of Canada and the United States.* London: Effingham Wilson, 1833.

Marryat, Francis. *A Diary in America with Remarks on Its Institutions.* (1839). Ed. Sidney Jackman. New York: Alfred A. Knopf, 1962.

Martineau, Harriet. *Retrospect of Western Travel.* 3 vols. London: Saunders and Otley, 1838.

———. *Society in America.* 2 vols. New York: Saunders and Otley, 1837.

Maxwell, Archibald Montgomery. *A Run through the United States, During the Autumn of 1840.* 2 vols. London: Henry Colburn, 1841.

Moore, George. *Journal of a Voyage across the Atlantic; with Notes on Canada and the United States.* London: George Moore, 1845.

Murray, Charles Augustus. *Travels in North America During the Years 1834, 1835, and 1836.* . . . 2 vols. New York: Harper and Brothers, 1839.

O'Ferrall, Simon Ansley. *A Ramble of Six Thousand Miles through the United States of America.* London: Effingham Wilson, 1832.

Power, Tyrone. *Impressions of America During the Years 1833, 1834, and 1835.* 2 vols. London: Richard Bentley, 1836.

Prentice, Archibald. *A Tour in the United States.* London: Charles Gilpin, 1848.

Reed, Andrew, and Matheson, James. *A Narrative of the Visit to the American Churches, by the Deputation from the Congregational Union of England & Wales.* 2 vols. London: Jackson and Walford, 1835.

Shirreff, Patrick. *A Tour through North America; Together with a Comprehensive View of the Canadas and United States. As Adapted for Agricultural Emigration.* Edinburgh: Oliver and Boyd, 1835.

Smith, Benjamin, ed. *Twenty-four Letters from Labourers in America to Their Friends in England.* (1829). San Francisco: California State Library for the W.P.A., 1939.

Stuart, James. *Three Years in North America.* 2 vols. Edinburgh: Robert Cadell, 1833.

Sturge, Joseph. *A Visit to the United States in 1841.* London: Hamilton, Adams, 1842.

Talbot, Edward Allen. *Five Years' Residence in the Canadas: Including a Tour through Part of the United States of America in the Year 1823.* 2 vols. London: Longman, Hurst, Rees, Orme, Brown, and Green, 1824.

Thomasen, A. See Bell, Andrew.

Thomson, William. *A Tradesman's Travels in the United States and Canada.* Edinburgh: Oliver and Boyd, 1842.

Trollope, Frances Milton. *Domestic Manners of the Americans.* (1832). Edited, with a History of Mrs. Trollope's Adventures in America, by Donald Smalley. Gloucester, Mass.: Peter Smith, 1974.

Tudor, Henry. *Narrative of a Tour in North America. . . . In a Series of Letters, Written in the Years 1831-2.* 2 vols. London: James Duncan, 1834.

Warburton, George Drought. *Hochelaga; or, England in the New World.* Ed. Eliot Warburton. 3d ed. rev. 2 vols. London: Henry Colburn, 1847.

Weld, Charles Richard. *A Vacation Tour in the United States and Canada.* London: Longman, Brown, Green, and Longmans, 1855.

Weston, Richard. *A Visit to the United States and Canada in 1833; with the View of Settling in America. . . .* Edinburgh: Richard Weston and Sons, 1836.

Wilkie, David. *Sketches of a Summer Trip to New York and the Canadas.* Edinburgh: Sherwood, Gilbert, and Piper, 1837.

Wilson, Charles Henry. *The Wanderer in America, or Truth at Home; Comprising a Statement of Observations and Facts Relative to the United States & Canada, North America. . . .* Thirsk: Charles Henry Wilson, 1824.

Wright, Frances. *Views of Society and Manners in America; in a Series of Letters from that Country to a Friend in England During the Years 1818, 1819, and 1820. By an Englishwoman.* London: Longman, Hurst, Rees, Orme, and Brown, 1821.

ANTHOLOGIES OF TRAVELERS' ACCOUNTS OF AMERICA

Carmer, Carl, ed. *The Tavern Lamps Are Burning: Literary Journeys through Six Regions and Four Centuries of New York State.* New York: David McKay, 1964.

Commager, Henry Steele, ed. *America in Perspective: The United States through Foreign Eyes*. New York: Random House, 1947.

Dow, Charles Mason, ed. *Anthology and Bibliography of Niagara Falls*. Vol. 1. Albany: State of New York, 1921.

Handy, Myrtle, and McKelvey, Blake, eds. "British Travellers to the Genesee Country." *Rochester Historical Society Publications* 18 (1940): 1–73.

Mau, Clayton. *The Development of Central and Western New York: From the Arrival of the White Man to the Eve of the Civil War. As Portrayed Chronologically in Contemporary Accounts*. Rochester: DuBois Press, 1944.

Nevins, Allan, ed. *American Social History as Recorded by British Travelers*. New York: Henry Holt, 1923. Revised and enlarged as *America through British Eyes*. New York: Oxford University Press, 1948.

Todd, C. Lafayette. "Some Nineteenth Century European Travelers in New York State." *New York History* 43, no. 4 (October 1962): 336–70.

Van Zandt, Roland, ed. *Chronicles of the Hudson: Three Centuries of Travelers' Accounts*. New Brunswick, N.J.: Rutgers University Press, 1971.

Index

THE NAMES of villages and cities of New York appear in **bold** type; the index registers only the current place name, ignoring variant spellings that appear in the text. All names of British travelers and tourists appear in *italics*.

UPSTATE TRAVELS

was composed in 10-point Compugraphic Times Roman and leaded two points
by Metricomp Studios,
with display type in Monotype Deepdene by J. M. Bundscho, Inc.;
printed by sheet-fed offset on 50-pound, acid-free Glatfelter Antique Cream,
Smythe-sewn and bound over boards in Joanna Arrestox B,
also adhesive bound with paper covers drawn on by
Maple-Vail Book Manufacturing Group, Inc.;
and published by

SYRACUSE UNIVERSITY PRESS

SYRACUSE, NEW YORK 13210